EL MUNDO ZURDO 10

SELECTED WORKS FROM THE 2024 MEETING OF THE SOCIETY FOR THE STUDY OF GLORIA ANZALDÚA

EDITED BY
SONYA M. ALEMÁN, RACHEL YVONNE CRUZ,
YAEL VALENCIA ALDANA,
AND ROMANA RADLWIMMER

aunt lute books

San Francisco

Aunt Lute Books, P.O. Box 410687, San Francisco, CA 94141
www.auntlute.com

Cover art: Miriam Flores © 2024
Cover design: Amy Woloszyn, Amymade Graphic
Text design: Amy Woloszyn, Amymade Graphic Design
Senior Editor: Shay Brawn
ProductionTeam: Isis Asare, Erin Edge, Maria Minguez, Emma Rosenbaum, and Golda Sargento

The production of this book was made possible by support from California Arts Council, the Council on Literary Magazines and Publishers, the Poetry Foundation, the San Francisco Arts Commission, Sara and Two C-Dogs Foundation, and the Zellerbach Foundation.

Printed in the U.S.A. on acid-free paper 10 9 8 7 6 5 4 3 2 1

CONTENTS

PART I: ESSAYS

PART II: CREATIVE WORKS

INTRODUCTION

LES ATRAVESADES DE SSGA OFFER LIGHT IN THE DARK

SONYA M. ALEMÁN, RACHEL YVONNE CRUZ,
YAEL VALENCIA ALDANA, AND ROMANA RADLWIMMER

Guided by the Anzaldúan commitment to forge a way through dark and troubled times, les atravesades that make up the Society for the Study of Gloria Anzaldúa gathered in May of 2024 at Trinity University. This two-and-a-half-day conference welcomed over 160 attendees who engaged in 60 sessions filled with dialogue, cultural work, theory-building, and/or testimonios, dedicated to coalition and bridge-building. Firmly grounded in an Anzaldúan cosmology that deconstructs in order to reconstitute, these eleven essays and six creative works resound with touchstones and insights for traversing hostile and repressive conditions, such as those triggered by the election of Donald Trump as the 47th president of the United States a mere six months after this dynamic gathering. Mired by the despotic and desperate actions of groups that have benefitted from white supremacist, imperial, colonial, heteropatriarchal and heteronormative ideologies to gain and maintain power and control, the atravesades featured in this collection serve as torchbearers, offering light, forbearance, and strength for these trying times.

The scholarly essays, for instance, address the foresaid challenges by offering means of overcoming them, primarily through acts and notions of solidarity. Three key questions serve as a thread through this set in the anthology: How does Anzaldúan thought foster coalitions in literature and philosophy, and which fruitful dialogues are established between them? What does Anzaldúa's theory mean for spiritual seeking and myth-making, and which contradictions and solutions emerge from it? What concrete impact do Anzaldúa's words have in the world, and how can her epistemology inform life paths and decisions? Accordingly, the essays in this volume are arranged around these three big complexes: firstly, literary-philosophic entanglements; secondly, spiritual options; and thirdly, comprehending the world with Anzaldúan theory.

Five scholars working in the fields of literature or philosophy engage Anzaldúan coalition building. Specifically, three articles reimagine literary texts—including contemporary Chicana and Puerto Rican, and early modern English literature—through an Anzaldúan lens. Laura López examines atravesada aesthetics in Belinda Acosta's 2010 novel *Sisters, Strangers, and Starting Over. López* draws parallels between the postmodern matriarch character Perla Sanchez and Coatlicue, the Mexica goddess theorized by Anzaldúa, analyzing how both figures are single mothers disparaged by their communities. Considering the long-lasting effects of colonialism, López argues that the patriarchal, misogynistic hegemony present in the novel structurally resembles the historic violence from the Mexica period and Spanish invasion, elements still woven into present day Latina/o/x gender norms presented in the novel. Alina Lugo's article proposes an Anzaldúan reading of Julia de Burgos's poetry, situating the Puerto Rican writer as a nepantlera who imagines decolonization and engages in self-transformation. Inserted into the broader context of third-world feminism, Lugo connects Burgos with Anzaldúa as a crucial step for decolonizing her writing and placing her within an intellectual community in which she no longer appears as the Other. For her part, Adrianna Santos, self-identified as a Chicanx studies scholar, dwells on the meanings of a "Borderlands Shakespeare." An intriguing question she frequently hears becomes the starting point of her inquiry: "Why Shakespeare?" Santos reflects on how Anzaldúan philosophy informs the reading of Shakespeare adaptations, and how it links borderlands cultures to academia.

Following these literary considerations, María José Ramírez Jiménez's and Diego Séval's essays examine Anzaldúan coalitions for hemispheric and intercontinental philosophical debates. Ramírez Jiménez studies the intersections between different decolonial projects, specifically how Gloria Anzaldúa's nueva mestiza and les atravesadxs, Enrique Dussel's transmodernidad and Rita Segato's relectura del mestizaje coincide in the central debate of raza in its colonial conditions. Ramírez Jiménez finds that ultimately all of them formulate useful options for transcending the framework of colonial legacy. Séval regards Anzaldúa's idea of rootedness as light in the dark as an alternative to problematic European conceptualizations which have been trapped by romanticized nationalist tendencies.

He sees Anzaldúa's New Tribalism as way to rethink the territories of community, which enables coalitions and the ability to regain and maintain political agency on both a local and a global scale.

A set of three contributions focus on spiritual communities. Rebecca Esho Greenslade sees the relationship between Anzaldúa's spiritual activism and the Bodhisattva Path undertaken by socially engaged Buddhist chaplains as a bridge between similar practices and epistemologies. In her eyes, both can actualize and nurture each other reciprocally to foster social justice and radical politics. Mark Hernández explores Anzaldúa's relational visions for theology. He makes the case that her notion of interconnectedness can help us to actively understand our positionalities and to develop an embodied understanding of the self, a sense of belonging, and a relational spirituality. Salvador Herrera meditates on Anzaldúan spirituality ex negativo, wondering what a "secular" reading of Borderlands might look like— one that is psychoanalytic and existential rather than metaphysical Herrera seeks to remedy any problematic implications of Anzaldúa's creative interpretations of Mesoamerican cosmologies, which might be understood as appropriative rather than imaginative or solidarity-oriented. By doing so, the author intends to make the ethics of spiritual activism more accessible to a broader audience.

The last set of essays in this section applies Anzaldúan theory as an instrument to better contemporary educational and labor institutions. Mónica Torreiro-Casal's essay describes a mental health initiative for undocumented students at the University of California, Davis. She presents the testimonios of Yaneyry Delfin Martinez and Karen Miranda Chavez. Together, the three voices produce a polyphone texture and a concrete example of what Anzaldúan coalition building may look like in the undocumented Borderlands. Christina Gómez Hernández chronicles how she embodies Anzaldúan theoretical constructs as an emergent bilingual educational leader. She links Anzaldúan quotes with personal anecdotes of the educational and political challenges she has overcome. Finally, Christian V. Ramirez investigates the cultural borderlands that separate homes of affluence and Latina domestic workers in South Texas. Grounded in an Anzaldúan intersectional understanding, the author notes how labor, gender, race, and citizenship overlap in domestic labor. Ramirez concludes that, while acting creatively to assert their own humanity, Mexican and Mexican origin domestic workers act as atravesadas navigating between South Texas barrios and affluent neighborhoods.

Methodologically speaking, the essays in this section map the seven stages of conocmiento (Gómez Hernández, Lugo), ponder myth-making (López, Herrera), or employ auto-historias (Ramirez, Gómez Hernández), or auto-historia-performance (Castillo, Medina De León, Sperry García, Sotomayor).

The creative contributions in the anthology continue Anzaldua's threads of community building via self-discovery, self-acceptance, and spirituality. The submissions vary from poetry, live performance, collective essays, zine making, illustration, and songwriting. Several of the creatives included here document their performative work in the conference space and how they connected with like-minded atravesades en comunidad.

The songs by Amalia Ortiz and poems by Yael Aldana further explore the concept of Anzaldua's new mestiza, the self that contains contradictions and ambiguity, and the concept of nepantla, the state in which the self is reimagined and reclaimed. In her lyrics, Ortiz establishes the whole self, the new mestiza going through the process of nepantla. In the song, "In Name Only," the speaker is torn down and apart by hypocritical people and organizations who are benevolent in name only. In the song "You Want to Kill Me," the façade of benevolence is gone, and the poem lays bare the ways society sought to kill the speaker, which is a stand-in for all women. The song "Hocicona, Peleonera" furthered the poet's nepantla journey as the speaker navigated societal injustices, first alone and then in community. The outside destructive forces tried to destroy the song's narrator, but as the self is fractured by discrimination and abuse, it is reborn and put back together as a stronger nepantla self. Aldana's "las mestizajes/ los mestizajes" echoed this nepantla journey and also engaged the unfortunately common theme of intolerance. The breaking of the self in this poem is in conversation with Ortiz's song. The speaker in this poem likewise formed a new, different, and stronger form through the destructive, then reclaimed nepantla process.

The performance and collective essay, "Now Let Us Shift Into the Light: A Generative Autohistoria-teoría Performance" by Avery Castillo, Esther Medina De León, Christen Sperry García, and Leslie C. Sotomayor II documents the multi-layered experience of uncovering and reconciling the individual and combined selves. In this piece, the four co-authors each offer an autohistoria-teoría, their respective stories told in in a way to draw in and build coalition and community. They explore the "brokenness" of the body, intergenerational traumas, and cultural memories, and how that can lead to evolving to a state of nepantla "wholeness." In the first section, "Somos Mujer / We Are Woman," the authors call on all women to be seen and come together in "wholeness." In the second section, Avery Castillo's auto-historia "Flesh & Needle," explores chronic illness, empathy, pain, and compassion, and draws on Anzaldúa's image of a cactus barb implanted in the flesh. Next, Esther Medina De León's auto-historia, "Heridas, Innocence Veiled, I am Esther," where she navigates her lived experiences of self-inflicted chaos as a woman and a mother. "La Casa Tract" by Christen Sperry García is a zine-based account. Sperry tracks her Coyolxauqui/ nepantla journey from romanticizing her ancestral homelands in Mexico and

San Diego to reconciling her relationship with her mother's "Mexican" cooking from an Iowa cookbook. The last auto-historia presented is "Pulling at my Umbilical Cord (Brincando el charco a Cuba)" by Leslie C. Sotomayor II. In this piece, Sotomayor bridges her life experiences with her limited knowledge of her mother's life in Cuba. These autohistorias shift from individual struggles to a collective nepantla "wholeness."

Another essay that reflects an effort to build community is "A Zine of Our Shared Reflection: Coalition Building Through Zines" by Brianna Glass and Daniel Alejandro González. The workshop described here aims to initiate forms of self-exploration and healing. Glass and González provide another example of the Coyolxauqui/ nepantla experience—the formation of a new personhood after pulling apart a sense of self.

Anzaldúa's Coyolxauqui/ nepantla journey is explored through visual art in Noreen M. Graf's "A Visual Interpretation of Gloria Anzaldúa's Unpublished Fable, Nepantla: Imagery and Analysis." Graf's visually completes Anzaldúa's fable with her striking drawings, aligning the Coyolxauhqui/nepantla journey of destruction and rebirth with Anzaldúa's and her own experiences.

In her paper, "The Destru/Creación of Songwriting: Atravesades en Comunidad," Rachel Cruz deftly describes her process as a songwriter as one of "destru/creación," the process of Coyolxauhqui and nepantla, emerging from an in-between space to pull oneself apart and reconstruct the self on a different level through her music and lyrics.

Although these creative contributions are expressed in a multitude of ways, the themes of Anzaldúa's Coyolxauhqui/nepantla journey of self-exploration, growth, and healing through fragmentation, reimagination, and reclaimation of self are present in all. Each work fosters coalition among atravesades en comunidad.

Moving through nepantla is not an attempt to escape this state: This journey should allow one to listen, to shed skin, to remember. As Gloria Anzaldúa writes in "Entering into the Serpent," transformation begins the moment we encounter what we have been taught to fear—when we step into the serpent's gaze, into the space between. To shed skin, as Anzaldúa teaches, is to release the roles, identities, beliefs, and expectations we inherited to survive—and to face the truths, wounds, and selves we have been taught to hide. Atravesades como nosotres do not survive in spite of the chaos but rather are shaped by it. Every offering in this anthology bears witness to that truth. Whether rooted in scholarly research and exploration, poetic or musical intuition, lived memory, or spiritual praxis, each contributor names and reclaims what has been fractured. Together, we pass through the darkness—not blindly or in haste, but with intention, each step an act of resistencia and renewal.

To live as atravesades—those who have been crossed, pierced, or marked—is a deliberate, embodied stance. Crossed by borders—geographic, cultural, linguistic, spiritual—atravesades navigate contradictions. Pierced by trauma, memory, and revelation, atravesades carry wounds that shape how we move through the world. Marked by race, gender, sexuality, class, and history, atravesades are visibly labeled—yet atravesades transform ourselves into symbols of resilience and survival. Atravesades are people of many genders and expressions, who inhabit the in-between: the corridor between worlds, the spiritual and cultural borderlands of identity, language, belonging, and belief. The writers, scholars, artists, and creators gathered in this volume offer narratives that move—intentionally, courageously, and necessarily—across, within, and through the spaces Gloria Anzaldúa called nepantla, where the real work of transformation begins.

To pass through nepantla necessitates surrendering to transformation. The contributors to this anthology do not bypass pain—they walk through it, barefoot and singing. They shed the skins imposed upon them—roles, beliefs, and expectations—and in doing so, embody what Anzaldúa called the new mestiza consciousness. What we find along the way is that the darkness holds knowledge, that pain carries memory, and that the stories we are told to silence often contain the very road maps we need to survive.

Each contribution in this anthology is a manifestation of survival. Whether academic or creative, visual or performative, what emerges is a shared commitment to resistencia, reclamation, and radical coalition-building. The atrevesades of the Society for the Study of Gloria Anzaldúa claim space here to unsettle exclusionary, racist systems. In this socio-political moment, we respond with generative action—rooted in community and sustained by a collective light that insists on shining through the dark. We are living in a moment of backlash, deliberate violence against our communities, our students, our bodies, and our truths. The pieces in this anthology show that resistance is not always loud. Sometimes, it is quiet and steady. A song sung at dusk. A poem read aloud to friends. A zine passed hand to hand. A classroom where a student sees themself reflected. As Noreen M. Graf's visual interpretation of Anzaldúa's unpublished fable reminds us, sometimes knowledge is not spoken but drawn, etched into image and symbol, transformation rendered in visual form.

This anthology is a threshold. A crossing. A mirror and a map. The voices gathered here do not conform to institutional expectations—they resist them. They carve space for the silenced and honor the labor of antepasades. This is the work of atravesades—creating through the struggles and learning, resisting and surviving in community.

EL MUNDO ZURDO 10

NAVIGATING THE NEPANTLA

EMBODYING ANZALDÚA'S VISION AS AN EMERGENT BILINGUAL EDUCATIONAL LEADER

CHRISTINA GÓMEZ HERNÁNDEZ

As a Nepantlera educator, I strive to be an advocate for emergent bilingual (EB) students, arguing for the need to integrate Mexican American studies into bilingual/dual language curriculum. As an emergent bilingual student, teacher, and educational leader, I believe incorporating Mexican American Studies (MAS) should be part of the third pillar of dual language curriculum, as it fulfills the sociocultural competence pillar (Howard et al.). Sociocultural competence allows individuals not only to learn about themselves but also to learn about others, essentially learning about other cultures (Arias and Medina). Incorporating MAS into dual language programs supports the goal of building the whole child and allowing the student to form a positive identity from an additive learning approach (Hernandez). While in a dual language program, the student becomes bilingual and biliterate. Adding MAS as part of sociocultural competence strengthens the students' bicultural/multicultural self.

As a daughter of an immigrant and a first generation Xicana, I have digested these experiences as part of my purpose to advocate as Nepantlera in the emergent bilingual world because I understand what it means to navigate schooling spaces that lack linguistic and cultural sensitivity. Anzaldúa's Coyolxauhqui Imperative allows for my reflection and healing process through auto-historia as a method to advocate publicly for MAS pedagogy for Emergent Bilinguals (EBs).

I often am torn between making this argument or changing current curricular practices while maneuvering places of systematic oppression. A guiding voice in my head is my mentor's voice asking: Do you fill the meter, or do you cause *desmadre* as a dual language and MAS advocate? At times, my commitment to giving space and voice in educational spaces to emergent bilinguals conflicts with the expectations of an educational leadership position. I recently asked myself, *¿puedo continuar con la lucha o necesito paz para sanar mis heridas que me ha causado mi trabajo?* [Can I continue in this struggle, or do I need inner peace to heal the wounds my work has caused me?]. Recently, I had to choose my emotional health and resigned from my leadership position in a toxic working environment.

Now that I am serving in a new leadership position that entails working with EB students at a regional level, I am reflecting on the conocimiento I gained, what I learned from my previous position to better serve EB students at a larger scale. I am paying particular attention to my understanding of space, location, language usage, culture, and power systems. These factors are important to analyze and process before making strategic moves that could yield manageable ways to uplift and empower the emergent bilinguals.

PURPOSE

In this autohistoria, I employ the seven stages of conocimiento [consciousness] (Anzaldúa 121-156) and Anzaldúa's Coyolxauhqui Imperative to theorize the lessons I learned from my efforts and the challenges I faced. The seven stages of conocimiento are Arrebato, Nepantla, Coatlicue State, Compromiso, Reuniting Coyolxauhqui, Conocimiento, Clash of Realities, and Shifting Realities (Anzaldúa and Keating 121-156). The Coyolxauhqui Imperative refers to the dismemberment of self wrought by colonization, and the re-writing and re-inventing of the self by recognizing and healing from these wounds. For each stage, I share an Anzaldúan quote and personal narratives or anecdotes. After moving through these stages, I demonstrate how I re-write and reinvent myself as a fuller EB advocate by facing and overcoming the trauma I experienced both as an emergent bilingual student and as a dual language educator. In this way, I hope to be a school leader who can improve the experiences of emergent bilinguals in the public school system.

COYOLXAUHQUI IMPERATIVE

In this portion of my auto-historia, I start with a quote about the Coyolxauhqui Imperative. I then transition into the seven stages of Anzaldúa's conocimiento theory.

> The Coyolxauhqui imperative is to heal and achieve integration. When fragmentation occurs, you fall apart...Coyolxauhqui is my symbol for the necessary process of dismemberment and fragmentation...is also...

> for reconstruction and reframing…an ongoing process of making and unmaking. There is never any resolution, just the process of healing. (Anzaldúa, *Light in the Dark*,19-20)

The first stage is the Arrebato stage, which I call the dismemberment of my linguistic identity.

FIRST STAGE: DISMEMBERMENT (ARREBATO)[1]

This section details the experiences that gutted my native language from my identity and caused chaos in my life. Anzaldúa's description of dismemberment can be applied to how my identity, once linked to my heritage language, Spanish, was severed:

> *Cada arrebatada* (snatching) turns your world upside down and cracks the walls of your reality, resulting in a great sense of loss, grief, and emptiness, leaving behind dreams, hopes, and goals. You are no longer who used to be… Exposed, naked, disoriented, wounded, uncertain, confused, and conflicted, you're forced to live *en la orilla*—a razor-sharp edge that fragments you. (Anzaldúa, *Light in the Dark*, 125).

Among my earliest memories around this trauma, this *Arrebato*, are the days when I wanted to play with my cousins after school, but I was stuck at the kitchen table with my mom. I sat at that kitchen table longing to go outside. I would peek through the gap in the floral window curtain the kitchen table sat against to see what they were doing outside. One afternoon, my mom was holding up a card from a deck of playing cards, and asked me, "What number is this?" I replied, "Nueve." Mom said, "nine." I asked mom, "¿Por *qué tengo que ser esto?* (Why am I having to do this?) My mom snapped out of frustration, "Because your teacher asked me to teach you English so you can pass to first grade!" I wondered why she did not question the teachers' request. After all, everyone in my kindergarten class was learning English just like me. At the time, I didn't know why my mom frustrated herself with yet another burden. She would come home from working her eight-hour shift to work another couple of hours to teach me how to read, write, and do arithmetic at the kitchen table. This must have taken a toll on her, considering she decided to only teach English to my two younger siblings.

This is where I pinpoint the beginning of the intergenerational trauma, one that originates from the public school system's policy regarding language. This mandate compromised my family's cultural and linguistic identities to the

1. Anzaldúa calls the first stage "El Arrebato." I use the word "dismemberment" to describe what happens when one figuratively breaks into little pieces from a traumatic event, much like what is described in the Coyolxauhqui Imperative.

point where my youngest sibling cannot speak Spanish today. Instead, I am the interpreter and translator between my father and younger siblings. I relate this painful disconnection to what Anzaldúa calls *el arrebato*.

My positive identity and connections with my family were impacted early on, an effect I began to recognize when I received my first affirmation as a ninth-grade student. Reflecting back, I realized that this experience in kindergarten shaped how I saw myself and my place in the world, and it was only in high school that I truly understood its influence on me.

SECOND STAGE: NEPANTLA SELF-AWARENESS (NEPANTLA)[2]

> Living between cultures results in 'seeing' double, first from the perspective of one culture, then from the perspective of another. Seeing from two or more perspectives simultaneously renders those cultures transparent. (Anzaldúa, *Light in the Dark,* 127)

During my primary and early intermediate school years at Lone Star Elementary, academic intervention plans were made for me. My math intervention group was assigned a bilingual teacher aide who helped our group learn math concepts with Spanish support. The interesting part of this intervention was that services were provided to me and my cousin, but my cousin did not speak Spanish—I did.

In third grade, I was provided reading intervention in English. I remember having to walk to a portable building to receive additional support. Eventually, I met academic goals and no longer needed academic interventions after third grade. I received many unsaid messages that English needed to be mastered. These messages can be seen as "language terrorism," or in a sense, language erasure of my heritage language, Spanish (Anzaldúa, *Borderlands*, 80-81).

These messages affected my identity. It determined how I used language in different spaces, such as school and home. At first, I exclusively used Spanish at home and English at school, but things changed as I journeyed into my middle school years. Wanting to fit in and angered by my struggles, I stopped speaking Spanish at home with my father. Instead of developing my Spanish further, I subconsciously chose to acculturate to what the public school system valued: the English language.

During my adolescent educational years as an unidentified emergent bilingual student, I navigated between home, family, and school without understanding systemic power structures within schools and society. An unidentified emergent bilingual student is a student whose primary language at home is

2. Anzaldúa calls the second stage "Nepantla." I name this stage "Nepantla self-awareness" because here I am aware of what has happened to me in the past in the public school system. I make use of these experiences to learn and navigate the school system in hopes of making positive change.

another language besides English who enters the public school system without being identified as an EB and receiving language services to become English proficient. I did not question or challenge these events until I received my first affirmation as a high school student. This experience is important to mention because I did not know I needed this affirmation for my emotional health until I experienced it. As a *Nepantlera* educator, I now understand how to navigate school systems, academia, home, family, and society. I see the need to use my agency to advocate for EB students and place their needs above my emotion. From this more mature vantage point, I have learned to be strategic, rather than reactionary.

THIRD STAGE: DESCUBRIMIENTO (COATLICUE STATE)[3]

Autohistorias go beyond the traditional self-portrait or autobiography when telling the writer's/artist's personal story. It also includes the artist's cultural history—indeed, it is a kind of making history, of inventing our history from our experiences and perspective through our art rather than accepting our history by the dominant culture (Anzaldúa, *Light in the Dark*).

The next vignette illustrates my slow and long healing process of no longer being ashamed of speaking Spanish in a school context. Admittedly, I did not receive spoken messages stating you cannot speak Spanish in school, like my mother did during her schooling experiences between 1956-1970, but I understood the lesson loud and clear. My mother shared with me several times that she felt tasked with teaching me English and that she would never go through that again with my brothers. I felt my bilingualism was pushed aside due to these unsaid abrasive messages that had an immense impact on my linguistic identity. During my middle school years, I decided to no longer speak in Spanish to my father while at home. I would even skip Spanish I classes in middle school and yet ended up in Spanish II as a freshman at New Braunfels High School.

I was sitting in a New Braunfels Spanish II class as a freshman in a class full of juniors and seniors. Mr. Vidal, the teacher, announced to the class, "I graded the papers I asked you to write about a city or state in México. The only person who wrote in Spanish and is truly bilingual is Christina Hernández [while pointing at me]." I sat there feeling embarrassed because I was ashamed of my bilingualism and biliteracy skill set because in the schools I attended, it was seen as something to erase and not be proud of. I had never received praise from a teacher for my ability to speak or write in Spanish.

Therefore, when Mr. Vidal, who recently passed away, praised me for my linguistic gifts, I did not know how to react. Mr. Vidal returned my paper with an "A" circled in red ink and asked me to stand up and read it to the class. I stood

3. Anzaldúa calls the third stage "the Coatlicue state." I renamed it "descubrimiento" because this is when I became aware of my linguistic and cultural capital.

up because I respected him so much. He was a Chicano pillar in our community through his activism outside of school. I read my paper aloud in a strong loud voice. It was about my father's birthplace, Guanajuato, México. I read about my connection to Guanajuato and the places I visited. I looked up and saw Mr. Vidal smiling at me. I sat down, unsure whether to feel pride or insecurity. I just smiled and sat back down. From that day forward, I began to ask questions at home and practice my Spanish with my father.

Years later, I still remember this event and its profound impact on my life. In reflection, I realized Mr. Vidal instilled in me the sense of pride and empowerment that I deserved to feel in the public school system as an emergent bilingual. This is when I started to further explore my cultural, historical, political, and biological self. I continued being in this reuniting Coyolxauhqui stage, reconnecting my identity, language, and sense of cultural pride, during my college years at Southwest Texas State University (SWT) in San Marcos, Texas, where I learned to question systems of oppression and power. Thus, I began to rewrite my narrative while learning about my cultural history and heritage and reviving my linguistic gifts. Engaging in this process led me towards becoming the *Nepantlera* educator and leader that I am today. Centering the EB student is my focus in everything I do as an educational leader: elevating Spanish educational spaces, raising a bilingual and biliterate daughter, writing curriculum, and incorporating MAS content and pedagogy in my instructional delivery.

FOURTH STAGE: BECOMING A NEPANTLERA WARRIOR (COMPROMISO)[4]

> To be in *conocimiento* with another person or group is to share knowledge, pool resources, meet each other, compare liberation struggles and social movements' histories, share how we confront institutional power, and process and heal wounds. (Anzaldúa, *Light in the Dark*, 91)

To reclaim my Xicana culture and linguistic identity, I attempted to further connect to my culture as a college student. Movimiento Estudiantil Chicano/a de Aztlán (MEChA) is where I found my heart and passion within the organization's beliefs and principles. MEChA was founded in March of 1969 at the National Chicano Youth Liberation Conference (NCYLC) in Denver, Colorado, by Corky Gonzales, a leader in the Raza Unida Party (Baca Huerta). MEChA at SWT is a product of this important event from the Chicano Movement era. MEChA at SWT was a student organization focused on Xicana/o, Indigenous,

4. Anzaldúa calls the fourth stage "compromiso." I used the title "Becoming a Nepantlera Warrior" because I am becoming aware of my agency and learning how to advocate for emergent bilinguals.

and immigrant rights. I chose this organization because this is what I needed for my sense of belonging, understanding of self, and reimagining my identity (Anzaldúa, *Light in the Dark*, 74; Hernandez 22-23).

Being in MEChA helped me understand the process of organizing and developing cultural events that celebrate my ancestry as an Indigenous person and as a mestiza. I learned through MEChA that leadership and finding allies for the empowerment of marginalized groups would be a struggle worth advocating for. For example, I learned the importance of fighting for immigrant and undocumented rights, like those guaranteed by *Plyler v. Doe* (202). I learned through MEChA that Mexican American studies and dual language education are our rights. This case is outlined in the Plan de Santa Barbara (Baca Huerta 26).

As a *Nepantlera* Warrior, I advocate for MAS and dual language communities in academia, K-12 educational spaces, and home. In some spaces, the beliefs that fueled my advocacy are appreciated and encouraged; often, in public schools, I am seen as a troublemaker. I frequently challenge decisions made by personnel in positions of power with the hopes of helping EB students gain more access to opportunities, such as high school and college credit earned during their middle school years. Such advocacy has made me a target. Despite my good intentions, my actions have not been well-accepted by district leaders.

One of the skills I have developed as a *Nepantlera* warrior is how to see whether an educational space is ready for change.[4] I can determine if there is a desire to disrupt systems and practices currently in place that have little to no consideration of the EB student. Also, as a *Nepantlera* warrior, I need to recognize when it is time to move on from hostile or intractable spaces. Redirecting efforts to a different site often allows for new strategies to gain traction. Although I have exhausted what I could do to serve EB students in one particular educational space, I will not cease to serve EB students in another. This is how I have learned to navigate through educational spaces as a *Nepantlera* educational leader.

FIFTH STAGE: RE-ENVISIONING, RE-INVENTING, AND RE-WRITING SELF (REUNITING COYOLXAUHQUI)[5]

> Identity, as consciously and unconsciously created, is always in process—self interacting with different communities and worlds. (Anzaldúa, *Light in the Dark*, 69).

As an educator, I must question the systems of power and understand the power of their agency. After taking a deep dive into discovering myself as an

5. Anzaldúa calls the fifth stage "Reuniting Coyolxauhqui." I use "re-envisioning, re-inventing, and re-writing self" because this is where I realize the type of teacher I want to be. I am re-imagining my teacher identity.

undergraduate student in MEChA, I became the person I hoped to be. This new sense of identity then became the foundation of my educational leadership, a leadership that now serves the emergent bilingual student with a genuine authentic sociocultural approach within their school.

I knew I wanted to be the teacher I did not have but needed in the seventh grade. I just did not know what I wanted to teach. When I accepted my bilingual identity in high school, I assumed I would become a Spanish teacher. It was not until I worked with EB students and undocumented students that I realized I wanted to be a bilingual educator. This happened after running a free afterschool program on the east side of Austin. I enjoyed tutoring EB students with their homework because their native language functioned as a barrier.

Once I realized another path before me, I resigned from my Spanish teaching position and enrolled at the University of Texas at San Antonio to earn my master's in bilingual and bicultural studies. Rather than teaching, I wanted to focus on learning to become a better educator for my future students. I continued working with Spanish native speakers struggling in math at the secondary level while in my master's program. I also was hired as a tutor to give lessons in Spanish. During this time, I decided to take the bilingual composite and earn an additional certificate to teach bilingual children in public schools.

It became clear this is the kind of teacher I wanted to be. I wanted to be a *Nepantlera* educator and provide a different narrative for bilingual students. I wanted to teach them culture and history along with bilingualism and biliteracy. At the point of my realization, I began diving deeper into the different selves that make up my identity so I could develop into a culturally competent teacher for my future EB students.

SIXTH STAGE: BUILDING SELF AS AN EDUCATOR (CONOCIMIENTO)[6]

> Identity grows out of our interactions, and we strategically reinvent ourselves to accommodate our exchanges. (Anzaldúa, *Light in the Dark*, 75)

The following vignette is the story of when I began to re-imagine, re-invent, and re-write my linguistic and cultural self within the bilingual sixth-grade classroom I taught. I re-entered the public school system as a sixth-grade transitional bilingual teacher at an elementary school in central Texas. I officially became a certified bilingual teacher in the inaugural year of this elementary school that

6. Anzaldúa calls the sixth stage "Conocimiento." During this stage I am learning and engaging myself in self-professional development to become a culturally sustaining educator, thus, I name this stage "Building Self as an Educator." I learned to embed Mexican American Studies content and pedagogy in my bilingual classes.

served EB students from kindergarten to sixth grade. I was so excited to have my first group of EB students. I was eager to incorporate Chicanx authors, historical perspectives, celebrations, and community in my instructional delivery.

During that first year, I began reading *Jesse*, a book written by Gary Soto (1994), aloud to my students. I usually read a chapter every school day after recess to bring my students back to learning mode. Surprisingly, my students were attentive. I chose this book because it allowed me to translanguage within the text, and have students learn about farm workers and Cesar Chávez. Most importantly, they heard about two brothers who struggled yet continued their education at the high school and community college level. These main characters strove for a better future. I wanted to blend and connect historical and cultural content while teaching my students reading standards. The students connected to the text. Some stated, "In the summer, I took work in the fields with my family." Many of my students were undocumented or first-generation emergent bilinguals. They made connections to the book, and I shared my personal story with them knowing I only wanted them to succeed. I took this opportunity to read another novel from a girl's perspective, *Esperanza Renace,* authored by Pam Muñoz (2000). My students made connections to this book as well. I noticed they were more engaged as I shared material and resources they could connect with as a Mexican/Mexican American.

I continued to embed Chicanx-centric material using poetry, readers' theater, and novels by Chicanx authors. I began incorporating Mayan math in algebra extension lessons. I showed my students how to make *tortillas de maíz* while teaching them about the circumference of a circle. I included astronomy, pyramids, and Mexica origin stories in science. For me to engage in this type of additive teaching, I had to study on my own since school districts did not provide this type of sociocultural professional development. I learned about these sources of knowledge through my master's program on bicultural studies, through my own reading, and through traveling. That year, I visited Mexico City and climbed the pyramid at Tenochtitlan, where I stood with a humongous smile and took a Polaroid picture (Image 1). I felt proud to walk on the steps of my ancestors and more excited to share this story with my students.

Image 1: Hernandez_Nepantla Warrior

I continue to embed MAS content and pedagogy in educational spaces and encourage ways of knowing in my classrooms. As a *Nepantlera* educator, I understand that when students connect to content, they will strive to achieve more. I saw that in my classrooms and other classrooms that incorporated additive approaches to schooling for the EB student successfully. For example, EB students participating in a one-way dual language classroom that integrated MAS content and pedagogy in the Spanish language arts and social studies content outperformed mainstream students on assessments (Hernandez 4).

SEVENTH STAGE: MOVING FROM TRAUMA TO ADVOCACY (TRANSFORMATION)[7]

> The healing of our wounds results in transformation, and transformation results in the healing of our wounds. (Anzaldúa , *Light in the Dark*, 19)

Aware of the benefits of a culturally sustaining classroom within a dual language program embedded with MAS content and pedagogy, I wanted to create systems and structures that would support this curriculum at the middle school level. I wanted to move away from subtractive policies (Valenzuela 20) to additive schooling for EBs (Hernandez 14). As a district-level coordinator, I began my journey piloting a middle school dual language program and transitioned to proposing a MAS Spanish elective for the dual language program. I was asked to submit a course request that led me to write two units for this course plus a year-at-a-glance. The curriculum units were based on understanding the self through identity formation, oral history projects, research, and local San Antonio leaders.

I was asked to present these curriculum documents to executive directors and the assistant superintendent of curriculum After my presentation, one of the executive directors said to me, "I am surprised you were able to write a great curriculum in a short amount of time," which implied she doubted I had the expertise for such a task. I responded with a smile and said, "I am very versed in MAS studies, and I love to write curriculum." I perceived these hurdles as their way to obstruct moving forward with the course and getting school board approval, although their approval was not required. Despite the fact that the principal of the middle school was a MAS advocate and wanted to provide MAS courses for all, it was frowned upon at the district level.

A few weeks later, I had a conversation with the same individuals. The assistant superintendent of curriculum asked me if it was possible to embed the MAS curriculum in the dual language program courses instead of offering a standalone MAS course. I let her know it was possible to embed those lessons into the Spanish language arts and reading and social studies classes. At that point, I knew I had lost that battle for a standalone course, but I still needed to try.

A few days later, I asked the secondary executive director why the course was not moving forward. She curtly stated, "Because I am not allowing it to. I am not making the recommendation." I was irate but knew questioning the decision of my superiors would lead to other struggles.

I designed this curriculum with the intention of providing an additive MAS-based learning experience for students but ended up integrating the cur-

7. Anzaldúa calls the seventh stage "Transformation." I used the following terms, "Moving from Trauma to Advocacy," to describe this stage because this is when I encountered more oppression in an educational space. During this time, I reflect and learn how to navigate the next educational space.

riculum through socio-cultural competence within the dual language program. In the end, the curriculum was only offered to EB students, despite my efforts to make MAS studies available for all students.

After my efforts to advocate for this curriculum, I felt I was treated differently by colleagues. I noticed that individuals who once said hello to me and engaged in conversation no longer did so. This hostility made it harder to get ideas approved, but I continued to serve EB students, teachers, leaders, and students to the best of my ability. However, the trauma I experienced as a student resurfaced as new trauma caused by the same educational system. It stewed in me so much that it affected my mental health and I decided to resign after working faithfully to ensure the piloted dual language program reached the high school level. Grounded in my PhD training regarding systems of oppression, I am still learning from this experience so I can better serve EB students.

CONCLUSION

As a *Nepantlera* educational leader, I seek to disrupt and cause chaos in educational spaces so that our emergent bilingual students receive the education they deserve. I strive to encourage instructional leaders to keep the EB students as their focus, rather than as an afterthought in the process of school improvement measures. The goal is to provide a school culture and climate that is additive and affirming, instead of the historically subtractive schooling experience I endured as an EB student, which I am still healing from. I leave the reader with an Anzaldúa quote that exemplifies why I advocate for EB students as a *Nepantlera* educator and *lídere* in a way to dismantle oppressive structures in school systems:

> Ensuring that our acts do not mirror or replicate the oppression and dominant power structures we seek to dismantle, las nepantleras upset our cultures' foundations and disturb the concepts structuring their realities. (Anzaldúa, *Light in the Dark*, 83).

WORKS CITED

Anzaldúa, Gloria. *Borderlands/La frontera: The New Mestiza*. Fourth edition, 25th Anniversary, Aunt Lute Books, 2012.

—. *Light in the dark/Luz en lo oscuro: Rewriting Identity, Spirituality, Reality.* Edited by AnaLouise Keating, Duke University Press, 2015.

Arias, Beatriz, and José Medina. "Sociocultural Competence in Action." *Language Magazine*, vol. 20, no. 2, Oct. 2020, pp. 35–36.

Baca Huerta, Sandra. "*Towards a (r)Evolutionary M.E.Ch.A: Intersectionality, Diversity, and the Queering of Xicanism@.*" Master's Thesis, Kansas State University. 2013.

Hernández, Christina. "*The Gibbous and Crescent of la luna: Emergent Bilingual Educator Experiences in the K-12 Public School System as Student and Educator.*" Dissertation, Texas State University, 2023.

Howard, Elizabeth, et al. (2018). *Guiding Principles for Dual Language Education (3rd ed.).* Washington, DC: Center for Applied Linguistics, 2018.

Plyler v. Doe. 457 U.S. 202. Supreme Court of the US, 1982.

Ryan, Pam Muñoz. *Esperanza Rising*. New York: Scholastic Press, 2000.

Soto, Gary. *Jesse.* San Diego, Harcourt Brace, 1994.

Valenzuela, Angela. *Subtractive Schooling. [Electronic Resource]: U.S. - Mexican Youth and the Politics of Caring*. State University of New York Press, 1999.

SPIRITUAL ACTIVISM AND THE BODHISATTVA PATH

REBECCA ESHO GREENSLADE

This paper considers the relationship between Gloria Anzaldúa's cosmology—specifically her notion of "spiritual activism"—and the principles and practices of the bodhisattva path undertaken by socially engaged Buddhist chaplains. Undertaking this comparative analysis is a form of coalition building, an act of dialogue and bridging of spiritual epistemologies and practices that, to date, have had minimal engagement with each other. Through a consideration of how my own engagement with spiritual activist writings and praxis has enriched my understanding of how to actualize the bodhisattva path, I suggest that Anzaldúa's cosmology can augment how Buddhist chaplains might engage with social justice concerns through locating our bodhisattva vows and practice within more radical politics of spirit perspectives. Reciprocally, placing an ethical Buddhist framework—in this case, the Zen Peacemakers "Three Tenets"—in dialogue with Anzaldúa can offer further spiritual technologies through which to actualize Anzaldúa's feminist epistemological and ethical vision.

THE BODHISATTVA PATH

> Attention! Attention!
>
> Raising the Bodhi Mind, the supreme meal, is offered to all the hungry spirits throughout space and time, filling the smallest particle to the largest space. All you hungry spirits in the ten directions, please gather here. Sharing your distress, I offer you this food, hoping it will resolve your thirst and hunger.
>
> Supplication for the Raising of the Bodhi Mind.
>
> Vow to feed the hungry spirits

I was introduced to this verse from The Gate of Sweet Nectar Liturgy—chanted in zendos across the world—by Roshi Eve Marko, a Dharma teacher with the Zen Peacemakers Order, during my Zen Buddhist Chaplaincy training. It has stayed with me since. What is this short verse referring to? I understand it to be an expression of a politics of care. It is an invitation to *all* those with hungry hearts—those hurting, those feeling lost, those feeling left behind or alone—to come and share a meal together. It is an aspiration to feed everyone, to tend to our thirsts. In this respect, the bodhisattva's intention is to become the supreme meal itself, a site of hospitality and accompaniment where no one leaves hungry.

What does it mean to *raise the Bodhi Mind*? Bodhi Mind is the enlightened mind. Zen teacher and founder of the Zen Peacemakers Order Bernie Glassman said the mind of enlightenment is for the sake of all beings. The raising of the Bodhi Mind is the awareness that we are all one interdependent body. What helps us realize this is practicing non-exclusion; it is through embodying an unedited existence in our everyday lives that we become the supreme meal. We become bodhisattvas of hospitality.

What do I mean by bodhisattva? Bodhisattva is a Sanskrit word that is a composite of *sattva*, or "being," and *bodhi,* or "awakened." The bodhisattva is anyone who, motivated by compassion, wishes to attain Buddhahood for the sake of all beings. The bodhisattva chooses to stick around in the material world—the world of suffering. Rather than following a solitary pursuit of meditating their way out of suffering, a bodhisattva meditates their way *towards* suffering. Two thousand six hundred years ago in Bodh Gaya, when Shakyamuni Buddha reached his right hand to touch the Earth, calling her to bear witness to his awakening, he did not then spiritually depart from this world. He stuck around for the next forty years, traveling and sharing his pragmatic teachings, before dying of dysentery by the side of a road. The Buddha died lying in his own shit. In Zen, Avalokiteshvara, the Bodhisattva of Compassion, is known as the "*Perceiver of the Cries of the World.*" She refuses to leave the material world until she can no longer hear a single cry. Although, I am sure that even Avalokiteshvara must be struggling right now as she listens to the live-streamed daily cries of genocides currently taking place in Palestine, Sudan, and Congo. The bodhisattva's awakened heart must also be, I think, a broken heart.

Now, of course, on one level, we could argue the vow to feed the hungry spirits is an impossible, even grandiose, endeavor. *Of course,* we can't feed all the hungry spirits. And yet, a bodhisattva vow is more than an impossible promise; rather, it is an expression of profound yearning, of active hope, an inexhaustible commitment not to stop practicing and serving until every single being is free from suffering. This vow represents an impossible, endless task, and yet, a bodhisattva enters this impossible work wholeheartedly. In this respect, through living by vow, the bodhisattva commits to imagining otherwise liberatory possibilities of our co-existence.

Zen teacher and climate activist David Loy describes the bodhisattva path as a "spiritual archetype that offers a new vision of human possibility" (Loy). This is a vision that is particularly counter to decades of neo-liberal mechanisms that separate us from each other, that keep us away from each other, that alienate us from each other's suffering, and that have removed the very commons that enable us to practice accompaniment and care. It is a vision that, I think, accompanies Gloria Anzaldúa's vision for the role of spiritual activist. Both are visions that are characterized by a recognition of our interdependent nature, by understanding the role, function, and impact of delusion, and, by a non-dual and loving politics. Both, I think, are characterized by a vision of becoming the supreme meal and vowing to feed all the hungry spirits.

SPIRITUAL ACTIVISM: INNER WORK, PUBLIC ACTS

The inner and outer work form bridges between the life of the mind, the life of the body, and the life of the spirit, as well as the life of the collective. In the moments of connection between the inner and outer worlds, the soul and the physical world come together and intersect. Spiritual activism stitches the two fabrics together (qtd. in Keating "Handbook," 203).

Throughout her writings, Anzaldúa centers a politics of spirit that insists upon the vital and reciprocal relationship between spiritual practice and social transformation. She refers to this radically inclusive politics as "spiritual activism." Whilst not the first to coin the term, her work has been pivotal in bringing it into feminist scholarship and praxis. She began to use the term "spiritual activism" more explicitly in her later writings to demonstrate her politics of spirit, which AnaLouise Keating describes as "a visionary, experimentally based ontology, epistemology, and ethics grounded in and based on a metaphysics of radical interconnectedness" ("Handbook" 203). Epistemologically, it is based upon a metaphysics of interconnectedness and relational ways of theorizing. Ethically, it involves specific actions that are designed to critique, challenge, and intervene in social injustice and forms of oppression. Spiritual activism is a call to action that necessitates us turning towards our interior selves in order to foster a depth of self-awareness and new ways of knowing (*conocimientos*) that enable us to see and intervene in social transformation. *Conocimiento* is a deeply reflective consciousness-raising practice that cultivates a seeing and opening towards—without attachment to—various constituent parts of the self. For Anzaldúa, this interplay of inner and outward actions is conducive to personal and social healing; it alloys the "traditional practice of spirituality (contemplation, meditation, and private rituals) [and] the technologies of political activism (protests, demonstrations, and speakouts)" (*Light in the Dark* 15). Therefore, spiritual activism is concerned with how spiritual practices and perspectives can be utilized to understand and intervene in systemic oppressions such as racism, ableism, and homophobia. As both theory and praxis, spiritual activism seeks to engage with social justice concerns and activist commitments.

Like Anzaldúa's conception of spiritual activism, for the bodhisattva, there are two reciprocal aspects of practice—the inner and the outer. I am now close to completing my second and final year of Buddhist Chaplaincy training with Roshi Joan Halifax and the faculty at Upaya Zen Center in Santa Fe. The first year of training is referred to as "inner chaplaincy." This has been the ongoing work of spiritual formation, studying and receiving the Sixteen Bodhisattva Precepts, sitting in Council practice together, reflective writing, daily meditation, and working with spiritual mentors to bring awareness to the wounds that speak our stories so that we don't serve others through them or from them. We undertake this "inner" work to understand that there is no inherent "me" that exists separately from the rest of the world. Therefore, there is no "other." And this wisdom, or insight, becomes actualized through how we live and act in the world. The second year is referred to as "outer chaplaincy," where we begin to explore areas of ministry and the pragmatics of serving from a Buddhist perspective. An important early Japanese Zen Master, Shih-t'ou, wrote a poem called "Song of the Grass Roof Hermitage." It contains the line: Turn around the light to shine within, then just return (Shih-t'ou). Shih-t'ou wrote this over a thousand years before Anzaldúa wrote "now let us shift—the path of conocimiento—inner work, public acts" ("now let" 540). Both are saying, turn the light towards yourself, illuminate what needs attention, and then return to serve. Act as Light in the Dark: inner work, public acts.

I have come to understand the bodhisattva path, and by extension, the work of a Buddhist chaplain, also as a bridge, an undertaking of the work of *bridging*, of spanning a divide, of creating and existing in moments of community—whether accompanying someone as they depart this material life; carrying a backpack with blankets, water, and a pocket-sized book of prayers for protestors; winding their way through segmented prison corridors to sit with an inmate; facilitating a restorative justice effort that holds both grace and accountability within a transgression that caused harm; or, even bridging—stitching together—the parts of ourselves that loudly surface in silent meditation, the Buddhist chaplain must practice so that they acquire the skills of a bridge builder, offering temporal bridges that might generate shift*s*, that might open, change and break hearts. The work of bridging is also central to Anzaldúa's worldview. For example, in "La serpiente que se come su cola," she writes, referring to herself in third person narration:

> "Her body was the bridge, the link between the external world and the inner one. She wanted to make that bridge a channel for the descent of the spirit. She wanted to reconnect her bonds of kinship with all life. She wanted a bridge of communication to the non-human world." (Keating, *Handbook* 26-27).

In Buddhism, we talk about "crossing the other shore." This crossing is, as Thich Nhat Hahn teaches, a journey from the shore of suffering to the shore of well-being. The vehicle, or boat, to get to the other side is *prajna*—meaning "wisdom"—the non-dual wisdom I have just described and which I find to be embodied within Anzaldúa's writings. In her preface to *this bridge we call home,* Anzaldúa tells us that "it's not just about one set of people crossing to the other side, it's also about those on the other side crossing to this side" ("(Un)natural" 4). Her words mirror the training Buddhists tempted to dwell comfortably on the shore of well-being receive—*not to stay there.* Our ethical commitments–our bodhisattva vows–are to find ways of helping others across, to build bridges. And, to build bridges, we have to understand why some folks want to stay where they are, what stories they are holding onto, and what wounds prevent movement. Like the spiritual activist, the Buddhist chaplain practices cultivating a justice-orientated awareness that imagines and invites ways of co-habitation—however momentary—that move beyond dualistic and binary modes of relating. And, as Thich Nhat Hahn reminds us in his simple, sweet language, "It's nice to cross the stream of suffering together, hand in hand" (Hahn).

Perhaps I am suggesting here that we might consider the bodhisattva as *la nepantlera*, one who tries to "facilitate passages between worlds" ("(Un)natural" 1), of seeing the world anew, actively *choosing* a constant process of undoing, of rupture and renewal, of ethical inquiry, of letting go of old narratives and opening to new ones that are rooted in commitments to social justice and transformation. Anzaldúa tells us that "for nepantleras, to bridge is an act of will, an act of love, an attempt towards compassion and reconciliation, and a promise to be present with the pain of others without losing themselves to it" ("(Un) natural" 4). Like *nepantleras*, can the bodhisattva embody a site of liminal possibilities where we pray for everything and also for nothing, where spiritual and material become indistinguishable, where we are guided not by prescriptive codes of conduct, but by these acts of will, love, and attempts towards compassion and reconciliation, *struggling* with the bodhisattva ethical precepts and living our way towards actualizing our Buddhist names?[1]

One framework for approaching this bodhisattva path is guidelines known as the "Three Tenets." Like Anzaldúa's spiritual activism, the Three Tenets are also rooted in epistemological and ethical commitments towards personal and social transformation and could offer further resourcing for the *nepantlera* also navigating the practice of staying upright and present when walking charnel grounds and confronting and crossing difficult thresholds.

THE THREE TENETS

There are two main lineages to the formation of Upaya's Buddhist Chaplaincy training and work. The first is the socially engaged Buddhism of Vietnamese Zen teacher Thich Nhat Hahn. The second is the teachings of Roshi Bernie Tetsugen Glassman, a Dharma heir of Japanese Zen teacher Maezumi Roshi, who merged spiritual teachings with social action, leading to the formation of the Zen Peacemakers Order. Both Thich Nhat Hahn and Bernie Glassman were teachers of Roshi Joan Halifax and have been formative in her actualization of a chaplaincy program that centers the bodhisattva as an activist, or as I argue, centers the bodhisattva as a spiritual activist. Roshi Joan understands Shakyamuni Buddha to have been a social reformer and calls for a revision of Buddhism based upon the misunderstandings that many white, western Buddhists have been caught in—namely, that Buddhism is an apolitical practice. Adopting perspectives of neutrality and apoliticality enables us to bypass suffering and social responsibility. By contrast, Roshi Joan teaches an interpretation of Zen Buddhist practice that is highly political and asks of her chaplaincy students that we also turn towards political engagement and social transformation as part of our practice. In this respect, interconnectedness is the basis for a political chaplaincy praxis. Here, I will speak to the key teachings of the Zen Peacemakers Order, known as the Three Tenets, placing them

1. In a formal ceremony known as Jukai, when a Zen student receives the Sixteen Bodhisattva Precepts, we are also given a Dharma name. I received the name "Esho" from Tenshin Roshi Fletcher in 2016, which means "wisdom blossoming." I received it as an instruction, as a precept to apply and an inquiry to embody.

in dialogue with Gloria Anzaldúa's spiritual activist vision[2]. The Three Tenets are non-linear, applied precepts for the socially engaged practitioner, guiding the work of Buddhist chaplaincy. These are *not knowing, bearing witness,* and *compassionate action.*

NOT-KNOWING: LETTING GO OF FIXED IDEAS ABOUT YOURSELF, OTHERS, AND THE UNIVERSE[3]

According to the Buddha, life is constantly in flux, which means it is constantly unstable. Yet, we look for and solidify belief systems that make life feel more solid than it really is. Not knowing is a practice to help us set aside our fixed points of view. Roshi Egyoku Nakao describes not knowing as "a flash of openness or a sudden shift to being present in the moment" (Nakao). *Now let us shift* ... When we open to presence, there is nothing to depend on. Rather than filling up with self-interest, differentiation, and opinion, not knowing empties us in order to meet what arises from a place of unconditioned openness rather than a place of conditioned reactivity. Non-knowing is a courageous, open mind that does not rely on conceptual knowledge or concepts. Perhaps this first tenet of non-knowing holds similarities with *la nagula's* phenomenological possibilities—a place of knowing that decenters the ego and is, by extension, less defensive, more open, and porous. Anzaldúa describes *la nagula* when "you give up investment in your point of view and recognize the real situation free of projections—not filtered through your habitual defensive preoccupations" ("now let" 569). In Zen, we call this *shoshin*, or beginner's mind. Not-knowing mind. When we cultivate *shoshin,* we shift into a new relational consciousness, one that supports personal and coalitional transformation.

Not knowing is not ignorance. But it *is* grounding ourselves in immediate experience, bringing full awareness without the fixation, centering ourselves in this boundless web of interconnection, which is so often severed because of fixed views. When we practice not knowing, we are able to expand our capacities for care *because* nothing is excluded. Zen students will often hear the phrase: *not knowing is most intimate.* This statement seems counterintuitive, yet I have come to understand that releasing our preconceptions and ideas about what's best for other people connects us more fully to them. We move beyond what we think we know into undiscovered, more intimate relational possibilities where instead of finding fault with the present, we meet it as it is, whatever it is.

---

2. Victoria Guentin's PhD thesis *Shifting Toward a Spiritualized Pedagogy: Gloria E. Anzaldúa and Thich Nhat Hahn in Dialogue* offers a useful discussion between spiritual activism and socially engaged Buddhism.

3. The sub-headings of The Three Tenets I am using here are as described by Roshi Egyoku Nakao..

The first tenet of not knowing aligns strongly with Anzaldúa's vision for alliances that are built out of a recognition of our interdependence rather than from the enclosure of fixed identities where differences are utilized to build walls, not bridges that can help us find our way to each other. Not knowing is the starting point for Buddhist chaplains entering a restorative justice process, for example, or meeting a prison inmate on death row for the first time. Not knowing as both principle and praxis enables us to open towards and to recognize the humanity in everyone. This practice of recognition is a consistent theme throughout Anzaldúa's work. She writes:

> This work of spiritual activism and the contract of holistic alliances allows conflict to dissolve through reflective dialogue. It permits an expansive awareness that finds the best instead of the worst in the other, enabling you to think of la otra in a compassionate way ("now let" 572).

Not knowing is one way to approach cultivating our capacities for this reflective dialogue and expansive awareness. It enables us to reach what Anzaldúa describes as when the slash between nos (us)/ostras (others) is dropped: "when the bridge will no longer be needed—we'll have shifted to a seamless nosotras" ("now let" 570). In this respect, not knowing becomes the very fabric of the bridge, built through a recognition of our interconnectivity that transcends yet does not erase identity categories. In fact, in *Light in the Dark,* Anzaldúa aligns the Buddhist teaching of non-self with *nos/ostros*. Not knowing is how we begin to see that we are not separate from others. It is also the precursor to bearing witness.

BEARING WITNESS: ATTENDING TO THE JOY AND SUFFERING OF THE WORLD

One of the simplest yet most impactful teachings I have received on my chaplaincy training is *strong back, soft front*. Can I center myself with equanimity (strong back) and stay open with compassion (soft front)? To bear witness is to bear witness not only to the suffering and joys of others but also to the suffering and joys of ourselves. It is continuous inner work and outer work. To bear witness is to find a center from which to live into the fullness of our humanity and to recognize that fullness in others–in all others.

Bearing witness is not being a bystander. But it is, to quote Roshi Joan Halifax, "about the courage to face the whole catastrophe, with humility, curiosity, and openness, and to let the situation enter you fully" (Halifax). For me, *letting the situation enter you fully* is such a feature of Anzaldúa's writing. Her embodied writing praxis demonstrates to us how bearing witness is not only to be affected but is also the capacity to host that effect *and* to inquire into that effect. We encounter this in her intimate reflections about her relationship to her body, sharing the shame and abnormality that accompanied a hormonal condition that caused her to menstruate from three months old and develop breasts at age six, and again in writing about the later devastation of a Type 1 diabetes diagnosis, another bodily betrayal and loss that, through her practice of autohistoria-teoría, she inquires into and integrates. As a forty-seven year-old woman currently navigating treatment for breast cancer, I have turned repeatedly to Anzaldúa's writings on illness in particular; her words are a steadying breath, a reminder to lean into my own treatment with eyes and heart wide open as new thresholds ask to be crossed. *Strong back, soft front.* Bearing witness is a refusal to collapse into our tendencies to turn away from suffering, and in Anzaldúa's case, manifests clearly in how she writes from and into her own sufferings.

Above my writing desk sits a citation from Anzaldúa: *when I write I hover* ("When I write" 238)."Hovering" has become an important spiritual practice for me. I have come to understand bearing witness to be an act of hovering, whether through sitting in daily meditation (zazen), paying close attention to what arises without intervening, or in the re-reading of a text, or leaning into the opaque edges of a nascent idea that is forming. Through learning to hover, I am learning to bear witness. Hovering is to let the situation enter us fully before turning towards the next new thing. Hovering is to bear witness to our tendencies to resist discomfort. It is to stay close to the nepantlera-bodhisattva dilemma when faced with a threshold to cross—do we refuse or do we transform? Hovering is the pause from which our discernment and capacity to act compassionately arises.

COMPASSIONATE ACTION: THAT WHICH ARISES FROM NOT KNOWING AND BEARING WITNESS

What is the effect of these two embodied practices? These practices help us learn how to "listen to the 'small still voice'" (Teish, 101) within us, which can empower us to create actual change in the world" (Anzaldúa "El Mundo" 195). And, when we do so, we are compelled to act. These practices help the Buddhist chaplain understand—and by extension *appropriately respond* to and intervene in—systemic oppressions such as racism, ableism, and transphobia. We begin to understand how Buddhism is not a neutral teaching. By committing to the inner work that enables us to see more clearly, we are transforming our relationship to what is known in Buddhism as the "three poisons"—greed, hatred, and delusion, cultivating what Zen teacher Frank Ostaseski refers to as a *fearless transparency.* And seeing more clearly, more fully, inevitably *compels us* towards compassionate action. This third tenet of compassionate action is rooted in intimate relations with our ancestors, to each other—human and other than human—to our communities. Compassionate action honors and reflects our intrinsic interconnectedness.

I am reminded of these two sentences from Anzaldúa in *La Prieta*: "I believe that by changing ourselves we change the world . . . a going deep into our self and expanding out into the world. And yet, I am confused as to how to accomplish this" (208). The first time I read this, I cried in relief at Anzaldúa's uncertainty, at her not knowing how to reconcile the contradictory and challenging aspects of her life and work, yet whilst at the same time meeting this uncertainty with the vulnerability and humbleness that infuse her writings. This radical interconnectedness that is foundational to her spiritual activism does not necessitate that we always know *how* to act in the world, yet we are compelled to do so. We are compelled towards compassionate action.

One of my favorite Zen teachings is when a young monk asked Master Ummon—a Chinese teacher in the Tang period—"what are the highest and most profound of all the Buddha's teachings?" Master Ummon replied, "an appropriate response." Out of *all* the Buddha's teachings, Master Ummon considered discernment and the capacity to make choices appropriate to the situations we find ourselves in to be more valuable than knowledge of the Buddhist *suttas*, hierarchies of spiritual attainment, or cosmological insight. This, for me, is a compassionate action. As chaplains, we must show up to a situation, not knowing what will be asked of us, not knowing if we can meet it, and, drawing on the resources of our spiritual practice, simply respond as appropriately as we are able to and trusting in the integrity of that response.

So, what does compassionate action look like? It might look like organizing, mobilizing, creating conversations, writing, offering a ritual or ceremony, sitting in silence, and sharing knowledge and resources to enable decision-making. It *is* perseverance. It might involve tending your own wound that a situation has pressed and opened so that you do not act from it. Compassionate action is rooted in the body and an everyday vernacular. It might mean the offering of a prayer and conscious, collective breath. It involves attending to the "we," not the "I." Sometimes, compassionate action is closing the bridge, putting up a barrier, when hostility and aggression will not enable alliance but harm it. But it is always the *public act* our *inner work* is in service of.

This paper has tried to show how Anzaldúa's theory and praxis of spiritual activism—"a visionary experientially-based epistemology and ethics, a way of life and call to action" (Keating "citizen" 242)—is in deep alignment with the bodhisattva path. So far, the reciprocity between these two spiritual practices has been relatively unexamined and, therefore, unrealized. Yet, coalition building requires us to build and cross bridges towards each other. When we do so, we encounter otherwise ways of (re)imagining our spiritual practices, learning from and with each other in our shared commitment to social transformation. We expand and enrich our epistemological and ethical frameworks, trying new ways and possibilities of thinking and practicing together. Engaging with Anzaldúa's scholarship has afforded me different perspectives through which to understand and actualize my bodhisattva vows. The rich and layered conversations that followed my presentation of this paper indicate that Anzaldúa scholars also see the benefit to considering spiritual activism through a Buddhist ethical framework, finding value in Buddhist teachings and practices. The charnel grounds Buddhist chaplains' step into and bear witness from are also *Borderlands,* unstable and passing-through places where possibilities of collation building arise, where the collective benefits of spiritual practices such as *zazen* meditation, compassionate presence, and ensoulment can compel us to act as *Light in the Dark.* And, through locating the bodhisattva path as a form of spiritual activism and by placing it in dialogue with Buddhist ethical frameworks, such as the Zen Peacemakers' Three Tenets, we expand the possibilities of how Anzaldúa's politics of spirit can be actualized, operating as both bridge and intervention into the separations and severances of contemporary life.

Dedication

I am grateful for opportunities to write where my relationship to Zen Buddhism is not sidelined as a personal, individual practice but rather as part of the broader, ongoing political commitment I undertake as a feminist psychotherapist and Buddhist chaplain. It underpins every line of this writing and is indebted to the lineage of Zen women who have preceded me and paved the way for this practice life. I include Gloria Anzaldúa in this lineage with deep bows for all she continues to show me in how to actualize my bodhisattva vows.

WORKS CITED

Anzaldúa, Gloria. "La Prieta." *This Bridge Called My Back: Writings by Radical Women of Color*. Ed. Cherríe Moraga and Gloria Anzaldúa. New York: Kitchen Table: Women of Color Press, 1983. 198-209. Print.

---. "El Mundo Zurdo." *This Bridge Called My Back: Writings by Radical Women of Color*. Ed. Cherríe Moraga and Gloria Anzaldúa. New York: Kitchen Table: Women of Color Press, 1983. 195-196. Print.

---. "(Un)natural bridges: Un)safe spaces." *this bridge we call home: radical visions for transformation*. Ed. Gloria Anzaldúa and AnaLouise Keating. New York: Routledge, 2002. 1-5. Print.

---. "now let us shift–the path of conocimiento–inner work, public acts." *this bridge we call home: radical visions for transformation*. Ed. Gloria Anzaldúa and AnaLouise Keating. New York: Routledge, 2002. 540—578. Print.

---. "When I write I hover." The Gloria Anzaldúa Reader. Ed. Ana Lousie Keating. Durham: Duke University Press, 2009. 238. Print.

—. *Light in the dark/Luz en lo oscuro: Rewriting Identity, Spirituality, Reality.* Edited by AnaLouise Keating, Duke University Press, 2015. Print.

Guentin, Victoria. *Shifting Toward a Spiritualized Pedagogy: Gloria E. Anzaldúa and Thich Nhat Hahn in Dialogue.* 2012. The Ohio State U, PhD thesis.

Halifax, Roshi Joan. "Practicing the Three Tenets and G.R.A.C.E. in our Imperiled World." 29th Nov. 2016. Web. 3rd May. 2024. <https://www.upaya.org/2016/11/practicing-three-tenets-and-grace/>

Keating, AnaLouise. *The Anzaldúan Theory Handbook*. Durham and London: Duke University Press, 2022. Print.

---. "I'm a citizen of the universe: Gloria Anzaldúa's Spiritual Activism as Catalyst for Social Change." *Feminist Studies* 34. 1-2 (2008): 53-69. Print.

Loy, David. "Enter … the Bodhisattva." Lions Roar. 16th April. 2006. Web. 7th May. 2024. < https://www.lionsroar.com/enter-the-bodhisattva-november-2012/>.

Nakao, Roshi Egyoku. "The Three Tenets."6+ *Zen Peacemakers*. Web. 7th May. 2024 <https://zenpeacemakers.org/the-three-tenets/>

Shih-t'ou. "Song of the Grass-Roof Hermitage." *DailyZen*. 22nd Dec. 1999. Web. 16th May. 2024. <https://www.dailyzen.com/journal/song-of-the-grass-roof-hermitage/>

Teish, Luisah. *Jambalaya.* New York: Harper & Row, 1988

Thich Nhat Hahn. "Going to the Shore of Non-Suffering. "*A Buddhist Library*. 13th Aug. 1997. Web. 28th April 2024. <https://www.abuddhistlibrary.com/Buddhism/G%20-%20TNH/TNH/The%20Other%20Shore/The%20Other%20Shore.htm>

HEALING OF CONOCIMIENTO

EXAMINING DISTORTIONS TO THE HUMAN PSYCHE THROUGH THE SPIRITUAL WISDOM OF GLORIA E. ANZALDÚA

MARK A. HERNÁNDEZ

> *To this day I'm not sure where I found the strength to leave the source, the mother, disengage from my family, mi tierra, mi gente, and all that picture stood for. I had to leave home so I could find myself, find my own intrinsic nature buried under the personality that had been imposed on me. I was the first in six generations to leave the Valley, the only one in my family to ever leave home. But I didn't leave all the parts of me: I kept the ground of my own being. On it I walked away, taking with me the land, the Valley, Texas.*
> *(Anzaldúa, Borderlands/La Frontera 16)*

In 1981, *This Bridge Called My Back* was first published, and Gloria Anzaldúa emphasized the need to correct the imbalance of "the rational, the patriarchal, and the heterosexual" in understanding the human person. She extended an invitation to "feminist-oriented men of all colors" to join the effort, alongside women, to reveal the injustices caused by male-dominated structures that erase and don't account for the lived experiences of women ("La Prieta" 50). Through her spiritual praxis, people who internalize hetero-patriarchal epistemology of the self, especially young men of color, are challenged to prioritize Indigenous, Queer, and embodied ways of knowing.

The importance of decentering the male body, male experience, and male-defined spirituality is critical for a holistic understanding of the self. Anzaldúa provides this roadmap for healing a dualistic understanding of sexual and spiritual energy through creative explorations of the self. Her non-dualistic spiritual anthropology integrates mind, body, and spirit by combating blank spots[1] in the human psyche. These blank spots are revealed through a spirit of openness and a willingness to engage in the creative writing process as a means of healing fragmented memories.

The goal of this discourse is to creatively engage with blank spots and distortions that exist in the human psyche using Anzaldúa's framework. In particular, focusing on ethnography as an embodied spiritual praxis, her Coyolxauhqui Imperative,[2] and seeking new perspectives with a nepantlera consciousness. As a result, sexuality as it connects to mystical spirituality can be seen as a complementary aspect of human development. The colonial, enslaver, and imperialist mentality embedded in dominant narratives fragments the spirit by distorting epistemologies through dualistic frameworks.

THE COYOLXAUHQUI IMPERATIVE AND NEPANTLERA CONSCIOUSNESS

Sacred storytelling is part of Indigenous Mesoamerican mythology and establishes a way to deepen the understanding of the self through autohistoria-teoria. Andrea J. Pitts outlines the key features present in Anzaldúa's autohistoria-teoria as collaborative, sensuously embodied, and productive. She states how, "Epistemic practices emerge via the forms of autohistoria that she describes, and require an interpretive community that can collaboratively render such experiences and forms of knowledge meaningful" (Pitts 365). Through analyzing the vision of Coyolxauhqui through a Queer and transformative lens, the sacred in the reinterpretation of this Indigenous anthropological story becomes visible. This story represents resistance to empire. This image is creatively explored by Heidenreich as she notes the different readings of the mythological text. She states, "While a patriarchal reading of the story can discourage action (the god of war is righteous, or, resist and you will die), this is not the reading that Anzaldúa

1. Anzaldúa refers to the distortions caused by dualistic consciousness as "binary thinking," "blank spots," and "Western dualisms." See Anzaldúa, Gloria E. "Geographies of Selves—Reimagining Identity: Nos/Otras (Us/Other), las Nepantleras, and the New Tribalism." *Light in the Dark/Luz en lo Oscuro: Rewriting Identity, Spirituality, Reality*, edited by AnaLouise Keating, Duke University Press, 2015, p. 82.

2. The term Coyolxauhqui (Ko-yol-shaUH-kee) is referring to the Aztec mythic goddess of the moon. Anzaldúa uses this folk story to show the importance of falling apart. She refers to this term as a process of dismemberment and dying to self. This process of integration, Coyolxauhqui imperative, ultimately "gives suffering a spiritual and soulful value." Anzaldúa, "Flights of the Imagination;" 29 see also Anzaldúa, "Geographies of Selves;" 92 and Keating, "Glossary." 243

and other feministas bring to the story. In feminista tellings, Coyoxauhqui's cause is righteous; her goal is to prevent the birth of the god of war" (Heidenreich 9). The body is distorted, fragmented, and broken by the heteropatriarchal gaze. This gaze influences and perpetuates violence toward women and people viewed as other. By critiquing dominant hetero-patriarchal narratives, the self can find meaning through this story encompassing human fragility.

The mythology of Coyolxauhqui represents her as the conquered and Huitzilopochtli as the colonial power. By analyzing Coyolxauhqui's position, from a Queer and Indigenous lens, it is apparent that Anzaldúa and feminist scholars critique gender norms, power dynamics, and repressive viewpoints. In contrast to the dominant filter placed in educational settings that prioritize Eurocentric hetero-patriarchal perspectives, Anzaldúa advocates a nepantlera (non-dual) consciousness "that does not rest on external forms of identification (of family, race, gender, sexuality, class, and nationality), or attachments to power, privilege, and control, or romanticized self-images" ("Disability & Identity" 302). The approach to letting go of attachments we have assimilated is a painful process and one Anzaldúa deems needed in our polarized time.

Anzaldúa refers to this path of liminal consciousness as becoming a nepantlera person. This person gains the spiritual, psychological, and physical tools to 1) connect with the body through performative creativity, 2) reject the limiting self-referential dualistic dominant narrative, and 3) challenge a monolithic understanding of Spirit that prevents human flourishing. Thus, these spiritual shape-shifters gain the ability to see the cosmic story and can become healers and bridge builders among contrasting beliefs, stories, and perspectives.

AUTOHISTORIA-TEORIA: CENTERING INDIGENOUS, QUEER, AND WOMEN OF COLOR ETHNOGRAPHIES

The narratives, writings, and stories of Gloria E. Anzaldúa provide new thoughts and perspectives that are relevant to exploring representations of the divine[3] depicted in non-dualistic, spiritual, and inclusive secular writings. Currently, the dominant spiritual practices in the Southwest borderlands are enmeshed with cultural Roman Catholicism. The dogmas present in Eurocentric methodologies give way to repressive storytelling that continues to erase and ignore the need for diverse secular literature to gain a deepened understanding of the human person. In this regard, M. Shawn Copeland states in the *Proceedings of the Catholic Theological Society of America* how these dominant narratives thus need to be recalibrated to heal the distorted consciousness of superiority

3. To align with Anzaldúa's terminology I will intentionally refer to God as Spirit, the divine, the sacred, and the universal consciousness. She discusses her efforts to find alternate words to describe the term "spirituality" as it is often misused. See Anzaldúa, "Within the Crossroads." 72-73.

and domination created in the human psyche that has "deformed not only our basic human living, but our religious, moral and intellectual praxis as well" (28).

Using autohistoria as a format for most of her writing, Anzaldúa represents a holistic model of encounter with the self and her community. She sees the writing process as a spiritual action and states, "The act of writing is the act of making soul, alchemy. It is the quest for the self, for the center of the self, which we women of color have come to think of as 'other'—the dark, the feminine ("Speaking in Tongues" 30). It is in and through writing that a spirituality of healing can be found for women of color and marginalized people. This writing process continuously reveals the self of the person writing.

There is a need to explore voices that have been systemically erased from spiritual, psychological, and embodied theoretical frameworks. Anzaldúa writings expand our understanding of the cosmic relationship to the inner wellspring of sustenance.

> When you're going through a lot of emotional pain and don't have anyone to support or help you, you're thrown back onto your own resources. You kind of surrender to the will of the universal consciousness, to God. Or you say, "I need help; I have to make changes in my life." You have to commit yourself through intention, so prayer is really good for that. . . . I had to find sustenance somewhere. I needed a connection with something outside myself that could sustain me but I was really fighting it. I didn't want to accept la diosa, that spiritual help—or maybe it's imaginal help, as it all takes place in the imagination. So when a woman or a group of women or men or a whole race has been oppressed historically, over and over, they have to create some means of support and sustenance in order to survive. ("Within the Crossroads" 72-73)

Liberation theology, in particular Womanist and Mujerista theology, takes into account the intersectionality of people's identity (Valentin 49; Mitchem 102; Pineda-Madrid 426). Liberation theology that centers marginalized voices seeks to delve into the lived experiences of people who experience oppression based on gender, language, and sex. To demand justice, it is imperative to showcase these voices and reveal the violence done to women, LGBTQIA+ people, and people of color. The need for such a liberative lens becomes evident when examining the widely circulated devotional text to St. Joseph, *Consecration to St. Joseph: The Wonders of Our Spiritual Father* (Calloway), which constructs a heteropatriarchal archetype of masculinity that erases the lived experiences of those on the margins and perpetuates theological violence.

In addition to a liberation theology, the writings of Irene Lara and Elisa Facio lay out the spiritual activism in Chicana, Latina, Indigenous, and Queer feminist activism-scholarship (3). Anzaldúa acknowledges that, although her relationship with the Catholic and Protestant churches was not fruitful, she states: "I couldn't really keep the spiritual down because I was always reading about mythology and religion. Then in college I took two courses: The Life of Christ, and The Bible as Literature. I'd read religion, but I just didn't believe what Protestantism and Catholicism were doing to the spirit" ("Spirituality, Sexuality, and the Body" 80). The institutional church, over time, has systematically failed to allow the human person to find wholeness through its dualistic catechetical lens, especially for the person who has been demonized through colonization and racism. This reality affects families and communities. Brenda Sendejo shares this relationship by stating, "Catholicism did not meet my political or spiritual needs, so I drifted away from it. I began to feel the need for some kind of spiritual practice. It was just something that I felt—the need for spirituality and the need for a deeper connection to my own spirit, something Catholicism failed to provide . . . I was angry at the patriarchal institution that had judged and oppressed me and those I love (82). Anzaldúa emphasizes the importance of finding nourishment for her spirit. These efforts are woven into her writings and her desire to find healing for herself, her community, and people seeking wholeness.

There can be a simultaneous educating of the human spirit to repressed memories and the cultivating of a society where belonging and inclusivity are paramount. Anzaldúa provides a solution to the dilemma of abusive rhetoric disseminated by people in power. Anzaldúa advocates for a form of resistance. This resistance consists of an active willingness to listen to new perspectives and develop a heart-centered facultad—one that fosters inclusivity, compassion, and the redemption of marginalized bodies.

At an early age, Anzaldúa developed a mature spirituality. This spirituality was heightened by the sudden traumatic death of her father, the bodily pain caused by early-onset of menstruation, and her developmental difference from her peers. All these occurrences developed her inquisitive nature, spirituality, and her sensitivity to the body. She found meaning and purpose through writing about and exploration of the self. Her efforts to bring healing are evident in her writings that center Queer, Indigenous and non-dualistic ritual practices.

In writing *This Bridge We Call Home*, Anzaldúa's intention is "to change notions of identity, viewing it as part of a more complex system covering a larger terrain, and demonstrating that the politics of exclusion based on traditional categories diminishes our humanness" (Anzaldúa, "(Un)natural bridges, (Un) safe spaces," 244). The path of spiritual shapeshifters is to inform consciousness through heart-knowledge and imagination. Exclusion based on external differences is destructive to human flourishing.

The new *mestiza* is a consciousness that is multi-ethnic, multi-racial, and not restricted to one mode of being. Remembering is necessary to help a person learn to shift among spaces. It helps a person make sense of their story, their trauma, and how these experiences have been repressed in people who do not look, speak, and act like white Eurocentric males. Combining theories from different marginalized groups is necessary to help bring justice for the violence inflicted on the human person when these narratives are not honored. Narratives play a pivotal role in transforming how we relate to one another. When we are willing to sit with the discomfort of someone else's story, we can expand our perspective and gain consciousness of our inherent blank spots.

THREE DISTORTIONS TO THE HUMAN PSYCHE

Healing conocimiento involves the lifelong process of being aware of the distortions that exist in the human psyche due to the narratives we listen to and absorb. Anna Blaedel states how Anzaldúa "describes conocimiento as a 'relational-onto-epistemology;' it represents a nonbinary, connectionist, transformative mode of thinking and being that tends to unfold within oppressive contexts and can assist with alliance-making" (Blaedel 354; Anzaldúa "Light in the Dark/Luz en lo Oscuro" 243).

Narratives play a critical role in the development of our understanding of self and the creative myth-making imagery of the divine. I describe these three distortions by outlining the process of healing fragmented narratives in the United States. This process is a thought experiment on how the writings of Anzaldúa can help reconcile cultural Roman Catholic faith with the development of an expansive, open-minded, and other-centered consciousness. The writings of Irene Lara, Diana Hayes, Cherríe Moraga, and Gloria Anzaldúa point to establishing a women-centered spirituality.

FIRST DISTORTION: SEPARATENESS TOWARD THE BODY

Living fragmented lives and choosing to ignore parts of our history is a root cause of developing distortions to the psyche. These parts that are ignored are seen as "our collective shadow" that we are invited to "confront and re-member" (Pitts 364). When speaking of our relationship to the divine I am rooting this discussion in our interconnectedness with all beings. The theologian and scholar-activist Robyn Henderson-Espinoza describes how Anzaldúa's understanding of the divine is ultimately seen as an interconnected spirituality in action. She states that,

> This turn inward toward the self as a potential relational spirituality is also a new and different epistemic feature that contrasts with the reliance of traditional god-worship and conventional religion on an external myth of God. It is from this bodily epistemic standpoint that we can begin to rethink relationality and re-imagine ourselves enfleshing a spirituality-in-acción (spirituality in action). (Henderson-Espinoza 111)

The need to inwardly reflect and spend time analyzing our behaviors and biases is central to rooting our connection to the sacred in the here-and-now. The distortions outlined below attempt to reveal internal blank spots[2] that must guide our reflection process. These blank spots often create harm to the self, our neighbor, and our relational spirituality. Using the Anzaldúan epistemology provided by Henderson-Espinoza, I will explore El Mundo Zurdo as the theological task of a "relational feminist theology of interconnectedness" (112). I make the case that this interconnectedness consists of actively understanding our positionality and examining blank spots that prevent: 1) embodied understanding of self, 2) interconnected sense of belonging, and 3) a relational spirituality.

The first distortion creates a separateness from our body. The body maintains an internal memory and holds trauma that the mind cannot repress. As the mind chooses to recreate stories, the body remains rooted in a fragmented and shattered state. The body can rebel against the mind by illness and seek to have us look at our wounds. Anzaldua emphasizes the need to develop an embodied resistance to the silence and erasure caused to marginalized peoples ("Haciendo Caras, Una Entrada" xxii).

Anzaldúa makes this point clear as she illustrates the connection of the inner and outer forces. These forces are in tune with each other. She shares how her relationship to the body and belief systems growing up prevented her from opening up to the body until she had a hysterectomy. She wrote about the disindoctrination process of unlearning the perspectives not helpful in seeking integration. She states:

> La curacion—the "cure"—may consist of removing something (disindoctrination), of extracting the old dead metaphors. Or it may consist of adding what is lacking—restoring the balance and strengthening the physical, mental, and emotional states of the person. This "cure" leads to a change in our belief system, en lo que creemos. No longer feeling ourselves "sick," we snap out of the paralyzing states of confusion, depression, anxiety, and powerlessness and we are catapulting into enabling states of confidence and inner strength. ("Metaphors in the Tradition of the Shaman" 122)

The stories we tell cannot be split from our body's reactions. Gloria Anzaldúa argues that there cannot be a story of healing that further divides the body, the mind, and the spirit.

By placing the theories of the Coyolxauhqui Imperative alongside the Genesis Story of Creation we can expand our anthropological lens. We live in a society that is fragmented and broken. This fragmentation is part of the human story. Creation stories and theories exist in religious traditions that seek to explain how the fragmentation happened. Even though these stories may be centered more on myth, they hold a more profound truth that we cannot discard.

In the Judeo-Christian narrative, the story of Adam and Eve forms the basis for Christianity's belief in humanity's broken nature. This creation story illustrates how the human person was disobedient to the will of the divine. This tale conjures theories of original sin, the Fall, and humanity's fragmented ways. Judaism and Christianity reference this mythological story found in the book of Genesis. Christianity, however, has taken a repressive view of the human body that leads to a distorted outlook on race, gender, sexuality, culture, and cognitive abilities (Copeland, "Scripture and Our Selves: Reflections on the Bible and the Body").

In Aztec mythology, the story of Coyolxauhqui (goddess of the moon) depicts the body of a female god being broken into many pieces and her decapitated head becoming the moon; the light in the dark. The Aztec myth portrays Coatlicue's[4] (mother of the gods) oldest daughter, Coyolxauhqui, convincing her 400 sisters and brothers to kill their mother who is impregnated with the god of war. Huitzilopochtli (god of war), nonetheless emerges fully armed as an adult form the womb, dismembering Coyolxauhqui and killing her siblings ("Let Us Be the Healing of the Wound"; "Putting Coyolxauhqui Together"). Coyolxauhqui's vision understands the gravity of having a god that brings war and division into the cosmic interconnectedness.

The myth of Coyolxauhqui influenced how Anzaldúa viewed the body and the non-dual approach she took to human fragmentation. She saw fragmentation as not something that needs to be feared or repressed. Instead, she saw healing and spiritual depth that arises from acknowledging our brokenness. For Anzaldúa, "Coyolxauhqui represents the psychic and creative process of tearing apart and pulling together (deconstructing/constructing). She represents fragmentation, imperfection, incompleteness, and unfulfilled promises, as well as integration, completeness, and wholeness" ("Border Arte" 50). Understanding Indigenous Mesoamerican mythology opens a pathway for Anzaldúa's non-binary thinking. She asserts the need to simultaneously deconstruct old ways of knowing and reconstruct new insights that bear healing for the human person.

The first step in bringing healing to our consciousness is by listening to the body, praying with the body, and experiencing a way to see the body rooted in the flesh and bones of our respective spiritual guides and ancestors. There needs to be a piecing together of the bodies numbed by physical, emotional, and patriarchal abuse. The bodies we inhabit need to be treated as sacred and revered.

Anzaldúa uniquely positions this healing method as a central pillar in her talk at Oregon State University ("The Difference, Power, and Discrimination Program" 1:46:36). She guides the people in attendance through a meditation practice rooted in the body, the earth, and the wellspring of knowledge that is present in the Spirit.

4. Pronunciation of Coatlicue (Kwat-LEE-kway). She is the earth goddess of life and death and mother of the gods. See Keating, "Glossary" 242.

See the feet as the roots of the tree, every time I breathe out visualize the root of my feet getting to the center of the earth; the cenote, my roots bring up the subterranean rivers from the middle of the earth, the nourishing waters flow from the center of the earth into my body. Bring up the cenote stream, I can visualize it orange or another color.

Take long, slow, deep breaths.

Think of all the mental activities happening in my mind and body; this is my first community, this is me. There is also an unconscious part that lies hidden in myself. I have both the positive and the negative. The inner self exists in my trunk, my roots, my branches, in the terrain around me.

Think of my mentors, my ancestors, my emotional community, this is my second community.

The third community—the special places I like to go to, the trees, the animals around me, the ocean, the wind, thunder, rain. Anzaldua goes to these things for calmness and sustenance.

The fourth community is the whole tree, this includes my whole family, aunts, uncles, ancestors from my family and the claims my family has on me, and the claim future generations have on me. Think of my immediate family.

The fifth community—my tree trunk, all the triumphs, mistakes, legacies of my ethnic group, this is where I struggle with racial prejudice, this is what keeps me upright.

The sixth community—a community of like minded people, a community that shares common interests, Anzaldua for example belongs to a community of writers, for example the Burger King club, or I own a Honda and I am faithful to Honda. Or I am in a community that watches the same tv show. I have a stake in this community and input. There are communities of interest that have nothing to do with ethnicity, or gender.

The seventh and outermost community—this is the geography Anzaldua talks about. My neighborhood, my city, my nation.

My identity is thus all these communities, not only ethnicity, class, etc.

My branches are going into the earth and getting substance from these places, there are little animals that live on me like birds and insects, there are vines that crawl up around me. We are all dependent on each other for sustenance and nourishment. It took all these different people to make the clothes I wear, the food I eat.

> *Think of myself as a tree that is near other trees, sometimes my branches will touch other trees. When I am in nature, I am really never alone. This concept of being alone and separate is a fiction. We think this because we are fragmented, our struggle is to bring us into harmony.*

Anlzaldúa's Coyolxauhqui Imperative and seeking to see in the midst of a dark reality, is a source of inspiration for people of the Southwest borderlands who have had their stories, experiences, and struggles erased, stolen, or fragmented. "Nuestra tarea is to envision Coyolxauhqui, not dead and decapitated, but with eyes wide open. Our task is to light up the darkness" ("Light in the Dark" 8).

Additionally, Davis states that "an intentional, embodied, ritualistic connection to spirit rooted in our Indigenous and cultural ways of being in relationship with ourselves and the world facilitates both resiliency and the healing of soul wounds caused by historical trauma. Therefore, intergenerational healing must require an examination into reclaiming and reimagining embodied spiritualities" (33).

SECOND DISTORTION: SYSTEMIC BIAS IN STORYTELLING

The second distortion is how we understand our narrative in relation to our neighbor. The institutions and social systems of the United States operate in a way that unconsciously and consciously privileges some narratives over others. Depending on the values, cultural milieu, and perceived benefits of some narratives, others get pushed to the side. Jesus' mission was to challenge narratives and engage people whose stories diverged from the Jewish tradition. There are three tendencies that reveal systemic bias in disseminating violent rhetoric: i.) the superior view of dominant narratives, ii.) misuse of energy to deconstruct dualistic renderings of the self, and iii.) the projection of the shadow self onto marginalized communities.

i. Inflated View of Dominant Narratives

The first tendency that causes the most harm is the superior view of dominant perspectives and narratives. This overinflation of the narratives from and about people in power creates a distorted view of the human person. Anzaldúa fights these injustices present in the overinflation of dominant narratives as she provides critical insight into the power of teachers to dismantle or perpetuate a repressive dominant ideology. This overlap shows the prevalence of how unjust teaching styles permeate secular and non-secular learning spaces. It becomes the lens from which we interpret the world and ourselves. This ability to silence voices in academia is expressed by a Chicana graduate student who shared with Anzaldúa her experience of racism in the classroom. She states that:

> Like many *mujeres*-of-color in graduate school, she felt oppressed and violated by the rhetoric of dominant ideology, a rhetoric disguised as good

> "scholarship" by teachers who are unaware of its race, class, and gender "blank spots." It is a rhetoric that presents its conjectures as universal truths while concealing its patriarchal privilege and posture. It is a rhetoric riddled with ideologies of Racism which hush our voices so that we cannot articulate our victimization. ("Haciendo Caras, Una Entrada" xxiii)

The importance of educators addressing the tendency to overinflate the Eurocentric dominant narratives by navigating diverse ideas and perspectives is pivotal for developing an inclusive consciousness. Acknowledging how some ideologies benefit some and hurt others is critical to seeking a liberative standpoint—one that allows us to bear witness and be capable of shapeshifting. This Spirit of belonging can reveal areas of growth, the need for a *corazón con razón*, and reveal particular blank spots in relating to perspectives of people on the margins. Perspectives that allow us to cultivate a compassionate worldview and be more sensitive to stories of difference. The Catholic spiritual anthropologist Copeland notes how the refusal to embrace difference limits our flourishing as she states, "In yielding to individual bias, these women and men not only stunt their personal affective and cognitive development, but their distorted experience becomes the foundation for aberrant understanding of others, impairs social relations, and affects cultural representation" (*Enfleshing Freedom* 14).

The refusal to be compassionate to people who are "different" will only damage our relationships with each other. The call for people seeking affective growth is to listen attentively to the voices that cry out with blood, sweat, and tears. We need to encourage teaching models that guide people to continual stages of psychic transformation. This healing of consciousness inspires a call to transform communities through compassionate acts of embracing differences.

Without critiquing dominant narratives, there becomes an overinflation of the self-narrative by people in power and a heightened fear of people whose stories do not align with these experiences. There is an indirect and direct silencing of everyone with an alternative viewpoint.

II. Misuse of Creative Energy

The second tendency is not as harmful to the cosmic narrative, but not the best use of energy. This tendency relies heavily on dismantling or only seeing the shadow side present in dominant narratives. Much of the mental and emotional resources that can be used to build networks of belonging are instead used to build political movements that rely on similar tools to those of the colonizer and forget to nourish the body, spirit, and mind. It uses the same dualistic patterns learned and can become misguided by the imperial tactics of imperial society. Anzaldúa expands on this distortion as she writes, "When marginalized groups fall back on defending identity as a strategy of resistance, when we cling to our identity as 'disabled,' 'immigrant,' or whatever and use identity as a basis for political mobilization, we inadvertently enforce our subordination" ("Disability & Identity" 302). Even though naming our identity is an important starting point for inspiring action, it must also hold within the beauty of communal encouragement, uplifting women mentors, and taking time to heal the self and pause the rat race. She describes how this may prove effective in the short term but questions its viability for long-term systemic change. This contention is relevant because it speaks to the act of healing consciousness from the perspective of marginalized people.

This tendency channels their efforts in the wrong direction, making it hard for this perspective to gain traction and provide long-term healing for the harm that has been done. While this route can be a much-needed release valve and venting space, it still results in an impoverished view of the self because it is not rooted in holistic, non-dual being-in-the-world.

III. Projection of the Shadow Self

The third tendency stems from people who inhabit multiple spaces and experience an internalized identity dilemma at an early age. This person has parts of their story in the dominant narrative and parts in the marginalized narrative. We see a trend in exclusionary political rhetoric that makes it easy for people who were once immigrants, foreigners, laborers to dissociate from parts of their communal story. Marcela García of the Boston Globe states, "It's an unconstitutional move that Abbott justifies using white supremacist language and rhetoric to describe an 'invasion' of migrants due to 'historic levels of illegal crossings.'" (García) This rhetoric creates an existential crossroads for people with intersectional identities. Society says their life will be easier if they align with the dominant narrative and forget and bury the marginalized, precolonized, dark-skinned, refugee, and migrant versions of their narrative. The marginalized narrative tugs at them throughout their lifespan, leaving them feeling incomplete, experiencing existential dread and a type of superficial façade that can consume them and lead to the projection of their repressed parts or "Shadow Self" onto marginalized communities. This person looks at themself in the mirror and denies their unique differences; as a result, they destroy their people through their gaze and inability to show compassion.

The way forward is to engage intersectional narratives as guides to become more at ease with holding the paradoxes and tensions of life. Anzaldúa refers to this consciousness in her theory of *nos/otras* (us/others). She states, "The future belongs to those who cultivate cultural sensitivities to differences and who use these abilities to forge a hybrid consciousness that transcends the 'us' versus 'them' mentality and will carry us into a nosotras position bridging the extremes of our cultural realities" ("Toward a Mestiza Rhetoric" 255). This hybrid consciousness is fostered in border spaces because, to survive, people need to hold the tensions of the dominant culture and, at the same time, remember their culture of origin.

Liminal narratives embrace the ambivalence and ambiguity that can be part of our everyday life. This shift toward learning to accept ambiguity is key to enacting networks of belonging. There are parts of the self that we can scapegoat onto people with diverse physical, sexual, and spiritual abilities. This false projection does not allow us to take ownership and responsibility for the areas of our lives that we must address, make manifest, and integrate into our whole personhood. This integration must seek proper naming of the areas that need healing within ourselves, before expecting our neighbor to adhere to all our preconceived notions of what constitutes acceptable spiritual, sexual, and interpersonal practices.

THIRD DISTORTION: MONOLITHIC IMAGE OF SPIRIT

The third distortion that arises from ignoring parts of our story is a distorted image of the divine. When we reject our story's gifts or limitations, we develop an impoverished view of ourselves. Integration comes with naming both our gifts and limitations. And in many instances, these aspects of the human person have meaning and significance for transformation.

By acknowledging only the giftedness of my nation, community, and social circle, I create an exclusionary viewpoint that tends to eliminate and erase anyone who does not have these gifts or reminds me of the failures of my ancestry that I have repressed. This viewpoint, in turn, leads to a misguided image of the sacred that excludes and is displeased with my limitations. A contemporary example of intentionally misguided imagery in widely used spiritual literature for lay Catholics is the book *Consecration to St. Joseph: The Wonders of Our Spiritual Father* which highlights the dehumanizing rhetoric toward gender identity and sexuality. The author states, "The times are tough. We're going through real confusion about things like marriage and family. People are confused today about what it means to be a man, a woman. Gender ideology has gotten a lot of people confused; people don't even know what bathroom to use… I contacted people all around the world. I asked people in France, Croatia and Poland" (Calloway, "It Takes a Father"). The images present in this text intentionally depict images of the divine as white, light skinned, overtly masculine males, and hidden within plain sight is language that takes a vehement stance and dehumanizes people on the margins and their families. This image can be dangerous as it can deeply wound the people that embody the limited parts of our story. This creates an impoverished worldview because we fail to see the self and our connection to others compassionately. This vision of the sacred is created from an orientation of fear of our perceived weaknesses and vulnerabilities. The distortion of a single narrative and erasure of a story can diminish our relationship to the self, neighbor, and the divine.

This false image of Spirit can lead to pessimism toward the self, my neighbor, and our cosmology. Anzaldúa's approach takes as its source her ancestors' mythical heritage and spiritual traditions to uncover the repressed parts of her history that colonial Catholicism has dismissed. She states:

> I propose a new perspective on imagining and a new relationship to the imagination, to healing, and to shamanic spirituality. Art, reading, and writing are image-making practices that shape and transform what we are able to imagine and perceive. In honoring the creative process, the acts of writing and reading, and border arte, I use cultural figures to intervene in, make change, and thus heal colonialism's wounds. I delve into my own mythical heritage and spiritual traditions, such as curanderismo and Toltec nagualism[5], and link them to spirituality, spiritual activism, mestiza consciousness, and the role of nepantla and nepantleras ("Flights of the Imagination" 44).

As a spiritual activist, Anzaldúa transforms colonized images of the divine by teaching us how to value non-binary thinking. The sacred holds the multiple parts of the self and wants us to find meaning in the continuous integration process.

It is hard to discover the authentic self if I am preoccupied with my limitations and embodied reality while losing track of the mystical embodiment and inheritance present in all things. This denial of one's gifts is a less painstaking process to overcome, yet is not an easy avenue for people who have endured physical, psychological, and spiritual trauma. These traumas such as global colonization, racism, slavery, xenophobia, sexual abuse, and objectification can leave a person distraught and unable to see the gifts they have been given because they have been robbed, tarnished, and vandalized by perpetrators of violence and hatred.

These three dispositions are meant to be continually healed and rejuvenated by telling our narratives in ways that do justice to the whole story. We bring these gifts and limitations together when we allow an Indigenous cosmology to inform the lens through which we view wholeness.

EL MUNDO ZURDO: CREATING NETWORKS OF BELONGING

Anzaldúa advocates a path to wholeness and addresses the gifts of education, spirituality, and psychology while acknowledging the need for intentional wrestling with the shadow parts of our personal and collective history. Anzaldúa also challenges our memory to fill in the gaps in the blank spots inherent in our cultural, societal, family, and experiential biases.

By unpacking the writings of a Mexican American of the southwest borderlands, we find pathways of dialogue, and a spiritual rootedness in self-transformation that is open to non-dual ways of thinking and living. Her exploration of liminal narratives demonstrates the power of autohistoria-teoría to grapple with conflicting perspectives through an embodied awareness of the self, integration with a women-centered anthropology, and an intentional spiritual praxis.

Anzaldúa's concept of El Mundo Zurdo (The Left-Handed World) is a great example of this, as this alternate world challenges colonial narratives that have misrepresented and, at times, demonized the stories of cultures that operate in non-dual ways. This new world fosters a space where diverse perspectives are prioritized, cherished, and celebrated.

As a Chicana woman writing from a liminal space, Anzaldúa maps out networks of belonging among marginalized communities. These networks require ongoing dialogue, transparency of privilege, and a desire to occupy the same spaces of communal exchange. Drawing from her lived experience, Anzaldúa documents new ways of communicating, healing trauma, preserving her roots, and actualizing her concept of El Mundo Zurdo.

El Mundo Zurdo not only challenges dominant and violent narratives, but it establishes a foundational interrelationality where belonging is central to human flourishing. The theme of belonging is present throughout Anzaldúa's co-edited work, *This Bridge Called My Back*. AnaLouise Keating states:

> For Anzaldúa, the left-handed-world represents a visionary form of community building where people from diverse backgrounds with diverse needs and concerns coexist and work together to bring about revolutionary change. El mundo surdo offers a methodology of relational difference and posits communities based on commonalities rather than sameness. (*The Gloria Anzaldúa Reader* 36)

These communities are formed through alliances, between women of color, people who are marginalized, and individuals cultivating a receptive consciousness. This left-handed world calls forward creative artists to break the rigid molds imposed by unchallenged patriarchy, sexist ideals, and racist practices. The new world proposed by Anzaldúa seeks to create networks of belonging through creative acts of compassion toward the self and our community. Through the retelling of stories, refiguring of bodies–both consciously and unconsciously harmed—and the embrace of an enfleshed spirituality, we can take steps to create an equitable world of relationships.

WORKS CITED

Anzaldúa, Gloria E. "Border Arte: Nepantla, el Lugar de la Frontera." *Light in the Dark/Luz en lo Oscuro: Rewriting Identity, Spirituality, Reality,* edited by AnaLouise Keating, Duke University Press, 2015, pp. 47-64.

—. "Disability & Identity: An E-mail Exchange & a Few Additional Thoughts." *The Gloria Anzaldúa Reader,* edited by AnaLouise Keating, Duke University Press, 2009, pp. 298-302.

—. "Metaphors in the Tradition of the Shaman." *The Gloria Anzaldúa Reader,* edited by AnaLouise Keating, Duke University Press, 2009, pp. 121-123.

—. "Flights of the Imagination: Rereading/Rewriting Realities." *Light in the Dark/Luz en lo Oscuro: Rewriting Identity, Spirituality, Reality,* edited by AnaLouise Keating, Duke University Press, 2015, pp. 23-46.

—. "Geographies of Selves—Reimagining Identity: Nos/Otras (Us/Other), las Nepantleras, and the New Tribalism." *Light in the Dark/Luz en lo Oscuro: Rewriting Identity, Spirituality, Reality,* edited by AnaLouise Keating, Duke University Press, 2015, pp. 65-94.

—. "Haciendo Caras, Una Entrada: An Introduction by Gloria Anzaldúa." *Making Face, Making Soul/Haciendo Caras: Creative and Critical Perspectives by Feminists of Color,* edited by Gloria Anzaldúa, Aunt Lute Books, 1990, pp. xv-xxviii.

—. "La Prieta." *The Gloria Anzaldúa Reader,* edited by AnaLouise Keating,Duke University Press, 2009, pp. 38-50.

—. "Let Us Be the Healing of the Wound: The Coyolxauhqui Imperative—La Sombra y el Sueño." *The Gloria Anzaldúa Reader,* edited by AnaLouise Keating, Duke University Press, 2009, pp. 303-317.

—. "Putting Coyolxauhqui Together." *Light in the Dark/Luz en lo Oscuro: Rewriting Identity, Spirituality, Reality,* edited by AnaLouise Keating, Duke University Press, 2015, pp. 95-116.

—. "Speaking in Tongues: A Letter to Third World Women Writers." *The Gloria Anzaldúa Reader,* edited by AnaLouise Keating, Duke University Press, 2009, pp. 26-35.

—. "Spirituality, Sexuality, and the Body." Interviewed by Linda Smuckler (1998). *The Gloria Anzaldúa Reader,* edited by AnaLouise Keating, Duke University Press, 2009, pp. 74-94.

—. "The Difference, Power, and Discrimination Program." *Oregon State University,* 24 Apr. 2003, Box 162, 7**. Time 1:46:36.

—. "Toward a Mestiza Rhetoric: Gloria Anzaldúa on Composition, Postcoloniality, and the Spiritual." Interview by Andrea Lunsford, 1996. In *Interviews/Entrevistas,* edited by AnaLouise Keating, Routledge, 2000, pp. 251-280.

—."Within the Crossroads: Lesbian/Feminist/Spiritual Development." Interviewed by Christine Weiland (1983). *Interview/Entrevistas,* edited by AnaLouise Keating, Routledge, 2000, pp. 71-127.

Ayala-Patlan, Andres. "Self-Change as Global Change: Spiritual Activism and Its Place in Gloria Anzaldúa's Legacy." *Journal of Feminist Studies in Religion,* vol. 36, no. 1, 2024, pp. 45-62.

Blaedel, Anna K. "Sacred Enfleshments: A Queer Theopoetics of Collective Liberation." 2024. Drew University, PhD dissertation.

Calloway, Donald H. *Consecration to St. Joseph: The Wonders of Our Spiritual Father.* Marian Press, 2020.

—. Interview by Joseph Pronechen. "'It Takes a Father': New Book Highlights Consecration to St. Joseph." *National Catholic Register*, https://www. ncregister.com/features/it-takes-a-father-new-book-highlights-consecration-to-st-joseph.

Copeland, M. Shawn. *Enfleshing Freedom: Body, Race, and Human Being.* Minneapolis, Minnesota: Fortress Press, 2010.

—. "Scripture and Our Selves: Reflections on the Bible and the Body." *America*, 21 Sept. 2015, www.americamagazine.org/issue/213/scripture-and-our-selves.

—. "The New Anthropological Subject at the Heart of the Mystical Body of Christ." *Proceedings of the Catholic Theological Society of America*, vol. 53, 1998, pp. 25-47.

Davis, Kimberly Jacinda. "Soul-to-Soul Healing: A Phenomenological Study on Reclaiming and Reimagining Embodied Spiritualities to Heal Historical and Intergenerational Trauma in Black Women." 2024. California Institute of Integral Studies, PhD dissertation.

García, Marcela. "Demonizing Migrants May Be the GOP's Most Consistent Platform. Just Ask Texas Governor Greg Abbott." *Boston Globe*, 15 July 022, https://www. bostonglobe.com/2022/07/15/opinion/demonizing-migrants-may-be-gops-most-consistent-platform-just-ask-texas-governor-greg-abbott/.

Heidenreich, L. "Sacred Heart of Coyolxauhqui: A Triptych." *El Mundo Zurdo 9: Selected Works from the 2022 Meeting of the Society for the Study of Gloria Anzaldúa*, edited by Sylvia Mendoza Aviña, Sonya M. Alemán, and Adrianna M. Santos, Aunt Lute Books, 2022, pp. 9-22.

Henderson-Espinoza, Robyn. "Gloria Anzaldúa's El Mundo Zurdo: Exploring a Relational Feminist Theology of Interconnectedness." *Journal for the Study of Religion*, vol. 26, no. 2, 2013, pp. 108-118. The University of Denver – Iliff School of Theology.

Lara, Irene, and Elisa Facio. "Introduction: Fleshing the Spirit, Spiriting the Flesh." *Fleshing the Spirit: Spirituality and Activism in Chicana, Latina, and Indigenous Women's Lives*, University of Arizona Press, 2014, pp. 3-18.

Keating, AnaLouise, editor. *The Gloria Anzaldúa Reader.* Duke University Press, 2009.

—. "Glossary." *Light in the Dark/Luz en lo Oscuro: Rewriting Identity, Spirituality, Reality*, edited by AnaLouise Keating, Duke University Press, 2015, pp. 241-246.

—. "Shifting perspectives: Spiritual activism, social transformation, and the politics of spirit." *EntreMundos/AmongWorlds: New Perspectives on Gloria E. Anzaldúa.* New York: Palgrave Macmillan US, 2005. 241-254.

Lopez, Christina Garcia. *Calling the Soul Back Embodied Spirituality in Chicanx Narrative.* The University of Arizona Press, 2018.

Mitchem, Stephanie Y. "Dialogue with Students: Teaching Womanist Theology." *Introducing Womanist Theology*, Orbis Books, 2002, pp. 101-102.

Pineda-Madrid, Nancy. "A Puerto Rican Decolonial Theology: Prophesy Freedom. Four Perspectives – III. History, Colonialism, and Imagination." *Horizons: The Journal of the College Theology Society*, vol. 45, no. 2, 2018, pp. 423-428.

Pitts, Andrea J. "Gloria E. Anzaldúa's Autohistoria-teoría as an Epistemology of Self-Knowledge/Ignorance." *Hypatia*, vol. 31, no. 2, 2016, pp. 352-368.

Radlwimmer, Romana. *Gloria Anzaldúa's Hemispheric Performativity: Pieces, Shuffles, Layers.* Springer Nature, 2023.

Sendejo, Brenda. "Methodologies of the Spirit: Reclaiming Our Lady of Guadalupe and Discovering Tonantzin Within and Beyond the Nepantla of Academia." *Fleshing the Spirit: Spirituality and Activism in Chicana, Latina, and Indigenous Women's Lives*, edited by Irene Lara and Elisa Facio, University of Arizona Press, 2014, pp. 80-101.

Valentin, Benjamin. "Strangers No More: An Introduction to, and an Interpretation of, U.S.Hispanic/Latino/a Theology." *The Ties that Bind: African American and Hispanic American/Latino/a Theologies in Dialogue*, edited by Anthony B. Pinn and Benjamin Valentin, Continuum, 2001, pp. 38-53.

CROSSING EL CENOTE

MEDITATIONS ON GLORIA ANZALDÚA'S BECOMING SERPENT

SALVADOR HERRERA

MEDITATION I: SACRIFICING THE SAVIOR

I was named after my father, and his father before him. In the Spanish tradition, to name a child "Salvador" is to recognize and honor Christ's sacrifice. "Salvador" means savior in English, and from a very young age I internalized a sense of responsibility to achieve as much as possible. Inspired by my parents' sacrifices, I wanted to help bring my family out from under the crushing cycles of economic precarity. This sense of responsibility extended to the way I perceive and navigate reality. I am primed to see racial and economic inequities in the world. I often feel it is my responsibility to take on the emotional weight of centuries of settler-colonial violence.

Even though my name has these religious overtones, I would describe myself as spiritual at best. This is part of what drew me to Gloria Anzaldúa's work when I was an undergraduate student. In *Borderlands/La Frontera*, I saw an alternative to organized religion, one that viewed the knowledge of colonized communities as legitimate sources of knowledge. I don't position myself as a savior or representative for any particular identity group. I am, instead, drawn to sacrificing aspects of my own identity and self-interests for a greater good. I believe we all have the capacity to act in ways that transcend the imposed boundaries between self and other. Rather than valorize the individual hero, Anzaldúa's work pushes us to form and act through an otherworldly sense of collectivity rooted in "spiritual activism": modes of self-care and solidarity that work toward social change (Keating 204-5). Spiritual activists tune in to what they perceive as the sacred force of life, one that permeates our existence but is thwarted by systemic injustice. In relational terms, spiritual activism acknowledges human differences but uses collective identity as a vehicle for transformation (205). Anzaldúa models a Chicana feminist practice of spiritual activism by reinterpreting cultural mythologies. Her reinterpretations refuse to compartmentalize spiritual belief from the natural and social sciences, including "psychotherapy" (40).[1]

Although Anzaldúa champions this bridge-building project across different modes of knowing, I believe that receptions of her work have been overdetermined by the spiritual aspects of her mythological hybridity. In her posthumous text *Light in the Dark (Luz en lo oscuro)*, Anzaldúa writes: "You hear la Llorona/ Cihuacoatl wailing. Your picture of her coiled serpent body with the head of a woman, shedding its skin, regenerating itself reminds you of the snake story in Genesis. A hunger to know and to build on your knowledge sweeps over you" (155). This perceived synchronicity—between Indigenous spirituality and the Christian bible through her symbolic reclamation of the "serpent"—allows Anzaldúa to honor forbidden feminine and Indigenous knowledge.

If we focus only on this spiritual analogy, however, scholars risk losing sight of colonial histories that imposed one mythos onto another. They also risk overlooking how oppressed peoples have resisted this practice of genocide through forms of cultural mediation which themselves alter the body, and therefore our "nature," at a material level. We overlook how snakes impress upon the human psyche at a neurological level, and in doing so model biological processes of transformation (e.g., "shedding its skin, regenerating itself…") that alter human behavior.[2]

Our coexistence with snakes is not purely symbolic. The reptilian, for Anzaldúa mediates the cultural connections between "Cihuacoatl," one of many serpentine fertility and mother goddesses of the Aztecs, "la Llorona," the folkloric weeping woman of Mexico who drowns her children in response to her husband's infidelity, and Eve, Christianity's first woman born of Adam's rib who was tempted by a demonic serpent in the garden of Eden. But serpents also mediate the false distinction between the spiritual scripts of culture and the secular taxonomies of

1. This process of reinterpretation and epistemological border crossing is part of what she refers to as "the path of conocimiento" (Light in the Dark/Luz en lo oscuro 121-159).

2. Anthropologist Lynne A. Isbell provides neurological evidence for the hypothesis "that the need to avoid snakes was ultimately responsible for the unique visual systems of primates," thus differentiating them from other species as part of an "evolutionary arms race" (12, 24).

nature endemic to Western modernity.[3] Consider, for example, the World Health Organization's logo involving a snake coiled around a staff. The symbol alludes to the Greek myth of Asclepius, a demigod who received his knowledge of the healing arts from his interactions with snakes. Asclepius was struck down by Zeus for fear that he would grant humans immortality. Under the healthcare system of the USA, we have substituted Zeus for corporate CEOs and shareholders.

And so, to counterbalance the Anzaldúan emphasis on the spiritual, I wonder what a "secular," psychoanalytic, and existential reading of *Borderlands* might offer contemporary audiences. By secular, I mean disciplinary modes of knowledge that distinguish themselves as not relying on metaphysical ideas to justify their methodologies and findings. I have in mind readers who might not appreciate Anzaldúa's creative interpretations of Mesoamerican cosmologies. Such readers may miss the significance of her philosophy of transformation when articulated through the "spirit world," especially as some critics view her myth-making as appropriative rather than imaginative or solidarity-oriented. Put another way, what would be the utility, if any, of a Chicanx ecofeminism without deities? How can Anzaldúa's methodology rupture inherited narratives and enable social transformation without requiring religious or spiritual belief on the part of political collectivities? How can "nature," rather than "spirit" per se, connect disparate interest groups who have a stake in revolution at a planetary scale?

Anzaldúa refuses to hold cultural phenomena "sacred" in Jamaican philosopher Sylvia Wynter's sense of the term (as in, transcendent, unchanging, and beyond critical reproach). I argue that Anzaldúa's repurposing of narrative is a secular strategy with the potential to make the ethics of spiritual activism accessible to a broader audience: one that places more faith in science than belief (45). In practical terms, I offer this meditative series of analyses as an example of how key Chicana feminist insights can be translated across discourses within and beyond the increasingly technocratic world-order of capitalism. Crossing disciplinary borders in this way makes room for "spiritual activism" to operate in multiple domains where power would otherwise dictate truth. This (post) humanist outlook inherent to Chicana feminism has the potential to make scientific knowledge more accessible, equitable, and impactful.

MEDITATION II: TRANSUBSTANTIATING THE SPIRIT

Having shared some of the significance of her work in my life, my second meditation probes the ramifications of the questions above by attending to the

3. The evolutionary framework of theologian Joshua M. Mortiz refuses the distinction "between moral evil and natural evil," and, therefore, the distinction between "instinct" and learned behavior (369-70). He instead takes up the idea of "moral emotional centers" as a cross-species capacity to harm and be harmed that predates humanity (367-68).

productive tensions between the secular and the spiritual in Anzaldúa's *Borderlands*. I draw attention to her chapters "Entering into the Serpent" and "La herencia de Coatlicue" in particular. In the first of these chapters, she writes:

> I know things older than Freud, older than gender. She—that's how I think of la Víbora, Snake Woman. Like the ancient Olmecs, I know Earth is a coiled serpent. Forty years it's taken me to enter into the Serpent, to acknowledge that I have a body, that I am a body and to assimilate the animal body, the animal soul (36).

By evoking Sigmund Freud and his theorizations on the unconscious, Anzaldúa stakes out an intervention in psychoanalysis. She ascribes a matriarchal and creative energy to the planet before the imposition of Western gender roles by evoking Olmec cosmologies. For the Olmecs, the serpent represented fertility, power, and the connections between the Earth and the underworld. Anzaldúa's "Snake Woman," then, would signal the interconnectedness of beings across multiple realms of existence. Furthermore, the Snake Woman would embody the endless creative potential of life to take on new forms. The spiritual element of this figurative understanding leads Anzaldúa to the utopian concept of "El Mundo Zurdo": a speculative space for those no longer oppressed. The "left-handed world" is one in which the mind, body, and spirit are reconnected after the ordeal of colonial compartmentalization.

However, there is a second valence, a psychoanalytic insight in her work that need not be limited to spiritual utopianisms. In secular terms, we can think here of the human brain stem and notions of pre-human instinct. This is the proverbial, palimpsestic "reptilian brain" said to predate the emergence of more complex mammalian structures.[4] We might also think of the ways in which embryos in the womb strongly resemble each other across multiple species. In this sense, Anzaldúa could be read as ascribing a serpentine sense of eroticism to nature. By this I mean an embodied sense of fluidity that precedes the social construction of gender, one that refuses to deny our animality.[5] Her shifts in consciousness enable her to see the interconnectedness of all things beyond national borders, cultural boundaries, and even species. This borderless consciousness allows Anzaldúa to develop a transformational sense of embodiment in line with actual snakes, rather than strictly relying on their spiritual symbology.

For example, Anzaldúa claims that, for the Olmecs, "the Serpent's mouth" is a "vagina dentata," a "sacred place," and "creative womb" in which life begins

---

4. The Triune Brain hypothesis has long been proven false, but comparative morphology is still useful for thinking about evolutionary history in relation to a common ancestor across species.

5. Consider Latinx Literary Studies scholar Suzanne Bost's brilliant discussion of Anzaldúa's fluid and "shape-shifting naguala" in relation to posthuman discourses (104–05). Bost reveals how Anzaldúa's speculative writings retool the power of the erotic in this sense (134).

and ends. But there is yet again a secular and psychoanalytic articulation of the snake's symbology that Anzaldúa makes available to us by recounting her childhood memories. She writes:

> After each of my four bouts with death I'd catch glimpses of an otherworld Serpent. Once, in my bedroom, I saw a cobra the size of the room, her hood expanding over me. I realized she was, in my psyche, the mental picture and symbol of the instinctual in its collective impersonal, pre-human. She, the symbol of the dark sexual drive, the chthonic (underworld), the feminine, the serpentine movement of sexuality, of creativity, the basis of all energy and life. (44)

In this reimagined scene, Anzaldúa's faculties are compromised and altered due to illness and her proximity to death. This proximity allows her to recognize the vision she has as a "mental picture" featuring a cultural "symbol," rather than the actual appearance of a deity in animal form per se. She recognizes the cobra as a manifestation of her unconscious, a manifestation of queer sexuality that was repressed until the "hood" of the snake encapsulated her entire being. The cobra stands not only for her "dark sexual drive" and the "underworld," but also for the erotic power of creativity inherent to the cyclical nature of life before the emergence of humanity. The cobra embodies this duality of good and evil, of life and death, which would otherwise be separated into mutually exclusive dichotomies by the moral orders of coloniality and modernity.[6]

Anzaldúa's experiences and research into ancient cultures lead her in the next chapter, "La herencia de Coatlicue." Anzaldúa's practice of Chicanx feminist reinterpretation enables her to understand Coatlicue, the Aztec fertility goddess with a skirt made of serpents, as an avatar of Tonantzin (a broader concept signifying multiple manifestations of the mother earth goddess). She then theorizes the "Coatlicue state" as follows:

> *Coatlicue* is a rupture in our everyday world. As the Earth, she opens and swallows us, plunging us into the underworld where the soul resides, allowing us to dwell in darkness...*la Coatlicue* is the consuming internal whirlwind, the symbol of the underground aspects of the psyche. (55)

I understand Anzaldúa's Coatlicue state as akin to depression, a temporary state of the body that slows us down before transformation, a state in which

6. Further along in "Entering into the Serpent," Anzaldúa explicates the significance of losing a cosmological sense of interconnectedness and duality not only to the rupture of colonization, but more gradually over the rise of the Aztec empire. She refuses to blame the fall of the Aztecs on Octavio Paz's condemned cultural figure of La Malinche (i.e., Malintzin, the enslaved and raped war-bride of Spanish conquistador Hernán Cortes). She instead considers the Aztec empire's own betrayal of other Indigenous groups through a culture of war that created class divisions and disenfranchised women.

we must interrogate, and integrate, insights from our experiences of trauma. By "plunging" into the "darkness" of the "underworld," Anzaldúa suggests that we must turn inward and sit with the uncomfortable contradictions at the center of our being as a "prelude to crossing." To advocate for the crossing of one's unconscious fantasies is to argue that marginalized populations have an unconscious at all. It is to assert that their psychic experiences are worthy of analysis, theorization, and care. Furthermore, to shift from Coatlicue as a deity of worship to an embodied psychic "state," marks the secular potential of Anzaldúa's theories of consciousness for altering humanity's self-perception.

Such a practice—of introspectively analyzing inherited cultural fantasies—is often painful. One must grapple with the existential threat of one's identity and name meaning nothing beyond what we construct in language. Anzaldúa reminds us that this psychic state of listlessness, while necessary, is not a way of life.[7] It is a stage leading to the reclamation of the self beyond imposed identities. One cannot "remain stone forever" (58). Anzaldúa aspires to a sense of self that is always in flux through a turn to universal, borderless consciousness. She does so by deifying the unconscious and re-symbolizing goddess avatars that have been hijacked by colonialism.

Still, there is yet another secular way of grasping Anzaldúa's philosophy of transformation, one that does not rely on mythological figures. She writes, "And suddenly I feel everything rushing to a center, a nucleus. All the lost pieces of myself come flying in from the deserts and the mountains and the valleys, magnetized toward the center. *Completa*" (60). Anzaldúa comes to understand her body as being composed of fragments of the earth that are held together by the invisible force of magnetism. The "nucleus" at her "center" is metonymically aligned with a planetary vantage point. In the face of the never-ending darkness of the cosmos, Anzaldúa no longer feels "alone." She no longer feels existential angst over what her identity means because she recognizes her body as literally made up of the natural ecology of the universe. This is what it means to feel "complete," for her, exemplifying the possibilities of Chicanx ecofeminism.

MEDITATION III: CREATING A WOMB WITHOUT BORDERS

After having considered Anzaldúa's women of color feminist and ecocritical approach to psychoanalysis, I turn now to my third and final meditation. Here, I will tie her theoretical concept of "el cenote," or "the sinkhole," to the "darkness" of the Coatlicue state. I explore the multiple definitions of this concept below. Broadly speaking, el cenote refers to the groundwater sinkholes of Mexico which

---

7. For more on the existentialism of Anzaldúa's work, consider philosopher Mariana Alessandri's exciting book which reflects on depression as a mode of knowing that has been disavowed by Western thought and toxic positivity culture (106–32).

are imbued with spiritual significance. Anzaldúa takes up these sites as a metaphor for the unconscious, as identified by Chicana philosopher AnaLouise Keating in The Anzaldúan Theory Handbook. El cenote bridges a series of dichotomies, including but not limited to conscious/unconscious, self/collective, and secular/spiritual. The word "cenote" does not appear in Borderlands, but it helps me conceptualize the gaps or voids that Anzaldúa traverses in said text. On the one hand, she literally crosses a hole in the fence between the U.S. and Mexico that attempts to divide land into nations (15–16). On the other, she pursues imaginative retreats into the dark abyss of herself as a form of psychic crossing.

Keating cites the first appearance of this conceptual thinking in Anzaldúa's unpublished autohistoria "Esperando la Serpiente con Plumas" (96). Written in 1982, Anzaldúa uses a depth model of psychology and the metaphor of "fishing" to describe the process of making repressed traumatic "objects" within herself conscious (99). This is essentially the goal of classical Freudian psychoanalysis—to make ourselves aware of our traumatic attachments and unconscious patterns of behavior so that we might live and "act" differently.[8] We can thereby understand Anzaldúa's *Borderlands* as conducting a psychoanalysis of multiple cultures across the Americas that have impinged upon her particular subjectivity.

Later, in 1989, Anzaldúa describes going into "el cenote" as a process of catching "the fleeting, fleeing images of events and feelings stored within the tissues of the body." Here, el cenote is not simply a cavern within the self, but a dispersed array of traumas that harden at acute points in the body like tension-filled knots. Crossing el cenote here would mean to "fish" for and reimagine one's relationship to memory. The space of flow and release created therein allows for the visualization of one's dynamic role in collective evolutionary processes. Hence the possibility of transcending the spiritual/secular binary or, at least, holding the two in tension.

Anzaldúa's concept continued to evolve into the 21st century. In 2003, she ascribed a sense of agency and aliveness to el cenote that spans multiple generations:

> El cenote, the well of inspiration, the source of our guiding voices, contains our depth consciousness, a greater knowledge that comes up/out in creative work and in moments of conocimiento. Their sources come from the generation of ancestors that live within us and permeate every cell in our bodies…Other sources are the higher centers within that we

8. In their Studies on Hysteria (1893-1895), Sigmund Freud and Josef Breuer offer two theorems toward this effect: that symptoms of hysteria have their roots in "precipitating trauma," and that the "affective strength" of said traumas of the psyche must be diminished through cathartic "abreaction and reproduction in states of uninhibited association" (7, 13, 228). In essence, it is not simply the reliving of trauma that brings relief, but its resignification in a safe setting where the patient can determine the meaning of an event on their own terms beyond what was originally encoded into the body.

> are not aware of because we are separated or exiled from them. We are in touch with only a small corner of the entirety of our inner universe. (97)

In this formulation, the knowledge stored within el cenote is inherited, but its memory has been closed off to us (i.e., repressed). She continues to toe the line between the secular and the spiritual, as our "ancestors" are both "cellular," biological beings, and transcendent voices that speak to us from beyond the grave. For Anzaldúa, this human inheritance is a form of knowing within the body that transcends everyday perception.

Anzaldúa describes two ways of accessing el cenote in this respect. The first is to engage in an aesthetic act through el cenote as a "creative womb," or, as a site of erotic imagination within one's self. The second method is more so a communal process of forming solidarity across differences in the form of what she calls "conocimiento." Latinx Studies scholar Theresa Delgadillo notes that this seven-stage process toward "social justice" is something of a middle ground between the secular and the sacred (9). The path of conocimiento is an invitation to those who do not have spiritual beliefs but nonetheless share similar political interests and are open to seeing life from new perspectives. Forms of cultural mediation put this ethos into practice across the discourses of psychoanalysis, Chicana feminist philosophy, and even the natural sciences.

The strength of Anzaldúa's formulation of "el cenote" lies in locating the unconscious in the body, but also everywhere else at once. For her, el cenote's potential lies in the yet-to-be-discovered insights of the universe that are contained within the smallest particles of our being. So, rather than dialing in a telescope and scheming to colonize Mars, Anzaldúa's cosmology sets her sights inward to reflect on the interpenetration of nature and culture. She adopts a speculative imaginary, comparable to the Earthseed religion in Octavia Butler's *The Parable of the Sower*. This imaginary understands all things as being made up of stardust in a state of constant flux. Neither of these worldviews is an apolitical, feel-good form of New Age spirituality. Anzaldúa insists that we engage with el cenote as it bridges the nation's modern nation with its dark colonial underbelly.

In the introduction to the conference proceedings from the 2007 meeting of El Mundo Zurdo, Chicana feminist philosopher Norma Alarcón notes the importance in Anazaldúa's work of engaging the Jungian "shadow" of U.S. politics in particular, given its position of power on the world stage (21).[9] This shadow is "el cenote," the unconscious, a site of silenced histories that our bodies carry at the cellular level. It is a site of repressed forms of interlinked oppressions around the globe that must be brought to light so that our relationships

9. See the work of Literary Scholar Matthew A. Fike to understand the distinctions between Jungian depth psychology and the work of psychologist James Hillman from Anzaldúa's "conocimiento" (63).

to trauma can be transformed. This cannot be achieved, however, without excavating the self so we can show up for others, and for ourselves, as needed.[10]

With respect to the concept of El Mundo Zurdo, I wonder whether its emergence and reach might be hampered by requiring its participants to subscribe to a spiritualist ontology (even if said worldview is open to multiple cultural manifestations). My meditation here is in dialogue with Delgadillo's thesis that the emergence of a "new mestiza conscious" requires "spiritual mestizaje" (1). This formative concept in the field of Chicana feminism refers to a critical, "self-reflexive," and "transformative renewal of one's relationship to the sacred." For Delgadillo, spiritual mestizaje is an embodied queering of spirituality that ruptures "oppressive discursive paradigms" (6–8). These ruptures break from colonial uses of religion and spirituality.

In thinking of Anzaldúa's serpentine transformation across el cenote in secular terms, I am not suggesting that one must choose between the secular and the sacred by any means. In fact, Chicana feminist principles of contradiction allow us to probe their intersections, and the concept of el cenote itself allows for discussions across both. Delgadillo has noted that both a culture of "postmodern secularism" and the secular politics of the state have lent themselves to the dismissal of Indigenous ways of knowing, and thus risk reinscribing patriarchal orders (18).[11]

Instead of critiquing or denying the spiritual aspects of Anzaldúa philosophy, in my meditations, I have turned to what I see as the repressed secular strategies of her spiritual concepts. Probing this intersection can broaden the audience that her ideas reach. Rather than interpret serpents as a sacred symbol of an otherworldly force, we might understand them as biological beings—sacred by virtue of their existence. These are beings that model for us the ability of all life in our ecosystem to transform as they shed their skin.

---

10. This step is a necessary prelude to what Anzaldúa calls "the new tribalism": a means of forging connections between seemingly disparate communities by sharing stories across our differences. The new tribalism is a means for inclusion that marks the boundaries between communities as permeable, rather than treating them as fixed borders in service of power.

11. In that respect, there is power to be found in collective spiritual movements that respond to the workings of both the state and capitalism. After a conference of Catholic bishops who congregated in Columbia in 1968, Peruvian priest Gustavo Gutiérrez published Theología de la liberación in 1971. This philosophy of liberation theology, when put into practice, encouraged clergy members to champion the poor and disenfranchised in the face of corrupt political establishments serving the rich elite across Latin America. Following the word of God as much as the word of Freud, Marx, and Hegel, Gutiérrez conceived of "First World" and "Third World" divides as marking zones of struggle over the meaning of history toward the experience of "dynamic liberty" (18). We might also consider the transnational "umbrella collective" Mujeres de Maiz, a "spiritual artivist feminist network" emerging during the 1990s in East LA after the Zapatista uprisings in México (González et al. 13).

This secular shift—from discerning the meaning of snakes to focusing on their functional capacities—takes us even further from the negative connotations ascribed to the serpent by colonial religious orders.[12] Such a cleavage can enable us to reshape our relationships to each other and the natural world from which we are made. We might then imagine forms of care and community that move beyond surviving under a capitalist system. And so, my lingering questions are: How can both spiritual and secular worldviews expand our collective ethical imaginations? In what ways is a Chicanx feminist and ecological worldview strengthened by the spiritual? Can our crossings of el cenote be guided by secular understandings that center the planet's survival?

My meditations ultimately suggest that the spiritual and secular are two modes of understanding the contours of reality, perspectives that need not be in opposition. Whether they articulate it as "spirit" or "nature," humans have the capacity to imagine collective political action that transcends the borders of the state and its economic systems of valuation. In the face of existential threats such as white supremacy, reproductive control, transphobia, and climate change, solidarity under, and synthesis across, the broadest epistemological framework is necessary now, perhaps more than ever. Rather than looking for figures of salvation, we must continue developing theories of transformation and putting them into practice.

For more practical models, we might turn toward Black feminist struggles for abolition, Indigenous struggles for land reclamation, and modes of body modification, gender-bending, and world-building emergent across trans* communities. Across these seemingly disparate domains, Anzaldúa's model of spiritual activism offers a bridge between the secular and the sacred, where both sides can be held together in all of their contradictions. By contrast, my secular application of her work demonstrates a mode of translating across disciplines. Both approaches are necessary to bring communities together and foster intersectional knowledge production—that we might cross el cenote, together.

12. In this respect, I am deeply inspired by the work of Sylvia Wynter and her method of decipherment (266).

WORKS CITED

Alarcón, Norma. "Introduction Becoming MeXicana with Gloria Anzaldúa." *El Mundo Zurdo: Selected Works from the Meetings of the Society for the Study of Gloria Anzaldua, 2007 & 2009*, edited by Norma E. Cantú and Christina L. Gutiérrez, 2010, pp. 17–21.

Alessandri, Mariana. *Night Vision: Seeing Ourselves through Dark Moods.* 2023.

Anzaldúa, Gloria. *Borderlands / La frontera: The New Mestiza.* 5th edition. Aunt Lute Books, 2022.

—. *Light in the dark/Luz en lo oscuro: Rewriting Identity, Spirituality, Reality.* Edited by AnaLouise Keating, Duke University Press, 2015.

Bost, Suzanne. *Shared Selves: Latinx Memoir and Ethical Alternatives to Humanism.* University of Illinois Press, 2019.

Delgadillo, Theresa. *Spiritual Mestizaje: Religion, Gender, Race, and Nation in Contemporary Chicana Narrative.* 2011.

Fike, Matthew A. "Depth Psychology in Gloria Anzaldúa's Borderlands/La frontera: The New Mestiza." *Journal of Jungian Scholarly Studies*, vol. 13, June 2018, pp. 52–70, https://doi.org/10.29173/jjs13s.

González, Amber Rose, et al., editors. *Mujeres de Maiz En Movimiento: Spiritual Artivism, Healing Justice, and Feminist Praxis.* University of Arizona Press, 2024.

Gutiérrez, Gustavo. *A Theology of Liberation: History, Politics, and Salvation.* Orbis Books, 988.

Isbell, Lynne A. "Snakes as Agents of Evolutionary Change in Primate Brains." *Journal of Human Evolution*, vol. 51, no. 1, July 2006, pp. 1–35, https://doi.org/10.1016/j.jhevol.2005.12.012.

Keating, AnaLouise. *The Anzaldúan Theory Handbook.* Duke University Press Books, 2022.

Moritz, Joshua M. "Animal Suffering, Evolution, and the Origins of Evil: Toward a 'Free Creatures' Defense." *Zygon*, vol. 49, no. 2, 2014, pp. 348–80.

Wynter, Sylvia. "Rethinking 'Aesthetics': Notes Towards a Deciphering Practice." *Ex-Iles: Essays on Caribbean Cinema Ex-Iles*, edited by Mbye B. Cham, Africa World Press, 1992, pp. 237–79.

READING PERLA SÁNCHEZ AS COATLICUE

REMEMBERING LAS ATRAVESADAS

LAURA M. LOPEZ

In the mid-2000s, writer Belinda Acosta published two young adult novels as part of a series called the "Quinceañera Club Novels" with plots that incorporate a quinceañera rite of passage for the Latina protagonists. To date, while other Latina YA novels[1] have approached the quinceañera topic through light-hearted plot or character development, Acosta's novels deploy the quinceañera as a ritual and space for healing broken family relationships. Moreover, in her second novel in the series, *Sisters, Strangers, and Starting Over*, the quinceañera is significantly overshadowed by the inclusion of a social justice theme focused on the Ciudad Juárez femicides.

In a previously published article on Acosta's second novel, I argue that elements in the plot structure construct a literary testimonio to set the record straight on silencing Latinas in the family; readers witness Perla Sanchez reinstated into the family narrative through the quinceañera ritual ceremony after twenty-five years of erasure.[2] This current article re-examines Perla's character through a different lens, one that draws from Mesoamerican Aztec mythology,

1. Novels such as Malin Alegria's *Estrella's Quinceañera* (2007), Veronica Chambers' *Amigas: Lights, Camera, Quince!* (2010), and Monica Gomez-*Hira's Once Up Quinceañera* (2021).

2. "Testimonio Witnessing of Gender-based Violence in Belinda Acosta's Sisters, Strangers, and Starting Over." *International Journal of Young Adult Literature*, vol. 3, no. 1, 2022, 1-15.

Mexica history, and feminist archaeology to connect Latine historical and cultural roots of misogyny to literary representations of violence towards Latina atravesadas in contemporary YA literature. In this new reading, I propose that Perla's character represents a postmodern, mythic atravesada echoing the ancestral Mexica atravesada goddess Coatlicue, the matriarchal Mexica goddess that legends recount was symbolically sacrificed, dismembered, and erased by both the Mexica and the Spanish conquistadores. Moreover, the novel restores the mythic Perla to her rightful place in the family through a matriarchal-led community ritual to correct the family injustice, and in doing so it links to the matriarchal ways of the Toltecs, precursors of the patriarchal, militant Mexica, who revered Coatlicue. Lastly, I propose that one of the legends of Coatlicue, documented by Fray Diego Duran, offers a Mesoamerican feminist manifesto for addressing systemic gender violence today.

A brief overview of the three legend strands surrounding Coatlicue reveals the history of patriarchal imperialism in Latine cultural roots. Around AD 1163, the Mexica invented a legend about the birth of their sun god Huitzilopochtli (the god of war), adopting Coatlicue as his mother and as the cosmic earth goddess who gives birth to all celestial beings. Historians, folklorists, and archaeologists have documented three major legends as (1) the birth of Huitzilopochtli and the plot to kill her, (2) Coatlicue's self-sacrifice to save Huitzilopochtli, and (3) an older Coatlicue, forlorn over her son's abandonment and prophesying the demise of the Mexica empire to Spanish conquistadores.

THE LEGENDS OF COATLICUE

In the first legend, recounted in Grisel Gomez Cano's *The Return to Coatlicue: Goddesses and Warladies in Mexican Folklore* (2010), Coatlicue gives birth to Huitzilopochtli who then plots to kill her. In the story, Coatlicue is impregnated by a feather that falls into her skirt. When her daughter Coyolxauhqui discovers the pregnancy, she urges "her 400 brothers to kill Coatlicue and the illegitimate growing fetus" (Gomez Cano 115). However, Coatlicue is warned about the scheme. Huitzilopochtli, growing inside his mother's womb, promises to protect her. When Coatlicue's offspring arrive to kill her, Huitzilopochtli emerges out of the womb fighting, dressed as a warrior. Armed with a fire weapon, he decapitates all of them. Coatlicue forgives her children and "transform[s] Coyolxauhqui into the moon and the other children into stars in the southern sky" (Gomez Cano 115).

In the second myth, Coatlicue sacrifices herself along with her four sisters to save Huitzilopochtli. Archaeologist Cecilia Klein's research on Mexica mythohistory through early colonial documents recounts the legend that Coatlicue and her four sisters voluntarily sacrifice themselves to give birth to and energize the sun (235). Klein argues that the famous statue of Coatlicue represents her as an important creator goddess who, prior to the Mexica leaving Aztlán, helped to create a habitable world (235). In their book *Queer Ancient Ways* (2018), Zairong Xiang challenges Klein's empowered view of Coatlicue by contending that her reading does not explain Coatlicue's "dismembered and decapitated appearance" (215), as depicted in the famous statue of the goddess in the Museo Nacional de Antropología in Mexico City.

The third legend, documented in Fray Diego de Duran's *The Book of the Gods and the Rites* in the late 16th century, depicts an older Coatlicue, depressed over her son's abandonment and the violence Mexica leaders exercise on neighboring communities. In this myth, a severe drought of more than five years compels Montezuma to send his troops and wizards to locate Coatlicue in the ancestral lands of Aztlán with gifts to regain her favor. They find her in filth, mourning at the peak of a magical hill. Coatlicue reprimands them for "having done many injustices to others, becoming cruel in their search for power, and abandoning their families" (Gomez-Cano 20). She predicts their doom: they will be driven from their land and possession, foreshadowing the arrival of the Spanish conquistadores. Gomez Cano contends that through this legend "Coatlicue condemns militarism and demands the restoration of old family values and harmony with the earth" (20). Moreover, Coatlicue's "concerns are similar to those of many women throughout world history who have experienced violence and family disintegration during periods of war and hunger: They want imperialism to end" (Gomez Cano 20).

During the period of the Toltecs (eleventh century AD), female goddesses like Coatlicue had positive attributes and were revered, especially in agricultural communities, characterizing a matriarchy that disappeared when the Mexica came to power. In *Borderlands/La Frontera*, Gloria Anzaldúa delineates some of the characteristics of Toltec society: "Matrilineal descent characterized the Toltecs and perhaps early Aztec society. Women possessed property, and were curers as well as priestesses. […] the royal blood ran through the female line" (33). The Toltecs revered Coatlicue but her attributes are later transformed by the Mexica, who revise her symbolically into a "ghastly, hostile force" (Castillo 10). By the time the Mexica dominate the area in AD 1324, the militaristic, patriarchal rulers have revised the stories of female goddesses to ones that instill fear in their people and enemies, emphasizing gruesome death rather than the fertile earth goddesses of earlier times. These revised Creatrix stories became demeaning and threatening representations used to justify women's subjugation and status in Mexica society, condoning violence towards women, in particular rape, enslavement, and sacrificial use of women's bodies to Mexica male gods. The new narratives supported the ruling powers and highly stratified social hierarchies of the time period, favoring male nobles over maidens. It was a system in which "males could enjoy sexual freedom, but women could not lose their virginity before marriage" or else they were subject to strict laws and punishments: "ridicule, ostracism, and death" (Gomez Cano 142). Symbolically, the patriarchal, militaristic, Mexica culture "drove the powerful female deities underground," says Anzaldúa, "by giving them monstrous attributes and by substituting male deities in their place, thus splitting the female Self and the female deities. They divided her who had been complete, who possessed both upper (light) and underworld (dark) aspects. Coatlicue, the Serpent goddess, and her more sinister aspects, Tlazolteotl and Cihuacoatl, were 'darkened' and disempowered [...]" (27). When the Spanish arrived, the conquest in 1521 bolstered and intensified gender and social discrimination. Over time, Spanish patriarchy establishes the cult of Marianismo, measuring women through the idealization of the Virgin Mary/Virgen de Guadalupe, and becomes the model for young women. That model was emphasized at home, schools, and churches, and one in which "women could easily bring dishonor to their families by losing their virginity" (198, 247). The Spanish deemed Coatlicue and other Mexica goddesses as antithetical to the Virgen Mary image and Spanish colonial norms for women, so they buried these icons literally and historically. When overtaking Tenochtitlan, the Spanish drove the female goddesses underground by building the Zocalo of Mexico City over Tenochtitlan's Templo Mayor. All indigenous religious icons, considered heathen and demonic representations, were intentionally stamped out of history to build the new colonial city as one imperial power took over another empire. The Spanish patriarchy targeted atravesadas even in their own people, such as Sor Juana Ines de la Cruz and St. Teresa de Avila. This Mexica/Spanish/Mexican history of stamping out of matrilineal heritage and positive female deities while creating a cultural system of female oppression, suppression, and control forms a deeply rooted, multilayered, reinforced patriarchal system of gender oppression within our culture that has endured for nearly a millennium. When Belinda Acosta writes the character of Perla Sanchez in *Sisters, Strangers, and Starting Over*, the story completely resonates with a long-standing tradition of Latine women silenced in their families and who are subject to acts of violence by the men in their own culture.

PERLA SÁNCHEZ, LA ATRAVESADA

Sisters, Strangers, and Starting Over centers on the developing relationship between its two main characters: Beatriz Sánchez-Milligan, an educated, mid-life Chicana living with her family in San Antonio, Texas, and her fourteen-year-old niece Celeste, who comes to live with her aunt after losing her mother, Perla, Beatriz's younger sister. The novel traces their lives as each main character comes to terms with emotional issues surrounding Perla's life and death. As a teenager, Perla's rebelliousness and unplanned pregnancy cause a rift between her and the family; unsupported during this crisis, Perla exiles herself to the Juarez border unbeknownst to the family. Decades later, she is killed in Juárez for her maquila labor activism. Perla Sánchez becomes one of the many females murdered in Juárez, Mexico, and thus the novel incorporates a social justice theme that, according to Acosta, was written deep in the background of the plot per the publisher's mandate to sideline it as the plot focus. Yet, the unfolding of Perla's mysterious disappearance and demise dominates the plot, and—particularly for those concerned about social justice—the theme begs to take center stage. Perla's carefully interwoven story emerges from the deep background to document the erasures of young Latinas and the violent consequences of breaking with traditional expectations for females in Latinx and Chicanx culture.

Without a doubt, Perla is an atravesada on many fronts. Anzaldúa defines los atravesados as the "prohibited and forbidden" inhabitants of the borderlands (*Borderlands* 3). Perla's character breaks the behavioral norms for women in her family, cultural proscriptions stemming from Mexica and Spanish patriarchal social structures established more than 500 years before. Yet, Perla is a millennial and her daughter Celeste is Gen Z. The setting is not ancient Mesoamerica or colonial Mexico; it's the contemporary Southwest United States, yet the same cultural norms are still operating in the story. Perla's premarital sexual activity is discussed in the plot but revealed through the unplanned pregnancy. No mention of Celeste's father in the story points to Perla's single-parent status. As an outspoken leader in Juárez, she draws attention to herself, which ultimately leads to her kidnapping and murder. Like Anzaldúa, who described herself as "kicking out with both feet" at anything that constrained her (16), Perla has been a rebel, an atravesada, her whole life.

The unfolding of Perla's story takes place through fragments embedded in the novel, revealed through key female characters in the book: her older sister Beatriz, her daughter Celeste, and a journalist working in Juárez named Josie. The reader's understanding of Perla develops slowly, and the reader must piece together fragments scattered throughout the story from those who had direct experiences with her. Since Perla's character is largely in the background and readers do not experience scenes with her, her story is told through second-hand accounts, which gives Perla's life a mysterious and mythical quality. We learn a bit about Perla's life as a young person from her sister Beatriz. The youngest member of the Sánchez family, Perla is described as "a little wild. Not bad, really, but so hardheaded" (Acosta 58). Beatriz and Perla are ten years apart and Perla looks up to her older sister. When Beatriz moves away to attend a university in Michigan, Perla loses her anchor and begins to have (undetailed) behavioral problems. By the time Perla is a teenager, her now elderly parents cannot control her. Perla bounces around different extended family homes with little direction (she is described as "lost"). Perla arrives at Beatriz's doorstep in Michigan, single and pregnant, having traveled 1200 miles to seek her help. Fearing Perla's troubled life will compromise her developing relationship with boyfriend Larry Milligan, whom she later married, Beatriz sends her on the first bus back to Texas. Essentially, Beatriz betrays her sister, and that is the last time Beatriz encounters Perla alive. No one hears of her whereabouts until 25 years later when Perla's daughter shows up on their doorstep in San Antonio. The reader discovers that Perla never returned home but exiled herself to Juárez, away from her birth family to the edge of the border region, to lead a nepantlera's life.

Beatriz's descriptions of the young Perla exemplify Anzaldúa's discussion of the effects of parental mirroring on the young child's developing identity: parents' responses to their children, the way they see them, can act as a mirror shaping how young people see themselves as loved and accepted versus judged and dismissed. Anzaldúa writes in *Borderlands*, "There is another quality to the mirror [aside from a portal for travelling souls] and that is the act of seeing. Seeing and being seen. Subject and object, I and she. The eye pins down the object of its gaze, scrutinizes it, judges it. A glance can freeze us in place; it can 'possess' us. It can erect a barrier against the world. But in a glance also lies awareness, knowledge. These seemingly contradictory aspects—the act of being seen, held immobilized by a glance, and 'seeing through' an experience—are symbolized by the underground aspects of Coatlicue, Cihuacoatl, and Tlazoteotl," which Anzaldúa calls the "Coatlicue state" (42). As a young child, Anzaldúa acquired the sense that there was "something fundamentally wrong" with her, "[b]y the worried look on [her] parents' faces" (43). Trauma experts like Bessel van der Kolk from *The Body Keeps the Score* assert that the quality of the first gazes from our parental figures during critical periods of childhood brain development are key to healthy self-development and even a sense of vitality as adults. Young children take pleasure in being seen and without it, our adult emotional health is affected. Writing about the shame over her bleeding disorder that made her feel different as a child, Anzaldúa's words could be coming out of Perla's mouth: "Her soft belly exposed to the sharp eyes of everyone; they see, they see. Their eyes penetrate her; they slit her from head to belly. Rajada. She is at their mercy, she can do nothing to defend herself. She has to learn to push their eyes away. She has to still her eyes from looking at their feelings—feelings that can catch her in their gaze, bind her to them" (43). "Ay mama, tan bajo que me he caido" (Anzaldúa 44). "She has this fear that she has no names that she has many names that she doesn't know her names … she won't find the way back" (Anzaldúa 43). Perla makes herself disappear after feeling abandoned by her family and once she is gone, they make her name and memory disappear in the family narrative.

As a young adult, Perla is disregarded by her family—unseen—that is, until she breaks their norms and she is judged unworthy. Since Perla has broken the norms of Marianismo, the family then rejects Perla and makes her invisible again. Even her favorite sister, Beatriz joins the rest of the family in their silence and ostracization of Perla, striking her very name from the family history. Rejected, Perla removes herself from the family and goes underground in the interstitial space of the borderlands. Subsequently, in her new community (Juarez), Perla asserts herself by standing up for the women of the maquilas, speaking out on economic injustice in a capitalist space of female exploitation. In the process, her atravesada behavior is judged once again as unacceptable and punishable; she is kidnapped and murdered, her final erasure. Atravesadas go through this continual process of being seen and unseen in an effort to assert their subjectivities in a family and culture that does not like differences or challenges to the imperialist patriarchal systems operating for millennia.

Perla's character echoes Coatlicue's own erasure post-Spanish conquest. Earlier, this essay summarized the history of Aztec gods and goddesses and polytheistic practices that were driven underground by the Spanish in 1521. Zairong Xiang's book chapter on Coatlicue Mayor recounts that two hundred years after Coatlicue's statue was uncovered in 1721, it was taken to a science university to be examined. "Friars and professors of the university soon regarded the statue as a demonic presence of Aztec paganism [...] so dangerous that the 'idol' might contaminate the Mexican youth. For this reason, this 'satanic symbol' was soon buried again" (Xiang 211). In 1803, German scientist Alexander von Humboldt received permission to view the statue; it was unearthed and quickly buried a third time because "'the presence of the terrible statue was unbearable'" to him. Coatlicue's statue literally went through a process of being seen and unseen, along with other Mexica goddesses, whose stories were revised because the patriarchy was threatened.

During the lost years of Perla's life when she exiles herself to the border, the Sánchez family labels Perla as "the black sheep," someone "to be ashamed of" (Acosta 257). An unspoken family rule develops in the Sánchez familia that forbids the mention of Perla's name over the 25-year period. "Even Beatriz didn't know how that rule came into being or when it was understood that she would not be included in talk of old times or mentioned in the family tree. She knew it was wrong—to have Perla's name erased from their tongues, even if she was alive in their memories—but she went along" (Acosta 122). Like Coatlicue, whose story is silenced and whose statue is buried underground, Perla is silenced in her own family for what she represents, a threat to the norms for young Latinas.

Rosalinda Fregoso argues that "intracommunity silences" acts as a linchpin of the Chicano familia romance to preserve its problematic gender ideology in the culture. *Sisters, Strangers, and Starting Over*, challenges the patriarchal ideology of the Chicano familia romance.

Through Celeste, the reader learns that Perla moved to the El Paso-Juárez border after the rejection from her family to create a life for herself and her daughter. We learn that she was a caring and thoughtful mother. We also learn about her demise. Celeste witnesses her mother's kidnapping and she is in a susto when she arrives at Beatriz's house. She carries with her a packet of documents and photos sent to the family by the journalist. The documents contained within are grotesque and horrific pictures and stories of Juárez victims. Beatriz's husband Larry Milligan wants to keep the packet unopened, hidden, and deeply buried because the pictures bother him; the information is disruptive to the idyllic life he has tried to create after his own humble beginnings in a working-class single parent family. He is possessive of Beatriz and feels threatened by the "dark" and "disturbing" Celeste. "*There was just something dangerous and, well, too foreign about Celeste that he couldn't shake*" (Acosta 164). The narrator reveals Larry's racial and gender prejudices, which are kept hidden from Beatriz through outward displays of liberalism.

In the chapter segment that focuses on Josie's experiences with Perla in Juárez, Josie's character fills in the gaps about Perla's life during the "lost" years. Perla has developed into an outspoken leader positively impacting a Latinx community in need. Perla eventually became a labor organizer in the electronic maquila where she worked in Juárez, and she also participated in charity work in El Paso with the surviving family members of murdered women from the U.S. side of the border (Acosta 93). Josie describes Perla as a petite woman with a large presence in Juárez due to her community organizing efforts. The young, outspoken, rebellious child had grown into an outspoken, fierce woman known as "la chingona" in the Juárez community because she was "a fighter, a survivor" (Acosta 93). Perla stands up for the women in Juárez, critical of the manner in which the media portrays their stories, sensationalizing the violence with no direct effect on the lives of the mujeres who continue to be killed. Emulating Coyolxauqui healing and assembling the pieces of her life together (Anzaldua and Keating 20), Perla has constructed a new life and identity for herself during this underground period. She acts for social justice, focusing on the community of women in Juárez, rather than on her own past experiences. Once again, Perla is an atravesada refusing to remain within the boundaries prescribed for Latine girls and women, stepping on the toes of patriarchal hegemony in Mexico, and, unfortunately, it comes with a cost.

Perla's visibility and credibility through her community activism in Juárez cause her to become a target. In Josie's words, "[t]here's nothing more dangerous than a woman who's discovered the full range of her power [voice]" (Acosta 103). Chicanx and Latinx cultural norms encourage females to remain silent, voiceless, invisible, and compliant with the mechanisms that control her. "Perla had moved beyond that" controllable, silenced woman (Acosta 103), and thus she became a victim of the oppressive violence she worked to expose. The details of her murder are not given, only that she is taken in the middle of the night and then later found dead. Perla's story becomes the story of the murdered Juárez women. The Juárez femicides have predominantly targeted young girls (13-18 years old) who work in maquiladoras. At the time Acosta was writing the novel, five activists were killed (in the 2010s). "There have never been as many femicides in Juárez as there were in 2010, when the city was controlled by the military at the height of Calderón's war on drugs." (Milz). Perla is a warlady, a threat to the capitalist system as a labor union activist and to the system of violence against Mexican women who have no voice, so she is silenced and murdered. This silencing has been enacted since the time of the Coatlicue legends, since Mexica revised the goddesses' myths, since the Mexica army kidnapped women from neighboring communities, enslaved them and then sacrificed them to appease the sun god Huitzilopochtli, and since the Spanish buried the statues of Coatlicue, Coyolxauhqui, and others. The level of violence towards women is prevalent today in Juárez, in Mexico, Latin America, the United States. *El Paso Matters* reports the continued waves of violent Juárez femicides. In January 2022, newspapers reported on the case of a U.S. Chicana lesbian couple from El Paso, living in Juárez, whose bodies were found dismembered in garbage bags and dumped on a public road (Kocherga). For Latine women, subjugation and dismemberment are baked into the goddess iconography of Coatlicue and Coyolxauhqui, their Mexica revised legends, norms and practices.

RECLAIMING PERLA THROUGH THE MATRIARCHY

In *Borderlands*, Anzaldúa delineates how Coatlicue intercedes on a Latina's behalf to conocimiento: "We need Coatlicue to slow us up so that the psyche can assimilate previous experiences and process the changes. [...] Coatlicue states which disrupt the smooth flow (complacency) of life are exactly what propel the soul to do its work: make soul, increase consciousness of itself. Our greatest disappointments and painful experiences—if we can make meaning out of them—can lead us toward becoming more of who we are. Or they can remain meaningless. The Coatlicue state can be a way station or it can be a way of life" (46). AnaLouise Keating writes that Anzaldúa later expands her ideas of the Coatlicue state into nepantla and the conocimiento transformation process in her posthumously published collection *Light in the Dark*.

Beatriz is in a depression for a large part of the novel, guilty over her betrayal of Perla 25 years before, over rejecting her sister Perla and choosing a white man over her, and over participating complicitly with the silence. "My resistance, my refusal to know some truth about myself brings on that paralysis, depression—brings on the Coatlicue state" (Anzaldúa 48). Coatlicue necessarily slows Beatriz down. This is how eventually, she is able to become in touch with her feminine strength, to stand up for her sister among the large group of family members and heal the family's betrayal. "'Knowing' is painful because after 'it' happens I can't stay in the same place and be comfortable. I am no longer the same person I was before" (Anzaldúa 48). This discomfort inspires Beatriz to enter a level of consciousness that awakens her loyalty to Perla. The day of the quinceañera, Beatriz takes action to correct the injustices to her younger sister. As in the Coyolxauhqui imperative, Beatriz re-members and reconstructs Perla's position in the family through a process of community healing during the quinceañera ritual. At the novel's conclusion, Acosta crafts the quinceañera scene in a way that shatters the silence around Perla's name and counteracts her erasure from the family history. Beatriz ceremoniously breaks the family silence when she introduces Celeste as Perla Sánchez's daughter in the presence of the entire Sánchez-Milligan family. As Celeste makes her entrance, Beatriz opens the ceremony:

> "I don't have much to say except that I am so grateful to see this day come, when I can present to you, mi sobrina, Celeste Josefa Sánchez, the daughter of our dear, departed sister..."
>
> For a split second, Beatriz could sense the catch in her throat, as if all those years of imposed silence might cut off her breath and keep the words from coming out. But Beatriz was tired of being silent, tired of feeling guilty, tired of not saying the name of her sister.
>
> "Perla Sánchez, en paz descanse," Beatriz said proudly. (Acosta 298)

After a moment of silence, Beatriz begins a call and response sequence, shouting the name "Perla Sánchez!" over and over until each family member begins to respond "Presente!", ending with the entire family roaring "Presente!" in unison (Acosta 298) and "[t]he guilt that had suffocated [Beatriz] all those years had been cleared like cobwebs and let loose to fly off and away" (Acosta 299). Through the shattering of the silence, Perla becomes reinstated into the family's history, and Beatriz is able to move forward from the guilt. She is no longer stuck, embrujada. Thus, Acosta employs Celeste's quinceañera as a vehicle for reinscribing Perla back into her Chicanx family history. The intracommunity silence within the Sánchez family is broken, creating a counternarrative. Beatriz's character sets the record straight, repairs the past betrayals by breaking the silence, seeing and naming Perla, and thus reinscribing her narrative into the family history. At the conclusion of the quinceañera, Celeste also participates in the reinscription and reconstruction of her mother's memory and the women of

Juárez's when she symbolically marks the close of the ceremony by placing a rose on two empty chairs. Celeste condemns the violence of Juárez femicides using a symbol of nature and the earth. She reinscribes her mother's rightful place in the family ceremony, while simultaneously connecting her death to Juárez femicides and condemning the violence through one final symbolic gesture. Both sister and daughter take action in the renaming of Perla, in her reassembly and her reintroduction to the family. This act is a powerful symbolic act of matriarchal, female-led efficacy, the complete antithesis of Coatlicue's most well-known Mexica legend, that of the matricide plot led by her daughter and the slaughter of all Coatlicue's children by Huitzilopochtli as punishment. Daughter against mother, woman against woman, brother against sister, and family against family are sanctioned through this Mexica cultural myth.

In the novel, Acosta uses a matriarchal network of mostly strong female characters—sister/daughter/friend (Beatriz/Celeste/Josie)—to restore Perla's mythic narrative, to basically bring justice to Perla's mistreatment by the family who adheres to the patriarchal cultural scripts for Latinas. Anzaldúa believed that "it is imperative that mestizas support each other in changing the sexist elements in the Mexican-Indian culture. ...the struggle of the mestiza is above all a feminist one.... The first step is to unlearn the virgen/whore binary and to see 'Coatlapopeuh-Coatlicue in the Mother, Guadalupe'" (*Borderlands* 84). Recalling the third legend of an older Coatlicue documented by Fray Diego de Duran, we encounter an angered and emotionally distressed Coatlicue, disturbed by the Mexica violence and community injustices to build an empire in the name of her son Huitzilopochtli. "Coatlicue condemns militarism and demands the restoration of old family values and harmony with the earth. Her concerns are similar to those of many women throughout world history who have experienced violence and family disintegration during periods of war and hunger: They want imperialism to end" (Gomez-Cano 20). Repairing family and cultural injustices through a matriarchal, female-centered value system is the "Coatlicue imperative," a feminist manifesto for combating imperialist dogma and patriarchal practices. Coatlicue's matriarchal manifesto calls for social justice for women violated or erased like Perla, a break with the binary Western ways of thinking that create Perla as an atravesada while her sister Beatriz is normative, and anti-imperialist ways that prioritize family and relationships over greed, power, and domination. It is imperative that young Latinas today learn about the historical roots of the cultural norms that operate in their lives as if they existed since time immemorial. It is also imperative they read YA fiction with social justice themes like Acosta's work that go beyond the cultural rituals that may obfuscate and reinforce the binary beliefs and customs that keep patriarchal and constraining structures for Latinas in place.

Las atravesadas, like Coatlicue, Sor Juana, Gloria Anzaldúa, Perla Sánchez, Belinda Acosta, and others, are simply asking for the controlling silence and violence towards all atravesadas to stop. The gift of novels like Acosta's, writing like Anzaldúa's and Castillo's, and research like Gomez-Cano's, is the gift of knowledge and stories that uncover the hidden realities of las atravesadas, dismantle patriarchal structures deeply entrenched in a patriarchal culture, re-envision them, and inscribe new possibilities. They are calling for harmony, peace and justice for all; for families not to turn a blind eye to the rebels who kick outward and to hold up the mirror—to see the true worth in atravesadas who push boundaries; for the nation states of Mexico and the United States not to turn a blind eye but to bring justice to the Juárez femicides and to stop the violence. Coatlicue is still lamenting the injustices of imperialistic ways inflicted upon women and children. Addressing these injustices by returning to matriarchal ways of knowing and being is imperative to preserve our cultural ways, our people, and the earth through more millennia.

WORKS CITED

Acosta, Belinda. *Sisters, Strangers, and Starting Over*. Grand Central P, 2010.

Anzaldúa, Gloria. *Borderlands/La Frontera: The New Mestiza*. aunt lute books, 1987.

—. *Light in the Dark/Luz en lo oscuro. Rewriting Identity, Spirituality, Reality*, edited by AnaLouise Keating, Duke UP, Durham, 2015.

Brumfiel, Elizabeth. "Figurines and the Aztec State: Testing the Effectiveness of Ideological Domination" in *Gender and Archaeology*, ed. R.P. Wright, 143-166. U of Penn Press, 1996.

Castillo, Ana. *Massacre of the Dreamers: Essays on Xicanisma*. 20th Anniversary edition. UNM: 2014.

Fregoso, Rosa Linda. *meXicana encounters: The Making of Social Identities on the Borderlands*. U of California P, 2003.

Gomez Cano, Grisel. The Return to Coatlicue: Goddesses and Warladies in Mexican Folklore Xlibris, 2010.

Klein, Cecilia. "A New Interpretation of the Aztec Statue Called Coatlicue, 'Snakes-Her-Skirt.'" *Ethnohistory*, vol. 55, no. 2, Spring 2008, pp. 229-50. Kocherga, Angela. "Recent Killings of Women in Juárez Spark Protest, Dispute Over Gender-based Violence." *El Paso Matters*, 2022.

Milz, Thomas. "'Oasis of horror': In the Mexican border town of Ciudad Juárez, women and girls have been dying and disappearing for the past 30 years." *Neue Zürcher Zeitung*. 2022.

Xiang, Zairong. "Coatlicue Mayor: Or, Other Ways of Rereading the World." *Queer Ancient Ways: A Decolonial Exploration*, Punctum Books, 2018. pp. 203-40.

JULIA DE BURGOS

SELF-TRANSFORMING VERSE BY VERSE

ALINA S. LUGO

INTRODUCTION

Gloria Anzaldúa's words resonate with the life and work of Julia de Burgos, a Puerto Rican poet from the early 20th century. Burgos questioned her socio-cultural surroundings through writing, created new avenues for self-understanding, and followed her own path. During her lifetime, Puerto Rican society repressed feminine multiplicity, thus leaving Burgos outside of literary, nationalist, and feminine circles. Similarly, Anzaldúa faced multiple boundaries without knowing "which side to turn to, run from" (*Borderlands* 216). Connecting Burgos with third-world feminists like Anzaldúa and others is an essential step for decolonizing her writing and placing her within an intellectual community, in which she is no longer an *otra* (other). Rather, Burgos is a *nepantlera* who writes to express her multiplicity, imagine decolonization, and engage in self-transformation.

While some critics may focus on the political, cultural, erotic, or feminist aspects of Burgos' work separately, applying Anzaldúa's seven stages of *conocimiento* demonstrates that each component is inseparable and strengthens one another. Like *Coyolxauhqui*, Burgos has been ripped apart and split in many ways. Anzaldúa also wrestled with the problem of writing "without being inscribed (reproduced) in the dominant white structure" (*Light* 7). Thus, this paper aims to apply Anzaldúa's theories to Burgos' work to achieve a decolonized perspective.

While the essay primarily focuses on Anzaldúa's writings, it also draws on other third-world feminist theorists because they often overlap and coincide with each other. For instance, the additional Chicana/Xicana lens of Emma Pérez applies to the Puerto Rican context for her approach to nationalism, colonialism, and identity. In addition, contemporary critics of Burgos' poetry, including Consuelo López Springfield, Vanessa Pérez Rosario, and others, work towards a decolonized image of her. The following overview provides an explanation of the seven stages of *conocimiento* as it applies to Julia de Burgos' life and work, as well as the essay structure. Overall, the essay demonstrates how Anzaldúan concepts, especially the seven stages of *conocimiento*, and third-world feminist theory demonstrate Burgos' multiplicity and self-transformation.

AN OVERVIEW OF BURGOS' LIFE AND WORK THROUGH ANZALDÚAN THEORY

In *Light in the Dark/Luz en lo oscuro: Rewriting Identity, Spirituality, Reality*, Gloria Anzaldúa outlines seven stages of *conocimiento*, which overlap and are not chronological. To begin, Anzaldúa describes the rupture stage as a shattering and questioning of reality (124-5). Due to her social landscape, Burgos experienced many ruptures. Therefore, this essay categorizes them along the following lines: colonial, national, gender, and imperial. Additionally, this essay identifies the following intermediary spaces: true vs. false self, feminine vs. political voice, one-dimensionality vs. multiplicity, and us vs. others. The *nepantla* stage, according to Anzaldúa, is composed of intermediary spaces where tension, transformation, and healing occur (2). Hence, for this essay I combined the rupture and *nepantla* stages to address Burgos' complex social reality and subsequent subversive strategies.

"Putting *Coyolxauhqui* together," according to Anzaldúa, is a stage of reconstruction that also happens in all stages (140). Since eroticism and the decolonial imagery matter for the comprehension of Burgos' work, in the essay, I divide the "Putting *Coyolxauhqui* together" stage into two sections. Further inspired by Hélène Cixous' and Emma Pérez' theories, I explore how eroticism and the decolonial imaginary inform reconstruction.

I interspersed the remaining four stages of Anzaldúa's seven stages of *conocimiento* throughout the essay. The "call" is a stage of brief, temporary awareness, where "longing for your potential self is an ache deep within," according to Anzaldúa (135-6). However, when we heed the "call" and test these beliefs, they may fail. Anzaldúa identifies this experience as the "blow-up" stage (123). The

Coatlicue stage embraces contradiction and plunges the subject into a process of destruction and construction that leads to completeness and knowledge (*Borderlands* 68-73, 96). Lastly, according to Anzaldúa, spiritual activism is an internal and external stage that shifts realities, transforms, and develops alliances (*Light* 150).

The ruptures in this essay are ordered chronologically, according to developments in Puerto Rican history, with an additional gender rupture. Together, they form a spine from which other stages are explored in this unchronological process. Hence, the analysis begins with the colonial rupture.

THE COLONIAL RUPTURE: FALSE VS. TRUE SELF

The colonial rupture occurs when Julia de Burgos grapples with Puerto Rican history and social restrictions. Spanish colonization of the island dates back to the turn of the 15th century, which included relying on the forced labor of indigenous populations, who were then replaced by enslaved Africans (Stark 20-1). Hence, Burgos often explores the *nepantla* between social constructions and freedom, or the false and true self, by identifying with the marginalized, rejecting social norms, and connecting emotion with knowledge.

Burgos' poetic voice does not identify with the elite colonizers, as demonstrated in "Yo fui la más callada" ("I Was the Quietest One"): "No ships heavy with opulence carried me, / no oriental rugs supported my body" (111). Furthermore, this marginalized position is regarded as superior because the poetic voice is at peace with their conscience and can express their truth "with no more weapon than a verse" (Burgos 111). Another example is "Ay, ay, ay de la grifa negra" ("Ay, Ay, Ay of the Kinky-Haired Negress"), in which the poetic voice declares that their grandfather was a slave, as opposed to the master (Burgos 33). However, from a third-world feminist perspective, this *nepantla* can also be interpreted through Pérez's conception of hybridity as "two halves, the colonial decayed self and the decolonized free self" (113). Hence, Burgos can also move between both sides.

Burgos navigates this *nepantla* through *naguala* in poems such as "A Julia de Burgos" ("To Julia de Burgos"). Anzaldúa defines *naguala* as "the imagination's power to shift" from one identity to another (*Light* 84). "A Julia de Burgos" ("To Julia de Burgos") is written in first person and the poetic voice declares: "You are the cold doll of social lies, / and me, the virile starburst of the human truth" (Burgos 3). The poetic voice often shifts between the two selves:

> You are a housewife, resigned, submissive,
> tied to the prejudices of men; not me;
> unbridled, I am a runaway Rocinante
> snorting horizons of God's justice. (Burgos 3)

Anzaldúa's concept of double-seeing also applies because a split in awareness helps reveal myths (*Light* 127). In Burgos' case, the myth is social conformity as the ideal truth.

In response to colonial divisions, Anzaldúa opts for the Aztec connection between writing and wisdom that can occur through poetry and image as "a bridge between evoked emotion and conscious knowledge" (*Borderlands* 91). For instance, in "A Julia de Burgos" ("To Julia de Burgos"), Burgos uses metaphor to equate herself with "a runaway Rocinante," which represents untamed, beastly freedom. Hence, through poetry and her knowledge of *Don Quijote*, Burgos arrives at the wisdom that she does not fit within a socially constructed house. The poetic voice opts for borderless horizons instead, thus initiating the "call" stage.

THE "CALL"

In "Transmutación" ("Transmutation"), the poetic voice declares:

> Here there is no geography for hands nor spirit.
> I am over the silence and in the silence itself
> of a transmutation
> where nothing is edge… (Burgos 65)

The poem is an example of the "call" stage because, according to Anzaldúa, the body is more than categories and freedom occurs "by widening the psyche/ body's borders" (*Light* 134). *Conocimiento*, as defined by Anzaldúa, also applies because it occurs when our ways of living no longer accommodate our identity. As a result, you ache to expand past these limits and "take responsibility for consciously creating your life" (*Light* 118, 136). For Burgos, the "call" is about pushing these borders, reconceptualizing identity, and rethinking the past and present.

The path towards *conocimiento* includes opening the body and all senses; in Anzaldúa's case, "Something flutters its feathers, stretches toward the sky" (*Light* 120, 136). Similarly, in "Poema del minuto blanco" ("Poem of the White Minute"), it starts with "an attitude of ecstasy" and ends pushing her to the sky (Burgos 103). However, pushing boundaries is not only an outward process but ultimately aids in arriving at oneself. In "Intima" ("Intimate"), the poetic voice's body morphs, inverts, tightens, and recedes, leaving her intimate (Burgos 7).

The poem "Río Grande de Loíza" traces the poetic voice's life stages in relation to the river. Similarly, according to Anzaldúa, identity is akin to a river (*Light* 135). The poem opens as follows: "Río Grande de Loíza!...Elongate yourself in my spirit / and let my soul lose itself in your rivulets" (Burgos 9). Returning to Anzaldúa's analogy, identity is always in transition and differs upstream from downstream. Hence, in the "call" stage, you "define yourself in terms of who you are becoming, not who you have been" (*Light* 135). After the river bathes the poetic voice's body, she wonders: "Who knows in what rainfall of what far land / I shall be spilling to open new furrows" (Burgos 9). Thus, the poetic voice recognizes that she will not remain in the original location but rather continue flowing and charting new paths.

The "call" stage, along with others, helps one to reinterpret the past and shape the future, according to Anzaldúa (*Light* 136). An example is the poem, "Confesión del sí y del no" ("Confession of the Yes and the No"). The poem begins by stating that the past is threatening the moment, yet slowly each obstacle loses its previous sting: "The edges guarded by thorns / that pricked my steps toward the infinite paths of light, / dissolve today before the rolling pulses of my spirit" (Burgos 293). As a result of this new perspective, the poetic voice is at peace and ready for new beginnings, as evidenced by the first line of the last stanza: "Nothing disturbs the fertile dawn of the moment" (Burgos 295). Across the selected poems, there is a push for transformation to reimagine life without limits. Nevertheless, the "call" is often brief and shattered by outside forces, such as political narratives, which can also act on the mind and body. In Burgos' case, an additional rupture is caused by Puerto Rican nationalism.

THE NATIONALIST RUPTURE: FEMININE VOICE VS. POLITICAL VOICE

Julia de Burgos was active during the literary era of the *Generación del 30* (Generation of the 1930s). In response to North American imperialism, this era established literature and a national identity based on Antonio S. Pedreira's *insularismo*. This nationalist concept rejected *mestizaje*, privileged Spanish heritage, and constructed land-based boundaries for nationhood and "authentic" cultural production (Rivera Villegas 445; Pérez Rosario 1-2). Nationalist narratives, according to Maria Lugones, are "a complex series of fictions" that impact reality to achieve unity by shaping the minds and bodies of citizens (464). Hence, questioning these fictions as a female writer leads to the rupture stage. Caught in a *nepantla* between her feminine and political voice, Burgos utilizes *naguala* to shift between overt and covert political statements by aligning with or subverting nationalist narratives, as well as using poetry to write from within.

The *Generación del 30*, according to Áurea María Sotomayor, elevated "[Burgos'] feminine voice over her political voice" (66). This is an example of Burgos being an intersectional outsider in her own nationalist group. Hence, according to Lugones, these members "are marginalized through erasure" (474). Burgos was further silenced due to her alignment with the marginalized, disapproval of elite interests, and rejection of hegemonic feminism that upheld racialized social hierarchies (Pérez Rosario 16-7, 22, 25, 29). As a result, poems like "Despierta" ("Awaken") contrast with other poems that extol personal truth and freedom in order to align with nationalist narratives. The poetic voice calls for Puerto Rican women to rise in defense of "the innocence of your homeland" by rejecting the "destructive perfumes of vice…" in favor "of liberty that offers you dignity and redemption" (Burgos 487).

Conversely, poems like "Somos puños cerrados" ("We are Closed Fists") are combative and politically aligned with the marginalized: "Let us launch the offensive / in a superb proletarian push" (Burgos 447). Poems like "Amaneceres" ("Dawnings") take it a step further, because Burgos mixes politics with eroticism:

> When the intimate door is opened
> to enter one's self,
> what dawnings!
> ....
> and let it hang all the songs of bourgeois ways
> and break its seconds in a million proletarian hymns. (Burgos 23)

Nevertheless, despite Burgos' nationalist sentiments, she was reduced to the symbolic role of "la novia del nacionalismo" (nationalism's girlfriend) (Sotomayor 77).

Within masculine cultural and political contexts, poetry provides an alternative site for survival and engagement by allowing women to write from within (Sotomayor 88; Cixous 350, 357). Therefore, according to Pérez Rosario, Burgos could only express her true desires through poetry and letters (33). In "Se me ha perdido un verso" ("I Have Lost a Verse"), the poetic voice is caught between silence and self-expression. The poetic voice laments the loss of her verbal and cerebral life yet rejoices once it returns: "Revolution which shatters the curtains of time! / / In your Yes, inevitable world revolution, / I have found myself, upon finding my verse" (Burgos 19). Patriarchal narratives, according to Pérez, idealize and romanticize women by reducing them to "only metaphor and object" (122, 124). Yet, Burgos was able to navigate these spaces through poetry and *naguala*. Additionally, the tools provided by the *Coatlicue* stage allow Burgos to lament, as well as face these contradictions and the pain that accompanies them.

LA COATLICUE

"Entretanto, la ola" ("Meanwhile, the Wave") is a lament as the poetic voice cries out: "I am defeated… / Dawn so far away, / that even my shadow is frightened at its shadow" (Burgos 183). The poetic voice's experience closely aligns with *la Coatlicue* because it gets plunged into depression, isolation, and paralysis; nevertheless, this disintegration also signals growth (*Light* 129, 131; *Borderlands* 68-9, 70). In Sotomayor's analysis, the themes of contradiction, transformation, death, and rebirth are recurrent in Burgos' poems. The poetic voice seeks emancipation, transforms through waters, and experiences emotions from ecstasy to pain (Sotomayor 81-2). Thus, this stage includes growth, the death/eroticism connection, which I explain below, and finding one's self.

In "Voz del alma restaurada" ("Voice of the Soul Restored") the poetic voice cries, feels wounded and restricted, yet opts for growth: "I will open my conscience / with this tenuous rain that will make the wave grow / and will drag the hand denied to my path" (Burgos 107). *La Coatlicue*, according to Anzaldúa, offers completeness to repair the harm caused by divisions, in favor of a life without borders (*Borderlands* 95). An example is "Canción para llorar y amar" ("Song for Crying and Loving"), in which the poetic voice sees how the sobs are "purifying the breeze of your path and my path" (Burgos 123). Moreover, the poetic voice acknowledges the power of pain: "From there, / pain and love carry / my emotion tied" (Burgos 125). Therefore, in the *Coatlicue* stage, Burgos' poetic voice grows and is strengthened.

The poetic voice contemplates the death and rebirth of a star in "Poema de la estrella reintegrada" ("Poem of the Restored Star"). Pain and love then descend upon the poetic voice, as she cries out: "How immense is being, when you thought yourself dead!" (Burgos 197). Death is part of the transformation cycle and intimately linked with eroticism. For example, Burgos can turn erotic symbols of nature into metaphors for death (Portalatín Rivera 12, 134; Pérez Rosario 66). Nannette Portalatín Rivera highlights the psychoanalytic duality and erotic connection between Eros and Thanatos, the impulse towards death. Furthermore, within this context of eros/death, writing remains linked to the body, as in Burgos' "Naufragio de un sueño" ("Shipwreck of a Dream"): "it expires me in the verse... // Run, because it is dying, / and it has asked for my body!" (Burgos 187).

In Burgos' "Intima" ("Intimate"), the poetic voice experiences a series of deconstructions and constructions: "I began getting lost atom by atom of my flesh / and slipping little by little to the soul. /.../ and I arrived at myself, intimate" (Burgos 7). During Anzaldúa's *Coatlicue* state, her body collapses unto itself until she feels "everything rushing to a center" and then she is complete (*Borderlands* 73). Similarly, the poetic voice finds herself after experiencing "... immense solitude..." and "...suicidal temptation..." in "Poema con un solo después" ("Poem with a Single Afterward"):

> But the laughter returned in sweet serenade
> of knowing itself whiter.
> The earth takes refuge in all its auroras
> and offers me infinities where the sob expires. (Burgos 223)

While the poetic voice finds restoration, Burgos has another rupture to navigate due to gender.

THE GENDER RUPTURE: ONE-DIMENSIONALITY VS. MULTIPLICITY

Carlota Caulfied argues that Julia de Burgos' identity as a female writer is essential because her identities as a woman and writer inform each other as she explores what prohibits her from developing herself (119). Burgos was caught between restrictive patriarchal structures that articulated one-dimensional norms of womanhood and a desire for multiplicity that would accommodate all aspects of herself. Maria Lugones defines multiplicity as defying the logic of control and engaging in "an art of resistance, metamorphosis, transformation" (478). Facing and questioning these obstacles thus leads to the rupture stage and gender-based *nepantla*, in which Burgos wrestles with her multiplicity, is a figure of "sexile," and escapes inwards.

The poem "Momentos" ("Moments") demonstrates the poetic voice's desire for multiplicity as it declares: "Me, multiple, / as in a contradiction, / tied to a sentiment without edges" (Burgos 15). Yet, the expectations of her as a writer can create unwanted, painful splits, as in "¡Oh lentitud del mar!" ("Oh, Slowness of the Sea!"): "I have had to give, multiply myself, / shred myself into complex orbits… /…/ And still they ask me to trade songs for words" (Burgos 201). The poems end by lamenting stagnation and death, respectively. Hence, these poems problematize the desire for multiplicity, especially when it cannot be achieved on Burgos' own terms.

This gender-based *nepantla* goes hand in hand with Vanessa Pérez Rosario's application of "sexile" to Burgos's life. The concept applies because Burgos is expelled "from the immediate family of the nation" due to her gender, thus compelling her to use escape routes and create spaces for her multiple identities (Pérez Rosario 3, 52). Burgos directly addresses her (s)exile in poems like "Mi alma" ("My Soul"): "The madness of my soul /…/ of the free thinker, who lives alone, / in quiet exile" (51). Patriarchal structures, according to Lugones, seek to control multiplicity because it is powerful and "[threatens] his own fiction," specifically that which is "gendered, racialized, and 'cultured'…tainted by need, emotion the body" (467-8).

Societies that do not recognize women as writers leave them feeling not only constricted by societal norms but even physically and mentally sick (Gilbert and Gubar 26, 29). Yet, Burgos finds the strength of her escape routes in "Mi símbolo de rosas" ("My Symbol of Roses"): "Forty open roses, open in my soul, / sustain my life in continuous escape inwards" (Burgos 43). Burgos also uses her imagination for female agency in poems like "El vuelo de mis pasos" ("The Flight of My Steps"): "(There is no anchor that resists / the flight of my steps /

that row daylights.)" (97). Burgos' rejection of one-dimensionality is a testament to being an active subject. She chooses to piece together her own narrative, thus initiating the next stage: "putting Coyolxauhqui together."

"PUTTING *COYOLXAUHQUI* TOGETHER": EROTICISM

Julia de Burgos' desire to embrace her multiplicity also corresponds to the stage of "putting *Coyolxauhqui* together." This stage involves reconstruction and moving from passivity to agency, according to Anzaldúa (*Light* 140, 143). Therefore, eroticism provides a key lens of analysis. Eroticism, as defined by Cixous, impacts our lives, from physical to psychic and emotional needs, thus empowering women to consciously make decisions and take actions (340). For example, eroticism plays a role in the poetic voice's development in "Armonía de la palabra y el instinto" ("Harmony of Word and Instinct") because she begins as "a word, still virgin" to then transform into a "liberated soul" and "an unthought scream" (Burgos 83). There is ample insightful scholarship on Burgos' erotic voice, therefore, the focus for this paper is how eroticism pushes the subject to be their true self by rejecting social norms, affirming multiplicity, and being fearless.

In "Víctima de luz" ("Victim of Light"), the poetic voice instructs their lover to forget their paths and instead opt for light (Burgos 159). In Portalatín Rivera's analysis of Burgos' poetry, the poetic voice seeks multiple lovers, such as water, man, and nation; yet, the union is between subjects who have shed societal restrictions and oppressions (82, 92-3, 123-4). For example, the poetic voice declares in "Cortando distancias" ("Cutting Distances"):

> And a crazy and savage goodbye to us
> in rituals and norms and gestures and masks.
> ....
> And let it be more intimate than all the phrases
> of all the times, of all the races. (Burgos 21)

In other words, the poetic voice actively rejects social norms in favor of erotic plenitude.

Scholars have studied how Burgos subversively emphasizes process, affirms shifting identities, and reclaims multiplicity by using water imagery as tides or an active, erotic subject upon the poetic voice (Hey-Colón 180, 183; Portalatín Rivera 84, 87). Yet, the poetic voice takes a different approach in "Alta mar y gaviota" ("High Sea and Seagull") because it is both the ocean water that does not belong to any nation and a bird in flight. The poetic voice also assures their lover: "I love you amidst human doors that tie you" (Burgos 91). As a result, both the poetic voice and their lover can grow, multiply, and vibrate (Burgos 91). In other words, part of the poetic voice's multiplicity involves both being acted up and taking action to transform both parties.

Eroticism does not exist separately from other parts of us, but rather operates together with knowledge, according to Audre Lorde and Anzaldúa. Both scholars also agree that after transformation, the subject is no longer the same by choosing to let go of fear, refusing powerlessness, and living from within (Lorde 341-2; *Borderlands* 70). In "Paisaje interior" ("Interior Landscape"), the poetic voice wrestles with their emotions yet opts for transformation: "Oh nudes of restlessness, /…/ in the transmutation of my soul / toward the un-lived…!" (Burgos 323). Therefore, eroticism is fundamental to the seven stages of *conocimiento* because it provides strength to be our true selves. "Putting *Coyolxauhqui* together" occurs in all stages; therefore, eroticism also permeates all stages, even in moments of doubt that occur within the "blow-up" stage.

TESTING, TESTING, "BLOW-UP"

Burgos' poetic voice sometimes doubted her path as in "Poema de la íntima agonía" ("Poem of the Intimate Agony"): "How many times have I seen it on useless paths /…/ Believing myself a seagull, seeing my flight split, / giving myself to the stars, finding myself in the puddles" (Burgos 179). The poetic voice experiences pain for following their beliefs, yet this disillusionment is part of the process. Creation and reconstruction, according to Anzaldúa, requires a sacrifice and leap of faith that are then met with another challenge—the "blow-up" (*Light* 97, 123). Throughout her life, Burgos faced both personal and professional "blow-ups."

Vanessa Pérez Rosario's work provides excellent insight and helps paint the complex landscape that Burgos faced. When Burgos divorced, she changed her name to "de Burgos" to signify that she belonged to herself, which in turn damaged her public image and compelled her to flee Puerto Rico (Pérez Rosario 28). Neither was Burgos' bold messaging accepted by middle-class, criollo feminism due to her alignment with the working class (Pérez Rosario 33). In Anzaldúa's case, a feminist conference was a "blow-up" because it was supposed to be a safe, common ground but instead became a battlefield (*Light* 144).

There were different camps at the feminist conference, according to Anzaldúa, each with their own fears, hurts, desires, and demands (*Light* 146). Similarly, Burgos was inadvertently split by the "Latinidad Feminista" movement. Pérez Rosario draws attention to how some writers "preserved, rejected, and modified parts of [Burgos'] story" in relation to their personal development (106-7). In other words, these individual interpretations silenced certain aspects of her voice while emphasizing others. However, in "Soy en cuerpo de ahora" ("I Am Embodied in Now"), the poetic voice responds to the centuries that want to knock her down by affirming that "my ambitions are not yours, my flights are not yours" (Burgos 45).

Instead of running away, Anzaldúa negotiates between the opposing feminist camps as a *nepantlera* (*Light* 148). Similarly, the poetic voice in "Vuelta al sendero único" ("Return to the Only Path") chooses to continue, despite the pain: "Miracle of having come close to my life! / I start to move on the endless path that pierces / my own heart in space" (Burgos 269). Nevertheless, this occurrence is part of the seven stages of *conocimiento*, in which ideals are put into action, yet they "explode in your face" (*Light* 147-8). Hence, Burgos continues the journey of self-transformation and "putting *Coyolxauhqui* together," this time with the help of the decolonial imaginary.

"PUTTING *COYOLXAUHQUI* TOGETHER": THE DECOLONIAL IMAGINARY

The poetic voice tells us that "My symbol has memories and anguished flowers. / It knows live hopes in a horizon of tenderness / and tall palm trees grown by my imagination" (Burgos 43). These lines from "Mi símbolo de rosas" ("My Symbol of Roses") demonstrate how, according to Anzaldúa, the new stories that we create for ourselves both "depict your struggles" and "celebrate the workings of the soul that nourish us with visions" (*Light* 142). Moreover, in piecing together her narrative, Julia de Burgos engages in the decolonial imaginary as defined by Emma Pérez. Desire has been constructed through colonialism, yet the decolonial imaginary serves as a third-world feminist practice for resistance (Pérez 103, 110). The decolonial imaginary, according to Pérez, "challenges power relations to decolonize notions of otherness to move into a liberatory terrain" (110). Through new narratives, the decolonized subject's body remembers, operates within an in-between space, and fantasizes.

Pérez argues that "[t]he body is historically and socially constructed" and that its memories become a part of its desires (108). For example, the first line of "El encuentro del hombre y el río" ("The Encounter of the Man And the River") frames the poem as a memory: "I remember that the trees gathered their shadows" (Burgos 257). The connection between the body and memory is further exemplified when the poetic voice tells the man about the river: "I don't know if it was my breast that trembled with remembrance, / or if my eyes showed nostalgias" (Burgos 259).

The decolonial imaginary, according to Pérez, lies between the colonialist and colonized, a site for moving from colonial object to decolonized subject "by affirming a cultural sexuality with historical roots" (110, 116, 120-1). The poem "Ay, ay, ay de la grifa negra" ("Ay, Ay, Ay of the Kinky-Haired Negress") provides an example of decolonized desire within a liminal space, or *nepantla*, in which the poetic voice is like a black statue. She sculpts herself and wrestles with the legacy of slavery, between sadness and shame, in favor of a third option: "to be one for the future, / fraternity of America!" (Burgos 33). Burgos also represents the *nepantla* as desire between water and land in "Agua, vida y tierra" ("Water, Life & Earth"):

> I was a strong crash of the forest and the river,
> and voice between two echoes, I rose in the hills.
> From one side the water's hands reached for me,
> and from the other, the sierras planted their roots in me. (Burgos 249)

Hence, imagery allows the poetic voice to navigate desire in a decolonial *nepantla.*

In "Noche de amor en tres cantos" ("Night of Love in Three Cantos"), the poetic voice divides their fantasy between sunset, midnight, and dawn: "How the idea resonates in my soul / of a complete night in your arms" (Burgos 77). As a decolonized subject, according to Pérez, "women cast their own fantasies" (116). The desire further shapes the poetic voice's memories: "The night is already gone; the veil remains / that laces itself to the memory, tightened" (Burgos 81). Another example of fantasizing is "Pentacromia" ("Pentachrome"), a subversive poem about male victory over female passivity. The appropriation of male tropes, according to López Springfield, is used "to emphasize the subordination of women writers to male conventions" (707). Colonization, however, was followed by imperialism, which initiated another rupture and *nepantla* to navigate.

THE IMPERIAL RUPTURE: US VS. OTHERS

Two important turning points for Puerto Rico occurred when Spain ceded Puerto Rico to the United States and later when Puerto Ricans were granted U.S. citizenship in 1917 (Pérez Rosario 4, 85). Besides Puerto Rico, Julia de Burgos also lived in Cuba before going to New York for the second and final time in 1942 (Garcia). Burgos found herself in a new reality that she questioned, hence initiating a rupture stage that revealed an imperial *nepantla* between "us" and "others." Anzaldúa theorizes a third space to challenge the binary of "*nosotras*" (us) versus "*otros*" (others) by creating the slashed term: "*nos/otras*" (*Light* 79). Anzaldúa's concept parallels Carmen Rivera Villegas' interpretation, in which the colonized subject can invert their status from *otros* to *nosotros* within a metropolis (Rivera Villegas 451). Burgos navigated this dichotomy by calling for unity against imperialism, challenging borders, and shifting between assimilation and cultural preservation.

In "Ibero-América resurge ante Bolívar" ("Ibero-America Resurges before Bolívar"), the poetic voice denounces U.S. imperialism and the island takes a key role: "Puerto Rico is the sword / that will delay the advance / of the saxon empire!" (Burgos 427). However, according to Anzaldúa, "national boundaries dividing us from the 'others' (nos/otras) are porous, and the cracks between worlds serve as gateways" (*Light* 141). The "crack" for Burgos is the diaspora, which she includes in "Puerto Rico está en tí" ("Puerto Rico Is in You"):

The voice of independence that we follow with you
—those who live with honor refuse the alms
of a Puerto Rico "associated and ridiculous state"—
....
Take this message, Puerto Rican and mine:
your free brothers in New York are with you (Burgos 501)

Hence, Burgos calls for unity across borders, even as Puerto Rico finds itself in its own *nepantla*.

The multicultural metropolis, in this case New York, becomes a key site of identity formation. There we can observe the transformation that Anzaldúa describes as "becoming a geography of hybrid selves of different cities or countries who stand at the threshold of numerous mundos" (*Light* 81). For example, in "Canción a los Pueblos Hispanos de América y del mundo" ("Song to the Hispanic People of America and the World"), the poetic voice says: "You are a land of shelter from the sea to your name / whistling in continents through all the ravines. /…/ Explosion of horizons formed your breast" (Burgos 381). In other words, Burgos expands the borders of Hispanic people beyond nation-states. To navigate the imperial *nepantla*, Burgos also turned to other types of writing, including a short story and journalism.

Anzaldúa asserts that navigating between two extremes is necessary for survival: "assimilate/acquiescence to the dominant culture and isolation/preservation of our ethnic cultural integrity" (*Light* 79). An example is Burgo's short story, "En la cantina de la juventud" ("In the Youth Canteen"). According to Rivera Villegas, it reveals how conservative family formations continue on the mainland and place the responsibility of maintaining culture on women. Nevertheless, while the main character preserves cooking traditions, she also resists assimilation (Rivera Villegas 447). On the other hand, Burgos' coverage of female artists in New York challenges colonialist stereotypes, racial simplifications, and negative views on racial mixture by humanizing black femininity and intelligence (Rivera Villegas 452-3, 456). Therefore, Burgos seeks unity between people, a practice that can also be explored through the stage of spiritual activism.

SPIRITUAL ACTIVISM

Spiritual activism, as defined by Anzaldúa, is "the activist stance that explores spirituality's social implications" (*Light* 39). Hence, a return to Burgos' political voice can shed light on how she works on building connections and justice for all. Anzaldúa illustrates how *nepantleras* reveal, through *naguala* and connectionist faculties, the "interwoven kinship among all things and people" and "that beneath individual separateness lies a deeper interrelatedness" (*Light*

149-150). In addition to addressing interconnectedness, Burgos also engages in spiritual activism by providing language and transcending culture and time.

The poetic voice declares that liberty is collective and cannot coexist with any form of oppression. For example, in "A Rafael Trejo" ("To Rafael Trejo"), the poet voice proclaims:

> And Rafel, there will be no liberty in America
> nor can we talk about democracy invictus
> while there are tyrants that denigrate history
> and nations that have other lands enslaved. (Burgos 459)

This connection and concern for justice applies to the deceased, as well, as in "Las voces de los muertos" ("The Voice Of The Dead"). This poem includes the dead in Spain, China, Britain, Russia, and Germany, the last of which requests pity for being "born, raised, to kill" (Burgos 465). The poem ends with a call and an admonition from the "Universal Dead": "You who are alive, stop your orgy of machine guns; /…/ I am the most gigantic of the dead who will never / close his eyes until I see you saved" (Burgos 467).

Anzaldúa likens artists to *chamanas* (shamans) due to how they can use writing to gather "the scattered pieces of your soul back to your body" and imagination to impose "order on chaos" by providing language (*Light* 39, 155). In "Cortando distancias" ("Cutting Distances"), the poetic voice asks for the silent voices, in order to transform them into a scream (Burgos 21). On the other hand, in "Farewell in Welfare Island," the poetic voice is no longer its own but becomes one with its comrade's (Burgos 357). In addition, both poems are examples of engaging in *conocimiento* by healing wounds, transforming, and connecting people (*Light* 19, 153). In this case, healing occurs in terms of language; the wound is silence, it is transformed into screams or becomes one voice.

In "Saludo en ti a la nueva mujer americana" ("I Greet in You the New American Woman"), the poetic voice says: "We are of the new voice, stretched, instinctive / that will shake the language of progress" (Burgos 411). Thus, Burgos is also an example of how art, according to Anzaldúa, "makes a wider community, that transcends the artist's culture and lifetime" (*Light* 63). For instance, Pérez Rosario argues that Burgos' poetry helped lay the groundwork for Nuyorican writers in the 70s (12). Moreover, according to Hey-Colón, Burgos is the predecessor for "women writers for whom the rootedness of land is neither a given nor a birthright" (185). Lastly, the poetic voice's desire to transcend their lifetime is made clear in "Entre mi voz y el tiempo" ("Between My Voice and Time"): "Am I alive? / Am I dead? / Present! Here! Present…!" (Burgos 193).

CONCLUSION: JULIA THE IMMORTAL

Gloria Anzaldúa's seven stages of *conocimiento*, together with other theories, facilitates a unified and decolonial conceptualization of Burgos' work by embracing her contradictions and refusing to silence her as she was during (and after) her lifetime. Throughout this essay, common themes were explored across all stages, ranging from boundary pushing to escape routes and multiplicity to unity. Situating Julia de Burgos as a *nepantlera* who expresses her multiplicity, imagines decolonization, and engages in self-transformation fits into a broader context of third-world feminism. Hence, her work can serve not only as an inspiration but an invitation to engage in self-empowerment and spiritual activism. Burgos' engagement with historical narratives, including colonization and imperialism, can also be applied to postcolonial realities around the world.

This essay is only one step forward in a line of inquiry with a multitude of further applications. For instance, Burgos' poetry can lend itself to European feminism—through feminists such as Hélène Cixous—or to contemporary Latinx feminism. Burgos desired "artistic legitimacy" and her poetry manifested "a rhetorical quest to justify a female poetics" as a form of escape, resistance, and empowerment that would lead to wholeness and immortality (López Springfield 701, 704-5, 707). Hence, further study can analyze modern boundaries to artistic legitimacy for women and marginalized people in a digital age. In conclusion, situating Burgos within a third-world feminist body of knowledge, especially Anzaldúa's, provides a powerful rebuttal to restrictive narratives and calls for unity that is multifaceted and empowering for everyone.

WORKS CITED

Anzaldúa, Gloria. *Borderlands: La Frontera*. San Francisco, Aunt Lute Books, 1999.

—. *Light in the Dark / Luz en lo oscuro: Rewriting identity, spirituality, reality*. Edited by Analouise Keating, Duke University Press, 2015.

Burgos, Julia de. *Song of the Simple Truth: obra poética completa – The complete poems*, edited and translated by Jack Agüeros, Curbstone Press, 1997.

Caulfield, Carlota. "*Canción de la verdad sencilla*: Julia de Burgos y su diálogo erótico-místico con la naturaleza." *Revista Iberoamericana*, vol. 59, no. 162–163, 1993, pp. 119–126. *EBSCOhost,* doi-org.ezproxy.lib.uh.edu/10.5195/REVIBEROAMER.1993.5131. Accessed 27 Mar. 2023.

Cixous, Hélène. "The Laugh of the Medusa." *Feminisms: An Anthology of Literary Theory and Criticism*, edited by Robyn R. Warhol and Diane Price Herndl, New Brunswick, Rutgers University Press, 1997, pp. 347-361.

Garcia, Maira. "Overlooked No More: Julia de Burgos, a Poet Who Helped Shape Puerto Rico's Identity." *The New York Times*, 2 May 2018, https://www.nytimes.com/2018/05/02/obituaries/overlooked-julia-de-burgos.html. Accessed 30 Sept. 2024.

Gilbert, Sandra M., and Susan Gubar. "Infection in the Sentence: The Woman Writer and the Anxiety of Authorship." *Feminisms: An Anthology of Literary Theory and Criticism*, edited by Robyn R. Warhol and Diane Price Herndl, New Brunswick, Rutgers University Press, 1997, pp. 21-31.

Hey-Colón, Rebeca L. "Toward a Genealogy of Water: Reading Julia de Burgos in the Twenty-First Century." *Small Axe: A Caribbean Journal of Criticism*, vol. 54, 2017, pp. 179–187. *EBSCOhost*, doi-org.ezproxy.lib.uh.edu/10.1215/07990537-4272076. Accessed 27 Mar. 2023.

López Springfield, Consuelo. "'I Am the Life, the Strength, the Woman': Feminism in Julia de Burgos' Autobiographical Poetry." *Callaloo*, vol. 17, no. 3, 1994, pp. 701-714, doi.org/10.2307/2931846. Accessed 27 Mar. 2023.

Lugones, Maria. "Purity, Impurity, and Separation." *Signs*, vol. 19, no. 2, 1994, pp. 458-479, www.jstor.org/stable/3174808. Accessed 10 May 2023.

Pérez, Emma. *The Decolonial Imaginary: Writing Chicanas into History*. Indiana University Press, 1999.

Pérez Rosario, Vanessa. *Becoming Julia de Burgos: The Making of a Puerto Rican Icon*. University of Illinois Press, 2014.

Portalatín Rivera, Nannette. *Julia de Burgos y la tradición de poesía erótica femenina en Puerto Rico*. Ediciones Callejón, 2015.

Rivera Villegas, Carmen M. "'Detrás de la frontera': Julia de Burgos en *Pueblos Hispanos*." *El mito de la mujer caribeña*, edited by Dagmary Olívar Graterol y Jesús del Valle Vélez, Ediciones de la Discreta S.L., 2011, pp. 441-464.

Sotomayor, Aurea Maria. "El delito de Julia, la outsider." *Centro Journal*, vol. 26, no. 2, 2014, pp. 66–97. EBSCOhost, search.ebscohost.com/login.aspx?direct=true&db=a9h&AN=101137318&site=ehost-live. Accessed 27 Mar. 2023.

Stark, David M. *Slave Families and the Hato Economy in Puerto Rico.* University Press of Florida, 2015.

REESCRITURAS DE LA COLONIZACIÓN

PROPUESTAS PARA PENSAR LA MODERNIDAD DESDE UNA CONCIENCIA MESTIZA

MARÍA JOSÉ RAMÍREZ-JIMÉNEZ

Este ensayo es un primer acercamiento a los planteamientos de Gloria Anzaldúa, Enrique Dussel y Rita Segato. Pretendo que este primer paso me ayude a entender, analizar y visualizar los distintos puntos de encuentro entre sus propuestas; en un futuro este proyecto podría extenderse a señalar las similitudes en otros conceptos de los autores mencionados. Por supuesto, no pretendo aquí abordar las propuestas a profundidad, pues, por un lado, el espacio es corto y, por otro, pienso que se trata de una tarea mucho más grande que este breve texto. Sin embargo, quiero apuntar que ya existen esfuerzos como el artículo "El sujeto en los textos 'seminales' del Giro Descolonial: inventario, fuentes y significación" de Alfonso Rodríguez Manzano, publicado en 2021, sobre los textos seminales del giro descolonizador entre los que están *Borderlands/La Frontera: The New Mestiza* de Gloria Anzaldúa, así como *1492: el encubrimiento del otro* de Enrique Dussel (Rodríguez)—libro también mencionado y citado en el presente ensayo.

Para analizar y exponer la historia que atraviesa a las subjetividades del sur global (es decir, la historia de la colonialidad), es necesario reconocer que la Modernidad[1] se basa en el ejercicio de la subyugación de lxs otrxs, esto empuja a buscar nuevas formas de conciencia que permitan superarla. Algunas sugerencias para ello son: a) la conciencia mestiza de Gloria Anzaldúa; b) la *Trans-modernidad* de Enrique Dussel; y c) la *relectura del mestizaje* de Rita Segato. Estas muestran, por un lado, que el mestizaje puede tener otra cara, una que va más allá de la necesidad de homogeneizar y asimilar. Se trata de posicionarse en una perspectiva distinta de la historia: desde la de/lx subalternx, esa subjetividad liminar atravesada por los choques de culturas y la resistencia a la asimilación, esa identidad que debe cruzar las fronteras de lo "normal", característica impuesta por la cultura dominante. Por otro lado, estos tres acercamientos a la problemática de la Modernidad son una manera de repensar la experiencia subalterna, de legitimarla.

Para este ensayo, en el primer subcapítulo presento a cada unx de lxs autorxs, para luego exponer sus conceptos: la *nueva mestiza* y *lxs atravesadxs* de Anzaldúa; la *Trans-modernidad* de Dussel; y la *relectura del mestizaje* de Segato y afirmar que coinciden en el punto de partida: la raza. Asimismo, la exposición de los planteamientos se encuentra enmarcada por una reflexión sobre la Modernidad, en específico cómo la aborda Dussel. Aquí, cabe señalar que este planteamiento forma parte de una propuesta filosófica latinoamericana, conocida como Filosofía de la liberación.[2]

En el segundo subcapítulo, me dedico a profundizar sobre las similitudes entre los conceptos de lxs tres pensadorxs, a trazar una suerte de diálogo entre las propuestas. Por último, en las conclusiones señalo que Anzaldúa, Dussel y Segato pretenden no sólo reflexionar sobre la raza y su historia colonial, sino que con sus conceptos formulan una posible liberación o trascendencia de la Modernidad/Colonialidad.

---

1. Entendemos por Modernidad lo que Enrique Dussel denomina como el momento en que Europa puede confrontarse con el otro (1492), es decir, cuando logró definirse como un ego conquistador, descubridor colonizador de la Alteridad constitutiva de la misma Modernidad (1994 8). Recordemos que Dussel propone la fecha 1492 como inicio de la Modernidad, de una primera Modernidad; y sitúa las revoluciones francesa e industrial como parte de una segunda Modernidad. Sólo gracias a la invasión europea a América, occidente pudo erigirse como el centro de la Historia, ya que a la llegada de Portugal al Extremo Oriente en el siglo XVI como de España a América, la historia del planeta se torna una sola Historia Mundial, en otras palabras, gracias a estos hechos se arma lo que Wallerstein llamaría el sistema-mundo. Véase Enrique Dussel, 1492: el encubrimiento del Otro: hacia el origen de la Modernidad, 1994, pp. 7-37.

2. Según Patricia González San Martín, se trata de un movimiento intelectual, "un ejercicio de pensamiento que se vuelca críticamente hacia el sujeto (...) [donde se] lee críticamente a la historia del continente y, consiguientemente, se analizan las ideas, los conceptos, las categorías con las que se han justificado diversos proyectos civilizatorios" (46).

DE SUR A NORTE: TRES PENSAMIENTOS CRÍTICOS DESDE LA SUBALTERNIDAD Y SOBRE LA MODERNIDAD

En *Borderlands*, Gloria Anzaldúa plantea una conciencia que corresponde a una identidad mestiza; crea herramientas para que la entidad fronteriza pueda hacerse presente donde suele incomodar. El siguiente análisis pretende hallar las similitudes y los puntos de encuentro entre esta propuesta y las de Dussel y Segato: guías de resistencia para las subjetividades atravesadas por la Modernidad/Colonialidad.

¿Qué tienen en común lxs tres autorxs? Si bien Anzaldúa era originaria del Valle del Río Grande, Texas, y escribió desde Estados Unidos, ella misma representaba y construía una subjetividad racializada y subalterna. También fue activista, académica, docente, escritora y poeta, hija de trabajadorxs agrícolas (Cantú y Hurtado 4). Por su parte, Dussel, nacido en La Paz, Argentina, fue, además de un académico de renombre, reconocido filósofo y teólogo, activista político, pues formó cuadros de izquierda, como la Escuela de formación política Carlos Ometochtzin o su colaboración con el Instituto Nacional de Formación Política (INFP), ambas en México (Paizanni). Tanto Dussel como Anzaldúa dedicaron sus vidas a la docencia,[3] aunque en diferentes campos. Anzaldúa impartió talleres y clases de escritura creativa, su misión radicaba en ayudar a sus estudiantes a "get in touch with their root-self, the creative winner voice, and to speak and write from that place" (Anzaldúa Papers de UT Austin, caja 1 fólder 3). Pero el objetivo de Anzaldúa no era menor, sino político: ayudar a su alumnado a empoderarse y re/escribir su propia historia, crear autohistorias[4] y teorizar desde la propia experiencia. De acuerdo con Ricardo Vivancos, Anzaldúa se enfocó en escribir y enseñar escritura creativa en relación a una

3. Dussel ahondará sobre su experiencia docente en el documental Caminante no hay camino… un autorretrato documental, del 2015 dirigida por Sergio García-Agundis, en Vimeo https://vimeo.com/114714858. En la película, el académico recuerda su trayectoria como profesor en Argentina, su exilio en México y su incorporación como profesor en la Universidad Autónoma Metropolitana en la Ciudad de México. Asimismo, hablará también de las múltiples cátedras, lectures y conferencias que dio en distintas universidades del mundo, como Duke University, Auckland University, Universität Wien, entre otras. Toda su experiencia docente se encuentra condensada en su currículum, el cual puede ser consultado en línea. "Currículum", Enrique Dussel, fecha de consulta: 10 de febrero de 2025. https://enriquedussel.b-cdn.net/wp-content/uploads/2023/10/CURRICULUM_2023.pdf

4. Anzaldúa, acuñó los términos autohistoria y autohistoria-teoría para describir las formas en que las mujeres de color intervienen o han transformado la manera las formas tradicionales de crear/escribir textos autobiográficos en Occidente. La autohistoria, de acuerdo con Keating, "focuses on the persons life story but, as the autohistorian tells her own life story, she simultaneously tells the life stories of others" (Keating 319). De acuerdo con María del Socorro Gutiérrez-Magallanes, la autohistoria "se enfoca en la historia personal pero en la medida que la auto-historiadora cuenta su propia historia, simultáneamente cuenta las historias de otros" (Gutiérrez-Magallanes 55). Además, la académica señala que Anzaldúa llamó autohistorias a las autobiografías escritas por mujeres de color y las describió como textos con forma híbrida que transgreden los géneros (56).

formación de identidad; además de haber producido tres colecciones de poesía y una de cuentos, aunque muy pocos de estos proyectos han sido publicados (36).

Rita Laura Segato, originaria de Buenos Aires, es antropóloga, académica, escritora y activista feminista. Ha sido reconocida por su labor política, pues ha participado en investigaciones sobre violencia de género (feminicidios y violencia sobre cuerpos feminizados). Por ejemplo, fue perita en los juicios Sepur Zarco en Guatemala, donde se juzgó la violencia sexual (violaciones sistemáticas y esclavitud sexual por parte de militares) ejercida por el Estado. También fue jueza del Tribunal Permanente de los Pueblos en la Audiencia celebrada sobre crímenes contra las mujeres en Chihuahua, México (Ballón y Sánchez 234 y 238). Asimismo, en entrevista con Alejandra Ballón Gutiérrez y Dairo Sánchez-Mojica, rememora su encuentro con el mundo religioso afrobrasilero y su propio sentido de justicia, cuestiones que pueden notarse en su obra y su praxis política (230 y 231). Tanto Dussel como Segato han sido figuras importantes para la teoría decolonial en América Latina,[5] pero pocas veces desde nuestra región se reconocen las aportaciones de Anzaldúa a la decolonialidad.

¿Qué une a lxs tres autorxs? La categoría de raza es la que guía los tres conceptos de los que hoy hablaré. Por un lado, Anzaldúa habla de ser o de identidad asociados a los conceptos de colonización, raza, conciencia, entre otros. En el primer capítulo de *Borderlands* realiza un breve recuento histórico sobre México y su relación con Estados Unidos (hablará sobre la colonización de México, los aztecas, la guerra entre México y EU, así como el Tratado Guadalupe-Hidalgo, y relaciona estos eventos con la propia historia familiar) (Anzaldúa 23-35). Sin embargo, el proyecto de la autora no se enfoca sólo en la historia de la población chicana, sino también habla de la experiencia de las otredades de la otredad, es decir, las subjetividades queer dentro de una cultura colonizada y marginada por estigmas de raza, patriarcado y prejuicios de género. Una colonización perpetrada por el español y por el anglo, e incluso una dominación ejercida por el propio pueblo, o sea, por la propia comunidad chicana, desde los valores de una cultura que "traicionan" a las subjetividades femeninas o feminizadas y queer (Anzaldúa 37-45). Anzaldúa habla de una otredad que se vincula con una disidencia, señala que lxs habitantes de las fronteras son lxs atravesadxs:

> The prohibited and forbidden are its inhabitants. *Los atravesados* live here: the squint-eyed, the perverse, the queer, the troublesome, the mongrel, the mulato, the half-breed, the half-dead; in short, those who cross over pass over, or go through the confines of the "norm." (Anzaldúa 42)

5. Santiago Castro-Gómez, "Patriarcado de alta intensidad y mestizaje", video de YouTube, 26:01, publicado el 9 de julio 2022, https://youtu.be/7h4sPcn2fhU?si=OwRMQuKc4HJJfauD

Lxs atravesadxs es un concepto que se encuentra intrínsecamente ligado a la idea de la identidad mestiza y fronteriza planteada por Anzaldúa. La autora utiliza el término para referirse a aquellas subjetividades marginadas, porque no encajan dentro de las normas establecidas por la sociedad dominante, es decir, personas excluidas de la sociedad debido a su raza, género, orientación sexual, clase social, así como otras identidades no normativas (incluso podría agregarse aquí la situación migratoria). Subjetividades subalternas, que son vistas como anormales o diferentes, una otredad según los estándares sociales dominantes, y que a menudo enfrentan discriminación y violencia debido a su condición de atravesadxs.[6]

Anzaldúa destaca la experiencia compartida de opresión y marginalización entre lxs atravesadxs, así como su capacidad de resistencia y lucha por la liberación. Aboga por la solidaridad y la coalición entre los diferentes grupos atravesados, reconociendo que sus luchas están interconectadas y que juntos tienen el poder de desafiar las estructuras de poder, esto se hace más claro en el capítulo 7 de *Borderlands*, donde la autora apoya la historia de/lx otrx, el reconocimiento de las contradicciones de cada subjetividad y la tolerancia hacia la ambigüedad (Anzaldúa 99-113).

Desde lo propuesto por Dussel podemos entender que la cuestión de la raza viene ligada a la opresión y a la supuesta superioridad de la cultura blanca; el pensador argentino se ocupa de reflexionar cómo se ha construido la superioridad de la cultura europea/norteamericana sobre el resto. Dussel recuerda que para la entidad colonizadora, la población indígena estaba ligada a la servidumbre y a un estado de barbarie o inmadurez que la hacía víctima y culpable de una guerra contra ella (72-73). Además, señala que la masacre, la violencia y el sadismo contra estas subjetividades han sido justificados en diversas ocasiones. Muchas de ellas la justificación tiene una base racista. Enrique Dussel toma como ejemplo de esta defensa de la barbarie colonizadora el libro *De la justa causa de la guerra contra los indios* de Juan Ginés de Sepúlveda. En su conferencia "Crítica del 'mito de la Modernidad,'" Dussel explica que dicho mito se entiende como la autodefinición de la propia cultura como superior, en términos de mayor desarrollo, determinando a la otra cultura como inferior/bárbara. Entonces, considerando su

---

6. Como habitantxs fronterizxs, poseen en su corporalidad un signo, una herida abierta—"open wound [...] running down the length of [their] body" (Anzaldúa 24)—que les hará ser perseguidxs hasta ser exterminadxs o asimiladxs, como lo enuncia la autora chicana en el poema "To live in the Borderlands means":

> the mill with the razor white teeth wants to shred off
> your olive-red skin, crush out the kernel, your heart
> pound you pinch you roll you out
> smelling like white bread but dead (Anzaldúa 217)

inferioridad y su "incapacidad," "la dominación (guerra, violencia) que se ejerce sobre el Otro es, en realidad, emancipación, "utilidad," bien del bárbaro que se civiliza, se desarrolla o "moderniza" (Dussel, *1492* 69). Por ello, desde el punto de vista del colonizador, las guerras, las torturas y los asesinatos se hacen con una perspectiva emancipadora: se trata de llevarles el milagro de la modernidad a las civilizaciones inferiores, para salvarles de su ignorancia. En ese sentido, "la 'Modernidad' es justificación de una praxis irracional de violencia" (175), una dominación que produce víctimas, que sacrifica para llevar la salvación (176).

Hasta aquí me gustaría apuntar que ambos planteamientos, el de Anzaldúa y el de Dussel, parten de una necesidad de búsqueda de una identidad propia, o dicho en palabras de Dussel, "saber quién es uno mismo como angustia existencial" (Dussel, *Filosofías del sur* 282). Son propuestas que surgen de la toma de conciencia de una cultura otra y por tanto una identidad otra, ya sea latinoamericana (284) o chicana o mestiza (como la de Anzaldúa). Ese rastreo y comprensión de la identidad derivará en una búsqueda de otras posibilidades de ser-en-el-mundo, de existir, tanto de manera individual como en comunidad. Se trata de posibilidades de habitar en resistencia, a la asimilación, a la negación de una existencia otra, al blanqueamiento. De acuerdo con Anzaldúa: "The whites in power want us people of color to barricade ourselves behind our separate tribal walls so they can pick us off one at a time with their hidden weapons; so they can whitewash and distort history" (Anzaldúa 108). Esta misma preocupación por el blanqueamiento de la historia, o por el planteamiento de un sólo lado de la historia (la del vencedor), es la misma que llevará a Dussel a reflexionar sobre el mito de la Modernidad y las posibilidades de trascenderla.

Gloria Anzaldúa y Enrique Dussel coinciden en la importancia de la historia y la memoria. Ambos tienen esta preocupación por la identidad de las subjetividades subalternas, ya sea mexico-americanas o de color en EU o latinoamericanas, pero no se puede hablar de esta sin rastrear la historia y hurgar en la memoria. En el ensayo "The New Mestiza Nation," Anzaldúa destaca que la nueva mestiza trata de ver al pasado y examinar/analizar los aspectos culturales que han oprimido a la mujer). Pero el pasado se construye de muchas formas, cambia de una a otra época. Por otro lado, Anzaldúa reconoce que "the past has not been represented 'truthfully' in history books. Written by conquerors, history books distort and repress the histories of women and people of color" (Keating 215).

En el mismo ensayo, Anzaldúa habla de multiculturalismo, entendido más tarde como interculturalismo, y cómo este se debe interpretar como la inclusión de las historias de la diferencia. "Se trata de otras narrativas. It is about alter-narratives. The stories of multiculturalism are stories of identity, and narratives of identity are stories of location. A story is always a retelling of an older story.

This is my retelling" (Keating 216). Ese recontar o relatar la propia historia puede ligarse con la autohistoria. Así, para la autora es imprescindible incluir, leer y escribir historias/miradas de la diferencia, porque estarán recontándola desde una voz subalterna, desde abajo. Estas narrativas otras se erigen como la resistencia ante los embates del olvido, ese que proviene de la imposición de la historia oficial. Además, en la autohistoria-teoría lxs autorxs logran configurar escritos que no sólo se enfocan en la reflexión de la vida interior, sino que la entretejen con lo externo, cuestionando la cultura, la sociedad, las condiciones políticas, etcétera.

En el ensayo "Los cauces profundos de la raza latinoamericana: una relectura del mestizaje," Rita Segato también parte del concepto de raza, pues para ella éste "es el punto ciego del discurso latinoamericano sobre la otredad" (213). Se trata de una categoría de la que poco se quiere hablar, habla del fantasma de la raza, porque está en todos lados pero no está nombrada. Así, el mestizaje es el punto ciego de la otredad, porque para los no blancos el estado siempre es autoritario, dictatorial. Tomemos en cuenta que una buena parte de las identidades nacionales latinoamericanas se basan en la idea de un mestizaje homogeneizador, etnocida, donde se habla de una mezcla entre europeo (español o portugués) e indígena, pero donde la parte europea suele asociarse con mejores características y la parte indígena o negra suele negarse o invisibilizarse. Así, en distintas latitudes de nuestra región se ha negado la presencia de subjetividades otras, esas que no corresponden al mestizaje hegemónico u homogeneizador que corresponda a la identidad nacional, como lxs afrodescendientes, lxs negrxs o los pueblos originarios. Negar la existencia de esas otras subjetividades implica también la negación de sus derechos: al territorio, a la educación, a una vida digna, a la identidad.

Segato usa como ejemplo de negación de la raza a Brasil, donde buena parte de su población afrodescendiente y negra, así como de los pueblos originarios, deben sobrellevar distintas violencias, como la brutalidad policíaca, la falta de acceso a educación universitaria y el encarcelamiento. La académica llama la atención sobre el "Relatorio do Relator Espe de execucoes extrajudiciales, sumarias ou arbitrarias", donde es clara la falta de datos sobre la raza de las personas que llegan a ser asesinadas a manos de la "seguridad pública" (214). Negar este dato es negar que las operaciones policiales parecen planearse con el fin de matar jóvenes pobres, negros de sexo masculino. Además, su trabajo "El color de la cárcel en América Latina" señala que buena parte de la población carcelaria tiene ciertas características étnicas, sin embargo no hay censos que permitan identificar de manera precisa el número de personas no blancas encarceladas en Latinoamérica (215). Según la investigadora, la falta de reflexión sobre esta categoría en América Latina es "un síntoma, una ceguera sintomática, que se constata en los pocos informes disponibles que intentaron, de alguna forma, hablar sobre el color de los encarcelados en el subcontinente" (216).

UNA CONCIENCIA OTRA, EL MESTIZAJE Y LA *TRANS*-*MODERNIDAD* COMO UTOPÍAS

> Because I, a *mestiza*,
> continually walk out of one culture
> into another,
> because I am in all cultures at the same time,
> *alma entre dos mundos, tres, cuatro,*
> *me zumba la cabeza con lo contradictorio.*
> *Estoy norteada por todas las voces que me hablan*
> *simultáneamente.*
>
> —Gloria Anzaldúa (*Borderlands/La Frontera: The New Mestiza* 99)

Mientras el primer subcapítulo trata de los problemas de la Modernidad/Colonialidad y cómo lxs tres pensadores la conceptualizan, este apartado trata de las soluciones que ofrecen para trascenderla. Lxs tres pensadorxs se posicionan desde abajo para dar cuenta de la experiencia subalterna y proponer una solución a la Modernidad desde la perspectiva de la otredad.

En *Borderlands*, Anzaldúa busca crear herramientas para que la entidad fronteriza pueda hacerse presente en los espacios donde suele incomodar. Hacer visible lo que se quiere invisibilizar: una identidad encarnada en una corporalidad atrapada entre culturas (chicana, mexicana, afromestiza, norteamericana), que se vive de manera incómoda, es decir, con una guerra interna y una frontera atravesándola, desgarrándola para resignificarla. La conciencia mestiza es fronteriza, liminar. En ese sentido, la noción de *frontera* no se refiere únicamente al espacio geográfico que divide a México de Estados Unidos, sino que hace referencia a un no-lugar: el cruce entre culturas, entre lenguas, un espacio intermedio. Para Anzaldúa, la frontera "*es una herida abierta* where the Third World grates against the first and bleeds. And before a scab forms it hemorrhages again, the lifeblood of two worlds merging to form a third country—a border culture" (Anzaldúa 25, énfasis original). La herida se porta siempre abierta, no cauteriza, de su sangre emerge una cultura híbrida y un tercer país que es habitado por el sujeto fronterizo: como país (nación) tiene un lenguaje propio, una identidad, símbolos.

Anzaldúa enfatiza que la experiencia de la nueva mestiza implica un constante proceso de negociación y resistencia frente a las estructuras de poder dominantes. La nueva mestiza está en constante movimiento entre distintos mundos, adoptando y adaptando diferentes elementos culturales según contexto y necesidades, a esto se le llamará un estado constante de nepantlismo: "[...] torn between ways, la mestiza is a product of the transfer of the cultural and spiritual values of one group to another. Being tricultural, monolingual, bilingual" (Anzaldúa 100). La nueva mestiza puede atravesar diferentes cambios de conciencia, atraviesa distintos mundos, se sitúa en un estado llamado Nepantla. Estos cambios de conciencia requieren, a su vez, completa flexibilidad de la persona con esta identidad híbrida nepantlesca: la posibilidad de transitar en una dualidad, entre dos o más lenguas, diversas culturas. La autora chicana explica la subjetividad representada en *Borderlands* como:

> *[e]l choque de un alma atrapado entre el mundo del espíritu y el mundo de la técnica a veces la deja entullada.* Cradled in one culture, sandwiched between two cultures, stradling all three cultures and their value systems, la mestiza undergoes a struggle of flesh, a struggle of borders, an inner war. (100, énfasis original)

La nueva mestiza representa una identidad mestiza y fronteriza que desafía las categorías binarias y celebra la diversidad cultural. Es un concepto que invita a repensar las fronteras físicas y simbólicas, y a imaginar un mundo donde la diferencia sea valorada y celebrada.

Para Anzaldúa, la nueva mestiza representa a aquellxs que viven en la frontera entre diferentes culturas, lenguas, géneros, y formas de conocimiento. Esta identidad mestiza es fluida y dinámica, no se ajusta a las categorías binarias tradicionales, sino que abarca múltiples aspectos de la experiencia humana (Anzaldúa 101). Este concepto también implica una celebración de la diversidad y la hibridación cultural. Anzaldúa aboga por la valoración y el respeto de las múltiples identidades que componen la experiencia mestiza, así como por la creación de nuevos espacios y formas de expresión que reflejen esta realidad compleja y enriquecedora (Anzaldúa 102).

Enrique Dussel, por su parte, propone la *Trans-modernidad*; que se hermana con la de la conciencia mestiza en tanto que pretende visibilizar la otra cara negada de la modernidad, esa cara que es víctima, inocente (Dussel, *1492* 177). Además, en dicha propuesta, pretende un proyecto mundial de liberación. Algo que Anzaldúa también aspira con la conciencia mestiza: "The answer to the problem between the white and the colored, between males and females, lies in healing the split that originates in the very foundation of our lives" (Anzaldúa 102), cuando la autora habla del problema entre la raza blanca y la de color, o del conflicto entre hombres y mujeres, puede entenderse como una serie de problemáticas que no sólo son propias del territorio estadounidense, sino de magnitud global; para la poeta y académica chicana, el trabajo de la conciencia mestiza permitirá romper el pensamiento dualista (blanco/de color; mujer/

varón), el primer paso para iniciar una lucha que permita el fin de la violación, la violencia y la guerra (102).

Pienso que hay varios puntos en los que convergen Dussel y Anzaldúa, por ejemplo, cuando el filósofo señala que se puede superar la razón emancipadora/liberadora:

> [...] cuando se declara inocentes a las víctimas desde la afirmación de su Alteridad como Identidad en la Exterioridad como personas que han sido negadas, como su propia contradicción, por la Modernidad. De esta manera, la razón moderna es trascendida (pero no como negación de la razón en cuanto tal, sino de la razón violenta eurocéntrica, desarrollista, hegemónica). (Dussel, *1492* 177)

Comparte con Anzaldúa la cuestión de la identidad negada, invisibilizada, borrada. También menciona la contradicción, que para la misma Anzaldúa es una noción importante, pues las alteridades deben lidiar con que ellas mismas están atravesadas por la ambigüedad y las contradicciones (Anzaldúa 101). Como la mestiza tiene múltiples identidades, vive en un estado de nepantlismo: "In a constant state of nepantilism, an Aztec word meaning torn between ways, la mestiza is a product of the transfer of the cultural and spiritual values of one group to another" (Anzaldúa 100). Así, tiene la posibilidad de transitar en una dualidad, multiplicidad, entre dos lenguas, diversas culturas.

De acuerdo con Dussel:

> El proyecto transmoderno es una co-realización de lo imposible para la sola Modernidad; es decir, es co-realización de solidaridad, que hemos llamado analéctica (o analógica, sincrética, híbrida o "mestiza") del Centro/Periferia, Mujer/Varón, diversas razas, diversas etnias, diversas clases, Humanidad/tierra, ... (Dussel, *1492* 177)

Anzaldúa también llama a una solidaridad, a que las diversas alteridades se unan para explicarse y conocer entre ellas sus historias, pues sólo a partir de este (re)conocimiento es que se puede lograr una verdadera unión que apunte a un cambio social. Asimismo, apuesta por concientizar a la cultura blanca dominante, puesto que su ignorancia implica una amenaza para esa identidad mestiza/híbrida: involucrarle implica derribar prejuicios (Anzaldúa 108).

La *Trans-modernidad* surge como una crítica a la Modernidad y la posmodernidad, proponiendo una nueva época que trascienda las limitaciones y los problemas de ambas. En la perspectiva de Dussel, la Modernidad se caracteriza por su énfasis en la razón instrumental, la hegemonía de la cultura occidental, el colonialismo y la explotación. La posmodernidad, por otro lado, critica los metarrelatos y la idea de progreso lineal, pero tiende a caer en el relativismo y la fragmentación cultural.

La *Trans-modernidad*, según Dussel, busca superar estas dicotomías y dualidades mediante la integración de las diversidades culturales y epistemológicas. Propone una visión crítica de la Modernidad desde una perspectiva global y pluriversal, reconociendo las múltiples cosmovisiones y saberes existentes en el mundo (Dussel, *1492* 7-37). También, promueve el diálogo intercultural y la interconexión entre las diferentes tradiciones filosóficas y culturales. Se enfatiza la necesidad de una ética de la liberación que respete la diversidad y promueva la justicia social, la solidaridad y la equidad. En resumen, con este concepto Dussel propone una nueva época que trascienda las limitaciones de la Modernidad y la posmodernidad, abrazando la diversidad cultural y epistemológica para construir un mundo más justo y equitativo (Dussel, *1492* 69-81).

Rita Segato en su ensayo realiza una *relectura del mestizaje*, es decir una lectura en positivo de éste, pues lo piensa desde la subalternidad. El planteamiento de Segato tiene mucho en común con la conciencia mestiza de Anzaldúa, puesto que ambos conceptos hablan de una huella en el cuerpo mestizo, para Segato se trata de un signo racial (224), mientras que en Anzaldúa se trata de la frontera. Se puede pensar estas dos categorías como una herida colonial: una cicatriz que continúa abierta y que recuerda el pasado del cuerpo mestizo: la historia de la colonización se porta como una línea de color.

Segato, en su texto, enuncia:

> una tercera y nueva percepción del mestizaje se perfila, profundamente atravesada y sacudida por los proyectos históricos latentes y ahora emergentes en nuestra realidad: mestizaje como brújula que apunta al Sur. Un cuerpo mestizo en desconstrucción, como conjunto de claves para su localización en un paisaje, que es geografía e historia al mismo tiempo. (234)

Me parece que la propuesta es similar a la de Anzaldúa, en tanto que se habla de un cuerpo desmembrado, en "desconstrucción", "[d]espojando, desgranado, quitando paja" (Anzaldúa 104), solamente así será posible identificar lo heredado por todos los ancestros, distinguir entre lo que es realmente heredado, adquirido o impuesto (ibídem). El desmembramiento del cuerpo permite identificar las historias que lo atraviesan, su lugar en el paisaje que ha construido el proyecto de Modernidad.

Para Segato, "es necesario reoriginarse de otra forma, retomar los hilos de un panel histórico desgarrado, interrumpido por la interferencia, la represión, la prohibición, la intrusión, la intervención, la censura de la memoria" (241). En ese sentido, comparte con Anzaldúa el (re)conocimiento/rescate de la propia historia, de la memoria que ha sido negada, borrada y prohibida por la cultura blanca dominante. Como se mencionó anteriormente, sólo conociendo la historia de la cultura de la que se proviene y de las diferentes alteridades se podrá hallar un camino que derive en un cambio social, el cual primero deberá empezar como un cambio interno, en el pensamiento mismo del cuerpo mestizo, para que pueda manifestarse después en el exterior.

CONCLUSIONES, O DE CÓMO PENSAR MUNDOS DONDE QUEPAN MUCHOS MUNDOS, HOGARES PARA SUBJETIVIDADES DIVERSAS/ MESTIZAS

Para resumir, Anzaldúa con la nueva mestiza, propone una identidad fluida que abarca múltiples aspectos de la experiencia humana (Anzaldúa 101), en ese sentido representa las subjetividades que viven en la frontera entre diferentes culturas, lenguas, géneros, y formas de conocimiento. El estado Nepantla le ayuda a hacer malabares con las culturas. La nueva mestiza desarrollará una conciencia diferente, mestiza también, que le permitirá crear una nueva cultura, una nueva historia con una nueva mitología (Anzaldúa 102). La conciencia de la mestiza será el camino hacia una transformación planetaria, con ella la nueva mestiza se permite cuestionar las culturas que la atraviesan para resignificarlas, para poder crear una realidad mucho más incluyente. La lucha de la nueva mestiza es feminista y valora las acciones de la comunidad cuir en pro de un mundo más justo (Anzaldúa 103-112). Desde la conciencia mestiza llama a formas de colaboración entre diferentes identidades. Por su parte Dussel con la *Trans-modernidad* establece un proyecto de solidaridad, una forma de trascender las consecuencias de la Modernidad, en tanto que se reconoce a la alteridad como aquella que ha sido negada y llama a colaborar entre diversas razas, diversas etnias, diversas clases (Dussel, *1492* 177).

Por último, Segato realiza una *relectura del mestizaje* desde la subalternidad. Los conceptos de Segato y Anzaldúa hablan de una huella en el cuerpo mestizo. Mientras que para Segato se trata de un signo racial (Segato 224), para Anzaldúa se trata de la frontera. Estas dos categorías pueden pensarse como una herida colonial: una cicatriz que continúa abierta y que recuerda el pasado de la coporalidad mestiza: la historia de la colonización se porta como una línea de color. Es a través de este signo que las corporalidades racializadas pueden leerse desde su pasado histórico.

Las propuestas de estxs pensadorxs, intelectualxs críticxs, todxs ellxs situadxs "'entre' (in betweenness) las dos culturas (la propia y la Moderna)"[7] (Dussel, *Filosofías del sur* 317), son planteamientos de resistencia que llevan un proceso de maduración. Es decir, necesitan de tiempo y estudio para lograr una profunda reflexión sobre la cultura actual, la cual está compuesta por una diversidad

7. Dussel entiende por dos culturas lo siguiente: una, la propia (que en realidad está compuesta necesariamente por muchas otras (indígena, negra, mestiza)); y la Moderna (es decir la producida por la Modernidad, la colonial, de los colonizadores).

de culturas o expresiones culturales, y el enfrentamiento con la moderna dominante. Con ese proceso de maduración se da también una respuesta en la resistencia cultural, desde las creaciones (en la literatura, la pintura, el cine), hasta nuevos proyectos para transformar la cultura (políticas públicas). Dicho de otra forma, es a través de una reflexión que se puede pensar en otras formas de culturas que representen o den cuenta de una forma otra de ser-en-el-mundo. Desde Latinoamérica y las culturas latinoamericanas extendidas (dícese chicanas, nuyoricans, centro y sudamericanas en Estados Unidos) se han creado una serie de discursos u obras artísticas que son testimonios de una diversidad cultural que se contrapone a la cultura dominante. Toda autohistoria puede leerse como parte de esta resistencia cultural, así *Borderlands* y otros textos autobiográficos con fines políticos pueden leerse como obras que pretenden dar cuenta de la experiencia de una otredad y desde ese posicionamiento dan soluciones para sobrevivir a las amenazas de asimilación/aniquilación por parte de la cultura dominante.

Las tres propuestas convergen en que se trata de un paradigma otro, pues se trata de crear formas de pensamientos que critiquen a la Modernidad desde el lugar de lxs subalternxs/colonizadxs. Las tres, como paradigma otro, se conectan por una experiencia/historia común: el colonialismo. Promueven nuevas formas de pensamiento/conciencia que permitan atravesar/enfrentar los embates de la Modernidad.

De alguna manera, los planteamientos de Anzaldúa y Segato tienen en común con la filosofía de la liberación el posicionarse desde la experiencia o perspectiva de las subjetividades subalternizadas, puesto que como lo apunta Dussel, dicha corriente filosófica se trata de una toma de conciencia, de un diálogo donde se piensa desde la opresión, la exclusión y la otredad (Dussel, *1492* 8). Asimismo, Dussel señala que la filosofía de la liberación "descubría su condicionamiento cultural (se pensaba *desde* una cultura determinada),[8] pero además articulado (explícita o implícitamente) desde los intereses de clases, grupos, sexos, razas, etc. determinadas" (Dussel, *Filosofías del sur* 190). Entonces, dado que la nueva mestiza, la *Trans-modernidad* y la *relectura del mestizaje* son reflexiones que provienen de una posición subalterna, posibilitan que esa alteridad excluida intervenga y proponga fórmulas para trascender la Modernidad/Colonialidad.

---

8. Dussel aquí se refiere a la cultura dominada, la cultura latinoamericana que se edifica como cultura otra, esa que está compuesta por una diversidad de identidades y de expresiones culturales.

BIBLIOGRAFÍA

Anzaldúa, Gloria. *Borderlands/La Frontera: The New Mestiza*, 4ª ed., Aunt Lute Books, 2007.

Ballón Gutiérrez, Alejandra y Dairo Sánchez-Mojica. "Entrevista a Rita Laura Segato: autobiografía, pensamiento y políticas de la verdad." *Nómadas*, 53, julio-diciembre 2020, pp. 229-238. https://nomadas.ucentral.edu.co/nomadas/pdf/nomadas_53/53_13_Entrevista_Rita_Laura_Segato.pdf

Cantú, Norma Elía y Aída Hurtado. "Breaking Borders/Constructing Bridges: Twenty-Five Years of *Borderlands/La Frontera*. Introduction to the 4th edition", *Borderlands/La Frontera: The New Mestiza*, 4ª ed., Aunt Lute Books, 2007, pp. 3-13.

Castro-Gómez, Santiago. "Patriarcado de alta intensidad y mestizaje." Video de YouTube, 26:01. Publicado el 9 de julio de 2022. https://youtu.be/7h4sPcn2fhU?si=OwRMQuKc4HJJfauD

Enrique Dussel. https://enriquedussel.b-cdn.net/wp-content/uploads/2023/10/CURRICULUM_2023.pdf

Gloria Evangelina Anzaldúa Papers/Archivos, Benson Latin American Collection, Bibliotecas de la Universidad de Texas, Universidad de Texas en Austin, cajas 1, 5, 7, 8, 16, 32 y 33.

Dussel, Enrique. *1492: el encubrimiento del otro: hacia el origen del mito de la Modernidad*, Plural editores-Facultad de Humanidades y Ciencias de la Educación, 1994, pp. 7-37, 69-81 y 175-180.

__________. *Filosofías del Sur. Descolonización y Transmodernidad*, Akal, 2015, pp. 281-321.

García-Agundis, Sergio, dir. *Caminante no hay camino… un autorretrato documental*, 2015, en Vimeo, https://vimeo.com/114714858.

González San Martín, Patricia. "La filosofía de la liberación de Enrique Dussel. Una aproximación a partir de la formulación de la *analéctica.*" *Estudios de filosofía práctica e historia de las ideas*, vol. 16, núm. 2, diciembre 2014, pp. 45-52. ISSn 1515–7180. https://www.scielo.org.ar/pdf/efphi/v16n2/v16n2a04.pdf

Gutiérrez Magallanes, María del Socorro. *Autobiografía política chicana y latinoamericana: una producción cultural contrahegemónica. Proyectos culturales que revelan procesos sociales que difieren y escrituras que convergen (palabras, vidas y utopías de Gloria Anzaldúa y Roque Dalton)*, 2014, Universidad Nacional Autónoma de México, Facultad de Ciencias Políticas y Sociales, tesis doctoral.

Keating, AnaLouise, editor. *The Gloria Anzaldúa Reader*, Texas: Duke University, (2009), pp. 187-197 y 203-216.

Paizanni, Carlos. "Enrique Dussel, el filósofo que hizo pueblo." *Revista Tlatelolco: Democracia Democratizante y Cambio Social*, Programa Universitario de Estudios sobre Democracia, Justicia y Sociedad de la UNAM, 23 de noviembre de 2023. https://puedjs.unam.mx/revista_tlatelolco/enrique-dussel-el-filosofo-que-hizo-pueblo/

Rodríguez Manzano, Alfonso. "El sujeto en los textos 'seminales' del Giro Descolonial: inventario, fuentes y significación." *Sociocriticism*, XXXV- 2, 2021. http://interfas.univ-tlse2.fr/sociocriticism/3018

Segato, Rita. *La crítica de la colonialidad en ocho ensayos y una antropología por demanda*, Prometeo, 2015, pp. 211-243.

Vivancos Pérez, Ricardo. *Radical Chicana Poetics*, Colección Literature of the Americas, Palgrave Macmillan, 2013, pp. 29-49.

DOMESTIC FRONTERAS

"I HAVE A NAME AND IT'S NOT MAID"

CHRISTIAN V. RAMIREZ

INTRODUCTION

A house situated at the edge of Corpus Christi Bay in South Texas patiently waits to be vacuumed, swept, mopped, and organized. My mother often begins her daily routine of her job as a domestic worker in houses like this one. On this morning, a note with instructions and a list of duties—assignments that are customarily communicated by domestic labor employers—rests on the kitchen table. My mother, neatly dressed with her hair pulled back, arrives early to work. She finds the note left behind by her White employer. It reads: "Maid, please make sure the dog is let out before noon and that he is fed before you leave." Independently contracted, my mother maintains a certain level of autonomy in deciding who she works for, where she works, and to a certain extent her pay.

She intentionally responds with a follow-up note that read: "I have a name and it's not maid." This note was defiant, what Gloria Anzaldúa calls an act of an atravesada. This seemingly simple act of resistance, I learned, was an example of Las Atravesadas, or "those who crossover, pass over, or go through the confines of the 'normal.'"(Anlzaldúa 3). This concept of "atravecer" helps articulate the ways I understood the autonomy of domestic laborers and how Mexican-origin mujeres hired in the secondary labor market unsettle hegemonic ideas and notions of servitude.

This essay centers domestic labor and workers from South Texas. I use an auto-historia approach to situate instances that reflect atravesadas as anti-colonial forms of resistance and reject deeply embedded assumptions of Mexican-origin women in the U.S. Guided by Anzaldúa's particularized focus on Mexican-origin women along the borderlands, this method and focus on las atravesadas serves as a critique of the double-colonization and empire building along the South Texas borderland. It is also shaped by my own conocimiento about the intersection of race, gender, class, and labor as the son of a Mexican immigrant domestic worker.

Mexicanas, both immigrant and U.S. born, are gendered and racialized into specific labor parameters dictated by a colonial U.S. imaginary. Thus, an analysis of domestic labor necessitates a closer examination of the intersections of race, gender, class, and citizenship along the Texas borderlands. I argue that domestic work, in South Texas, is reserved for Mexican and Mexican-descended mujeres by a socially and culturally produced American imaginary that has been informed largely by a historic relationship of colonization. My own awareness of this relationship and understanding of inequality came by way of my mother's agency. The atravesada in her not only navigated the conditions of her workplace but also had a profound impact on my own conocimiento and acts of rebellion.

The theoretical work of Gloria Anzaldúa is appropriate as the point of departure because I am also employing an auto-historia teoría as a method of analysis to demonstrate how I experienced the way Mexican and Mexican-origin women working in domestic labor challenge hegemonic ideas of gender, reject notions of servitude, and access agency to negotiate work on their own terms. Documenting my own experiences growing up in South Texas serves as an intervention that creates an archive of the lived experience of those individuals raised by domestic laborers in Corpus Christi, Texas. Domestic labor has yet to be fully engaged as a source of knowledge in South Texas. What follows is a broad literature review of Latina domestic labor to better contextualize and focus on Mexican and Mexican origin mujeres' social place within domestic fronteras.

FRAMING LATINA DOMESTIC LABOR

In her book, *Domestica: Immigrant Workers Cleaning and Caring in the Shadows of Affluence,* sociologist Pierrette Hondagneu-Sotelo provides useful parameters and a definition of domestic work. For instance, domestic labor often includes the following three elements. First, domestic workers have several employers and clean particular homes on a weekly or bi-weekly basis at a flat rate. Second, workers are paid by the job instead of by the hour. Last, domestic workers experience atomized working conditions and privatized employer-employee relations, and they engage in a continuous search for multiple employers (Hondagneu-Sotelo, "Regulating the Unregulated").

Domestic workers have also been identified as reproductive laborers, as this term refers to the labor needed to sustain the productive primary labor force in postindustrial nations (Salazar Parreñas). Such work includes household chores, the care of the elderly, adults, youth, and the socialization of children. Domestic work from this perspective positions workers as the product and producers of a globalized experience along the intersections of gender, race, and citizenship in a post-industrial service economy. While South Texas is the focus of my analysis, domestic labor is a global phenomenon and extends outside of the U.S.

Those employed in the secondary labor market are part of a larger flow of what Rebeca Raijman et al. terms "global reproductive workers," who migrate into gender-specific jobs in Western capitalist societies. These include the newly industrialized countries of Asia and the oil-rich countries of the Middle East (Raijman et al.). Raijman et al.'s study provides empirical evidence of Latinas from South America being recruited to work in affluent households as far away as Israel. This suggests that the social and racial construction of Latinas actually extends beyond the cultural imaginary of the U.S. to a larger global economic and political system that positions all Latinas as ideal types for domestic work around the world.

In Northern Mexico, the image of Mexican women during and after the colonial period contributes to a gendered ideology of structural inequality. Antonia Castañeda identifies that "none of the historical literature refers to any women of color as bearers of culture and civilization." She identifies two dichotomous images of women of color within historical texts. "Good" women are characterized as light-skinned, civilized (Christian), and virginal while "bad" women are dark-skinned, savage (non-Christian), and sexually promiscuous. These gendered images have sustained unfair disparities not only between women and men but also between White women and their Mexican counterparts. The image of Mexicanas as "gentle tamers," a stereotype fed by colonial ideas about Mexicanas whose passive and nurturing helped to civilize the western and southern frontiers described by Castañeda, offers insight into the perception of racial and gender-based assumptions of Mexicanas as naturally positioned for domestic work.

What Hondagneu-Sotello, Salazar Parreñas, Raijman, and Castañeda emphasize is the racial nature of domestic labor as a global phenomenon and as a gender-specific job. The reproductive labor of Mexicanas and Mexican origin women in South Texas are woven into this larger global context. On one hand, my mother's lived experience as a domestic laborer reflects a hierarchy among racialized women. On the other hand, my mother's astute response to her employer challenges the entrenched assumptions that domestic workers are servants with limited agency. By refusing to be addressed as "maid" rather than by her name, she disputes social arrangements lodged in a history of Mexican subjugation. More importantly, it serves as a reminder that she has a history, a degree of agency, and the political incisiveness necessary to confront long held ideologies of colonization. The following section provides examples of rejecting these unequal relations between Mexicanas and their exploiters in South Texas.

REJECTING UNEQUAL RELATIONS EN LA FRONTERA

The U.S. coordinated control of land and labor not only through colonialism but also through commercial capitalism. As Ruth Wilson Gilmore explains in "Geographies of Racial Capitalism," all capitalism is racial capitalism: "Capitalism requires inequality and racism enshrines it." In South Texas, a colonized workforce and racially distinctive groups of people became the backbone of unequal labor relations. Mexican and Mexican-origin domestic labor are structured within this colonial and capitalist system of exploitation. Obfuscating these historical relationships relegates the material conditions of Mexican immigrant women in the U.S. to arbitrary images that assume their place in society as natural.

It is within this context of racial capitalism and exploitation that Anzaldúa writes herself into being in deep South Texas. Her poetry rejects these unequal relations between Mexicanas and their exploiters. In Anzaldúa's work, I find my own mother's voice to claim her name and her identity.

Anzaldúa's poem "To Live in the Borderlands" reads:

> Cuando vives en la frontera
> People walk through you, the wind steals your voice,
> You're a burra, buey, scapegoat,
> Forerunner of a new race… (Anzaldúa 194)

These words resonate with my memories of the social and structural dismissiveness towards my mother and other domestic workers. The informality of this job leaves many domestic workers without formal retirement options and health care coverage. They are often dismissed as unskilled burras. Oftentimes, these messages about their worth get internalized by the workers themselves. "Ay como soy burra," my mother would say, when, in reality, she and other domestic workers operated as entrepreneurs. I was fascinated by the vast social networks my mother maintained and how easily she could find a new home for newly arrived immigrants.

> In the Borderlands
> you are the battleground

where enemies are kin to each other;
you are at home, a stranger,
the border disputes have been settled
the volley of shots have scattered the truce
you are wounded, lost in action
dead, fighting back. (Anzaldúa194)

With her pronouncement, "I have a name and it is not maid," my mother conveys an understanding of an ontological battleground that privileges some bodies more than others, and that those without value are often unnamed. As Anzaldúa notes in her poem, in the borderlands you yourself are a battleground. The wound of not being referred to by her name, Yolanda, spurs my mother to demand being seen as a fully realized human being.

Anzaldúa reminds us:

To survive the Borderlands
you must live *sin fronteras*
be a crossroads.

My family has survived in the South Texas borderlands. The battlegrounds of race, class, gender, and citizenship were not dead ends. Rather, my mother and other domestic laborers live *sin fronteras* as they negotiate historic systems of inequality. *Ellas son las atravesadas*. My memories of the various neighborhoods my mother and her fellow domestic workers traversed are detailed in the next section.

UNA AUTO-HISTORIA DE DOMESTIC LABOR EN EL SUR DE TEJAS

Here, I use auto-historia to draw out the politics of my experiences to connect them to larger themes of domestic labor by Mexicanas and Mexican-origin women. My experiences at school, home, and as a first-generation immigrant are political in nature. Documenting the events surrounding my family's experiences from the mid to late 20th century historicizes and ground truths a particular Mexican immigrant experience in South Texas. I emphasize Mexican and Mexican-origin domestic labor because it is through this particular lens that I came to recognize my place in society. In this narrative, I express what it was to navigate between the working-class barrios to the extravagant and lavish homes of the affluent White families of Corpus Christi, Texas. What I share has been shaped by the dynamics of my gender, race, working-class background, and fluctuating citizenship status.

I witnessed the distinction of race and class differences inside the homes my mother cleaned. One obvious distinction was the size of these homes. Running through them seemed like an endless endeavor. Two living rooms? Who needed two living rooms? Our entire apartment seemed like it could fit neatly between the two. A private indoor gym led out to a backyard with a pool, hammocks, and a large mesquite tree. Other homes had direct access to the beach. None were owned by families like my own. White families hung their framed family photos with the popular Olan Mills logo stamped in the corner.

Growing up with access to the private spaces of these communities, I questioned why my family cleaned and cared for the upper-middle class White families in Corpus Christi. One thing that was irrefutable was my understanding that domestic labor had little to no social capital. I was ashamed of being associated with the occupation of my parents. When students or teachers would ask what my parents did for work, I often lied and said my mom was a stay-at-home mother and that my dad was in a high managerial position at Walmart. I learned that being linked to their real jobs as a domestic worker and custodian was something that produced *pena*. These negative messages were partially informed by popular media images of Mexican immigrants and other Latinas as poor, uneducated, undocumented domestic workers.

A few years ago, I asked my mother what career she had been interested in as a young woman. She replied, "I wanted to be a nurse to take care of little babies and old people. They are the ones that need the most attention and care." It made sense to me that although domestic labor was not her preferred profession she was in reality doing "care work." She raised children for other women while they concentrated on their careers and still continues to take care of an elderly woman through companionship and assistance with household chores. She cared for an elderly woman who had little contact with her extended family and provided friendship through her actions that went beyond taking care of her domestic duties. Though my mother is not a certified health care professional, she has made her profession reflect her ideal career choice.

Her migration to the U.S. and subsequent occupation is a result of the economic restructuring of world capitalism of the mid-1970s that would have a tremendous impact on my family's settlement in South Texas (Flores). By the 1980s, both of my parents had established themselves within the primary labor force in the highly industrial northern Mexican state of Coahuila. Prior to my birth and shortly thereafter, my mother worked in a textile plant that produced glass and tile. My father was a regional manager at a large national chain of gas stations. Neither of the two had more than a high school education but managed to sustain a comfortable working-class status in Mexico.

For them, the U.S. was not a potential or desired location for permanent settlement. However, their decision to relocate was brought about by larger social and structural forces. Beginning in the 1970s and through the 1980s, particular areas of the U.S., including South Texas, witnessed a dramatic resurgence of paid domestic work (Hondagneu-Sotelo, "Regulating the Unregulated"; Salazar Parreñas) as a result of several factors. The decade was one of income and occupational polarization, growth in management and professional positions, and the mass entrance of women into the formal labor force, all of which stimulated demand for the services of paid domestic work (Hondagneu-Sotelo, *Domestica*).

The economic shift in Mexico spurred by the devaluation of the peso and massive lay-offs, such as the dismantling of the company that employed my father, left my parents with few employment opportunities in Coahuila. We had extended family living in the U.S. who had established their residency in Texas in the decade before our arrival. By this time period, Latinas of all ethnicities had replaced African American women as the dominant group of domestic workers. The logic of the American imagination saw Mexican immigrant women and other Latinas as ideal candidates for what Hondagneu-Sotelo calls "care work" (*Domestica*). Women from Mexico and other Latin American countries were highly sought out for their perceived docile motherly nature, limited English proficiency, and lack of legal citizenship (Castañeda). The social-political and economic conditions of the 1970s and 1980s provided the conditions for entry into the secondary labor market my mother experienced as an immigrant woman from Mexico.

To this day, my mother works in some of Corpus Christi's most prominent homes along Ocean Drive, the thoroughfare that runs along the city's coastline, providing ocean-side views to the most affluent and privileged families in Corpus. The homes and neighborhoods along Ocean Drive are mansions, with perfectly hedged lawns, tall thin palm trees, and cars to match the economic status of the homeowners. Gated homes line the winding road along the coast with a perfect view of the sunrise and sunset. In the distance, the economic center of the city sits in plain sight; tall downtown buildings and a constant influx of import and export ships pass one another at the port of entry. The occasional jogger races by with a groomed dog and trendy tracksuit. It's a quiet space reserved for people who do not look like me or my parents. Our time in this neighborhood was limited and it expired once my mother provided her labor of care. It was within this space that I came to realize the economic privileges held by a group of people who I could not culturally identify with. Everything seemed to be neat, orderly, and policed to keep us at a distance.

Running through the long halls and broad beautiful gardens of these lush homes exposed me to stark class distinctions. The markers of my community did not exist within this space. For instance, pan dulce and ice cold paletas were only found on the west-side of Corpus, the other side of town. It was here, in the neighborhood known as Molina, where I felt distinctly welcomed, despite the hardships of poverty inflicted by decades of racial and class segregation in

Corpus Christi. My family and I lived in a small room that was part of a larger home behind our bilingual church. This neighborhood is predominated by Black and Mexican or Mexican American working-class families.

The Molina neighborhood is characterized by small wooden homes, with narrow cracked cement driveways dotted with the occasional portable basketball hoops where neighborhood children took turns playing three-on-three or a quick game of HORSE. You did not see joggers. Instead, there are gangbangers hanging out on front porches and grandmothers hanging clothes to dry. A loud ice cream truck with a siren announces its arrival. *Corridos* and hip-hop mixing into one another hang in the air. The local mechanic works on his ride. Never missing is the aroma of fresh made tortillas wafting through open windows. Many of the atravesadas my mother networks with live in neighborhoods like this that are throughout Corpus Christi.

The material conditions of this neighborhood and neighborhoods like it continue to be the result of colonization and capitalist exploitation. The predominantly Mexican-origin community in this space lacks control over the institutions of the barrio (Barrera, et al.). Interestingly, those living on Ocean Drive are largely dependent on the service work provided by those who live in communities like Molina. The contrasting social conditions of these neighborhoods are maintained by race-based exploitation. Each community has been historically shaped and developed by a racial, class, and gendered stratification. It is this relationship between communities that provides a microcosm of the experience of Mexican-descended peoples that results from the Spanish colonization of Mexico and the U.S capitalist development that further disenfranchised them from the land and its resources (Almaguer, "Chicano Colonialism").

It was the women of this barrio that introduced my mother to the social networks that enabled her to obtain a job. This network was exclusively composed of immigrants from Mexico who attended the Apostolic church located in the heart of Molina we attended. Most of these women had worked as domestic cleaners most of their adult lives in the U.S. I recall listening to their conversations discussing the long-term *casas* they cared for and sharing how one of their employers had a friend or relative that was looking for help. References were important markers of trust and entrepreneurship. Once a general trust was established, contracts between employers and employees were often verbal agreements. My mother and her *comadres* would regularly check in with one another to informally discuss their work conditions. Did they offer breaks? Were they hovering over them or allowing them to work without supervision? These were important questions they would ask one another.

Often, the type of "help" women like my mother provided included the supervision of children. Mary Romero points out that there is a racial preference for Latinas, especially Mexican immigrant women in Texas, as primary caretakers of children because of their perceived "natural ability" to care for young. I often hear my mother affectionately refer to the children in her care as "mi güerra" (my little white girl) or "mi güerro" (my little white boy). "Ya se nos hizo grande el güerro," (He grew up on us so fast) she would say to her employer. In this regard, these children came to be viewed as shared between parent and caregiver through a consistent career with a particular family.

The homes of affluence had more than one mother. More than one caretaker. More rooms to hold possessions that needed cleaning once a week. It was access to homes of affluence that I could visibly see that made me feel the inequality. These experiences influenced my decisions to take up sociology as my major in college and later Mexican American Studies as a graduate student at UT-Pan American. My mother's atravesadas were a key that unlocked my own *conocimiento.*

CONCLUSION

Anzaldúa reminds us that to survive the borderlands is to survive the empire and its design to dominate our lived experiences. She states, "I seek new images of identity, new beliefs about ourselves, our humanity and worth no longer in question." (Anzaldúa 87) From this perspective, Mexican and Mexican origin women in domestic work continue to challenge the racial, gendered and economic social arrangements set by hegemonic ideologies of the nation. This reworking of self and identity is at the center of being an *atravesada* en la frontera.

Reflecting on the spatial differences between Ocean Drive and Molina provided a lens to help me understand inequality without any formal education. As a child of a domestic worker, these intimate spaces were accessible and allowed me to situate the *atravesudas* of my mother. Demanding to be referred to by her name and not her profession is an anti-colonial form of resistance. Her decisions to work or not work with certain families according to her level of comfort demonstrated a degree of agency that I had not considered before. Through auto-historia, these realities reveal how domestic laborers in South Texas resist further exploitation and support each other through the networks they establish.

This essay is intended to serve as an intervention to create an archive of the lived experience of those individuals raised by domestic laborers in Corpus Christi, Texas. To the Mexican, Mexican-American, and Chicana/x children of South Texas: May we faithfully witness (Lugones) the labor of love our mothers create for us and others. Our collective response to a colonial history and current moment of capitalist exploitation happens in small acts. The self-assurance my mother demonstrated by claiming, "I have a name, and it's not maid," speaks truth back to power. Her radical atravesudas are stories worth archiving and retelling to future generations. We will be called by our names.

WORKS CITED

Almaguer, Tomás. "Toward the Study of Chicano Colonialism." *Aztlán*, vol. 2, no. 1, 1974, pp. 7-21.

Anzaldúa, Gloria. *Borderlands/La frontera: The New Mestiza*. Aunt Lute Books, 1987.

Castañeda, Antonia I. "Women of Color and the Rewriting of Western History: The Discourse, Politics, and Decolonization of History." *Pacific History Review*, vol. 61, no. 4, 1992, pp. 501-533."Geographies of Racial Capitalism with Ruth Wilson Gilmore - An Antipode Foundation Film." YouTube, uploaded by antipodeonline, June 1, 2020, https://www.youtube.com/watch?v=2CS627aKrJI&t=2s.

Hondagneu-Sotelo, Pierrette. "Regulating the Unregulated?: Domestic Workers' Social Networks." *Social Problems,* vol. 41, no. 1, 1994, pp. 50-64.

Hondagneu-Sotelo, Pierrette. *Domestica: Immigrant Workers Cleaning and Caring in the Shadows of Affluence*. University of California Press, 2001. Lugones, Maria A. *Peregrina Pilgrimages/Peregrinajes: Theorizing Coalitions Against Multiple Oppressions*. Rowman and Littlefield, 2003.

Raijman, Rebeca, Schammah-Gesser, Silvina, & Kemp, Adriana "International Migration, Domestic Work, and Care Work: Undocumented Latina Migrants in Israel." *Gender and Society,* vol. 17, no. 5, 2003, pp. 727-749.

Romero, Mary. "Conceptualizing the Latina Experience in Care Work." *A Companion to Latina/o Studies,* edited by Juan Flores, Renato Rosaldo, Wiley-Blackwell, 2011, pp. 264-275.

Salazar Parreñas, Rhacel. "Migrant Filipina Domestic Workers and the International Division of Reproductive Labor. *Gender and Society*, vol. 14, no. 4, 2000, pp. 560-580.

SPEAKING SHAKESPEARE IN THE BORDERLANDS

ADRIANNA M. SANTOS

For Romeo Santos, Sr. (1921-2019)

Reading Shakespeare as an awkward teenage girl in South Texas, I did not imagine I would one day be an Anzalduista in an English program in an era of renewed attacks on ethnic and gender studies. In this work, I consider myself a "Trojan mula," what La Gloria described as one "who has infiltrated in order to subvert the system," one of "[t]hose who have been educated and assimilated in the universities [who] run the risk of being white-washed in the academy's acid" ("New Mestiza Nation," 205). The struggle is real. I am a scholar with one foot in Chicanx Studies and one in Shakespeare Studies, ni de aquí, ni de allá, a nepantlera in an Hispanic Serving Institution in my hometown of San Antonio, Texas, who had more in common with her Southside students than with most of her colleagues when she started. As a recently tenured associate professor, I am attempting to reconcile warring parts of my scholarly identity (Chicana Feminisms and Shakespeare Studies) in which the personal remains political. As a student, I needed to both excel in the public schooling system and resist it in order to earn a Ph.D. from a research university in Chicana/o Studies. Thus, Anzaldúa's appropriation of a Greek tale that Homer recounts in *The Iliad* to describe her own subjectivity as a Chicana in the ivory tower resonates strongly with me.

Growing up, I was a seventh-generation Mexican American whose first language was English and whose parents frequently treated Spanish as a secret language, attempting to guard me from the trauma our elders experienced in the educational system. It was more important to them that I speak English well than to be able to communicate with mis abuelos en nuestra lengua nativa. As was the case with most public-school students, the study of works by the British writer William Shakespeare loomed large in my education, and I estimated, even then, that to be good at English, I needed to "speak Shakespeare." Unbeknownst to me, at the same time, marginalized artists had been appropriating Shakespeare to reflect the multilayered histories and present concerns of the U.S.–Mexico Borderlands. Brilliant playwrights from community theaters, university Theater Programs and Ethnic Studies programs were taking Shakespeare's plays and poems and interweaving their own languages and themes to meet the artistic and activist needs of their communities. Some of them included *The Language of Flowers* by Edit Villareal, and *The Merchant of Santa Fe* by Ramón A. Flores and Lynn Knight. The telenovelas of Borderlands Shakespeare relocate their settings and characters to reside within the hybrid histories, cultures, and languages of the La Frontera. Some take place during día de los muertos, some feature la Llorona, most are bilingual, and several were written with input from the local community in response to their own histories and social concerns (Gillen, Santos, and Santos).

When I decided to study Chicana literature in graduate school at the first Chicano and Chicano Studies Doctoral program in the country at the University of California, Santa Barbara, I thought I would abandon all my previous indoctrination to the Western canon, but, in the end, it was much more complicated. It would be more than a decade before I opened my *Norton Anthology of William Shakespeare*, a hefty tome, with the critical eyes of a Chicana scholar and for reference in relation to *The Tragic Corrido of Romeo and Lupe* by Seres Jaime Magaña, a bilingual *Romeo and Juliet* appropriation in which farmworkers in Pharr, Texas, rose up against the Anglo irrigation company that was exploiting the land and the people of South Texas. But with a reference to Gloria Anzaldúa's "herida abierta" in Act 1, Scene 7, I knew that there was an important phenomenon that I may be able to explore with my colleagues who were interested in Premodern Critical Race Studies, without whom I would not have paid attention. Intersections seemed unlikely to me at the time but have proven to be multitudinal. It was an unexpected leap, and, with the current state of public education and demand for literacy in the Eurocentric western canon still present, I ask myself: What does it mean to return to Shakespeare after years of training in Chicanx Studies? How does Anzaldúan philosophy inform my reading of Shakespeare adaptations and help to contextualize borderlands cultura to the academy? In this essay, I'll ponder what Borderlands Shakespeare has meant to me and what it can mean for young people today and attempt an answer to the question I get the most from raza scholars: Why Shakespeare?

As founders of the collaborative research project the Borderlands Shakespeare Colectiva and co-editors of *The Bard in the Borderlands: An Anthology of Shakespeare Appropriations en La Frontera*, my colleagues Katherine Gillen and Kathryn Vomero Santos and I are asked this question frequently. There are many answers to the query, but for the purposes of this essay, I will highlight just a few. First and foremost, the pedagogical potentials of smuggling Chicanx Studies through the vehicle of Guillermo Shakespeare are powerful. Borderlands Studies in "the ruff," if you will. The US southwest is home to the majority of Mexican American and Latinx school children. For better or worse, the cultural capital of Shakespeare is undeniable. He takes up a lot of space—in classrooms, in public theater, and in pop culture. When Chicanx playwrights can claim that space, they have access to a vast repository of knowledge, resources, and funding. Secondly, as many of the actors, writers, and directors we have worked with can attest, Latina/o/x actors are trained in Shakespeare, but they often have difficulty getting cast in traditional roles. Next, Chicana/o/x audiences, far removed from the contexts of Elizabethan theatre, might find it challenging to connect with the source material if the production makes no attempt to consider their lived experiences. It may even be a challenge to attract Chicana/o/x audiences to Shakespeare plays. Therefore, to address these lacunae, frameworks of Borderlands Shakespeare are recognizable, easily accessible, and free for acting companies who wish to draw on Shakespeare's cultural capital without compromising their own dramatic lineages in Teatro Campesino, Mexican satire, Theater of the Oppressed, radical performance protest, and more. As a symbol of whiteness, literacy, and status, Shakespeare signifies privilege and mobility. If you can "speak Shakespeare" you can more easily navigate social and cultural spaces. But this fluency is limited on its own.

Particularly if one is embedded in the Borderlands, a cultural reader must be able to speak multiple languages or at the very least comprehend their contexts. Borderlands Shakespeare thus offers a unique opportunity to explore the collisions and co-mingling of multiple worlds. One might argue that fronterizos are uniquely equipped to grapple with the complexity and drama of Shakespearean materials. The Borderlands are known for their "mestizaje," a term Rafael Pérez-Torres defines as "an affirmative recognition of the mixed racial, social, linguistic, national, cultural, and ethnic legacies inherent to Latino/a cultures and identities" (25). Borderlands Shakespeare takes to task all manner of social ills, evidenced in our multivolume, open access anthology of bilingual appropriations, *The Bard in the Borderlands*. We argue that the plays gathered therein "use Shakespeare to expose the material violence of ongoing colonization, [and] also emphasize the value, beauty, and restorative power of Indigenous and Mexican languages, mythologies, and rituals." However, "[They] do not simply reproduce Shakespeare in new contexts but rather use his work in innovative ways to negotiate colonial power, to reframe Borderlands histories, and to envision socially just futures" (Gillen, Santos, and Santos 1).

Since Shakespeare's "universality" as a playwright is rarely questioned in education, it is crucial that we figure out how we are going to challenge that as BIPOC communities. If they ban ethnic studies in schools, Shakespeare can help us to continue our decolonial work while we fight to restore it. Again, he takes up a lot of space. His plays are performed, by far, more often than any other playwright living or dead. If taken up with social justice aims, though, Shakespeare can be a vehicle for us to critique the very systems of white supremacy that his works helped to create and continue to reinforce, particularly as they shape our public humanities. Kathryn Vomero Santos describes how Borderlands adaptations "might serve as models for a future of Shakespearean public programming that is not interested in merely preserving Shakespeare and his whiteness but one that... works to destabilize the cultural authority of Shakespeare and does not simply radiate outward from the textual, institutional, national, linguistic, or racial center to the peripheries" (52-3). Borderlands Shakespeare can help us do this intentionally with our Chicana/o/x communities in mind. In *Young Latinx Shakespeares*, for example, Jesús Montaño argues that because of its prevalence in curricula for youth, Shakespeare can be considered Young Adult Literature and appropriations of it by Latinx and Queer writers allow for the interweaving of multiple identities as resistance to the hegemony of colonial spaces. Shakespeare plays and other so-called "classic" literature therefore has the potential to do both harm and good in Latina/o/x communities, depending on how it is implemented. For those who employ trauma-informed practices and culturally relevant pedagogy, centering works of Borderlands Shakespeare in the classroom can authorize students to tell their own stories by dismantling what is presented as canonical literature and taking up their own spaces and by amplifying the voices of their own communities.

My students at Texas A&M University-San Antonio are an excellent example of this type of negotiation. Often uniquely aware of their positionalities within the city and the performativity with which the history of the seventh largest city in the nation is sold to tourists, students yearn for culturally relevant texts. The Spanish fantasy heritage of the Riverwalk and Unesco World Heritage Mission reach brings in millions of dollars of revenue each year but does nothing to solve the educational inequities in our city. In fact, the eighteen independently funded school districts all but ensure educational inequality. San Antonio is still one of the most segregated cities in the nation, a reflection of its colonial past and economically divided population. Even after the gains of el Movimiento, the Mexican American Civil Rights Movement, our young people still struggle due to structural issues like economic and food insecurity, housing crisis and disenfranchisement, inequitable access to community services and resources, the fallout of redlining policies, the defunding of public education, and a general lack of culturally relevant pedagogies. This is not to say that there has not been an ongoing, valiant effort to address these problems. San Antonio is now home to the first Mexican American Civil Rights Institute, headed by Dr. Sarah Zenaida Gould. Educators and activists have worked tirelessly to meet the needs of our growing population of Mexican American children in the educational system by centering Mexican American Studies in K-12 education in Texas. As Josué Puente and Stephanie Alvarez argue, Mexican American Studies "provides an opportunity for Mexican American students to see that they are a part of the curriculum and gain an educational space to explore their own social and historical positions in the United States" (67). In her reflection on her leadership in the MAS for Texas Schools movement, Lilliana Saldaña notes that "this struggle for epistemic justice—the right to our knowledge in the face of white supremacy and U.S. settler schooling—is not a new movement. It's a movement that is at least 500 years old and is rooted in Indigenous resistance to the coloniality of knowledge and the coloniality of being," making direct connections to the history of community organizing and activism for educational equity through the nineteenth and twentieth centuries (10). The presence of Mexican American studies in schools is not novel, but it is a constant struggle to maintain in a perpetually hostile environment.

Recently, the attacks on DEI that Texas has been facing for decades, but especially the last few years, have come to national attention. If ethnic studies is banned in schools, maybe Borderlands Shakespeare can help us to continue our decolonial work with our Chicana/o/x communities in mind while we fight to preserve it. Since his "universality" is rarely questioned in education, perhaps Shakespeare can be a vehicle for us to critique the very systems of white supremacy his work has upheld. Ruben Espinosa argues that "As an icon of the English language, Shakespeare exists as a vehicle to define this view of legitimacy and to advance linguistic terrorism" ("Don't It Make My Brown Eyes Blue," 51). Extending Gloria Anzaldúa's *Borderlands/La Frontera* (1987) theory further in the context of Critical Early Modern Studies, Espinosa "offers an intervention that unsettles the critical frameworks that have, for far too long, reinforced the white rage and linguistic violence that sustain Shakespeare's white capital." He continues:

> Because of Shakespeare's deep interconnection with English, and with Englishness, he is often perceived to be less accessible to certain users,

> such as Latinxs. While apprehension surrounding the knotty nature of Shakespearean verse might partially guide these perceptions, attitudes about Shakespeare's place in the establishment of English linguistic and cultural identity certainly drive these views. ("Beyond The Tempest" 45)

Espinosa contends, "One can scrutinize Shakespeare as being a tool of colonial oppression while simultaneously recognizing that the colonial, postcolonial or neocolonial subject can appropriate that tool for themselves to offer anticolonial perspectives" ("Postcolonial Studies" 162). To be sure, Shakespeare and his texts are not above critique, reproach, and revision. Borderlands Shakespeare plays are particularly well suited for such grappling. In their musings on pedagogy, Katherine Gillen and Kathryn Vomero Santos write, "Rather than treating Shakespeare as sacrosanct, Borderlands Shakespeare plays take what is of use in Shakespeare and repurpose it to meet the needs of their communities and to imagine new futures. Reading Borderlands Shakespeare empowers students to do the same and to bring their own cultural, racial, and linguistic knowledges to bear on material often considered elite white property" (114-5).

Furthermore, in "Opening the Humanities to New Fields and New Voices," George J. Sánchez directly takes up the "crisis of the *public* in the growing work of the public humanities" wondering whether "our institutions of higher learning diversified sufficiently to readily bring expertise based on community knowledge, growing new scholarship, and passion to understand new perspectives to the world of the public humanities" (84). He argues, however, that there is a "larger movement to radically change the nature of graduate education" and "produce a new generation of scholar activists who do not structure their lives around scholarship solely for the disciplines they represent, but instead desire to engage the wider public in everything they do" (88). This kind of work "requires a full rethinking of the purpose of scholarship in the humanities for the twenty first century with a definition of the public that is much more expansive, multiracial, and class diverse than previous versions of civic engagement have been" (88). Because we are invested in community engagement and public humanities work as well as in more traditional scholarship, Drs. Kathryn Vomero Santos, Katherine Gillen, and I co-founded the collaborative research project the Borderlands Shakespeare Colectiva (BSC)—a growing group of scholars, educators, artists, and activists who engage with Shakespeare in ways that reflect the lived realities of the U.S.–Mexico Borderlands.

The main goals of the BSC include promoting Chicana/o/x and Indigenous literature, fostering culturally sustaining approaches to teaching canonical literary texts, making Borderlands Shakespeare texts and information about productions available to broad audiences, and generating pedagogical resources, scholarship and humanities programming on Borderlands Shakespeare. In describing our work, Gillen and Santos write, "Our collaborations with Borderlands artists and activists, moreover, have affirmed the importance of working outside our institutions, in community with a range of learners and knowledge creators throughout the Borderlands. We therefore see our projects not as attempts to reaffirm the value of Shakespeare but as part of a shared effort to create opportunities for liberatory learning, creativity, and social justice" (125). Funneling resources directly to Chicanx communities, whose artistic and theatrical talents have long been employed to make positive social change, give a meaningful approach to Shakespeare appropriation when applied in Borderlands contexts. This can be especially true when considering the bilingual, or even multilingual nature of these plays. Language politics matter.

Bringing it back to a reflection on my own literacy narrative, I realize that my story includes a lot of contradictions in my struggle to claim my ancestral inheritances and desire to see myself reflected in books, the world of the imagination that I so loved. This love of reading and world-making stemmed from my mother's influence, herself a public-school reading teacher. I was an only child, a shy kid who skipped a grade and attended Catholic School for most of my formative years. I was what Cristina Herrera calls a "Chicanerd." I was a bookish Mexican American chicanita whose grandparents were farmworkers. I attended school on the Northside of S.A. with a bunch of privileged kids, most of them white. I think that my parents were able to afford this because I was an only child. When I stayed with my tía on the weekends, in her Southside barrio, we would watch telenovelas together and sew clothes for my dolls. She spoke to me mainly in Spanish. I spoke back to her mainly in English. Communication was never an issue, though. We understood each other. My bilingual cousins teased me about my white girl accent, so I think shame kept me from fluency in these early years. It's an economically and racially segregated city, San Anto, and whenever I crossed the border from North to South and back again, I felt the familiar push and pull of different cultural literacies. I loved to sing and dance so I later became a child performer in community theater, which further isolated me from my Mexican American extended family who were more interested in football and wrestling. As a little girl with black hair, caramel skin and a Spanish last name, I was rarely cast in the lead role but often got to play the femme fatale in my teen years. It is not surprising to me now that the dark-haired mujer gets typecast as the bad girl, but that is another story. I basically grew up on the stage, spent my free time in rehearsals, and read with a voracious appetite for drama. As you may know, Shakespeare is the ultimate haunt of the mainstream theatre community. It was only a matter of time until I learned to use the phrase "The Scottish Play" inside the theater walls lest the current production of Macbeth be cursed, and to uphold Will's amalgamations of folklore, mythology, history, and tales from other parts of the world as the epitome of the modern stage itself.

Shakespeare was also a large part of my high school and college education, and I would venture to say that is true for most students of public education and perhaps even more so for private school kids. I read no less than four Shakespeare plays in high school and several more as an English major at the University of Texas at Austin. I even studied abroad at Oxford University and saw some of them performed at the Globe in London and by the Royal Shakespeare Company in Stratford Upon Avon, Shakespeare's place of both birth and death. At this point, however, I had only read one Chicana text in public school, *The House on Mango Street* (1984). While a beloved coming of age story of a Mexican American girl in Chicago, considered a modern classic of Latina literature, I would not get to see that novel adapted into a play until 2017 by The Classic Theater in San Antonio, right before I started on this Borderlands Shakespeare journey. With the majority of school-aged kids now identifying as Hispanic in Texas, we need to expand our culturally relevant pedagogy and offerings in Spanish. We had none when I was in high school. I was absolutely forming my own feminist consciousness but without access to the internet or a wide array of positive Latina role models in the media. I remember reading Macbeth sophomore year and being captivated by Lady Macbeth. She was an ambitious, fiercely loyal, fearless, sexual boss bitch chingona and I was there for it! Please, someone, write a Donkey Lady Macbeth. Coming into my own sexual awakening as an adolescent, I was grasping for any representation of female sensuality. Of course, she goes mad at the end, so that didn't make me too optimistic about my prospects for empowerment in that role. Not to mention Juliet—dead, Ophelia—dead, Desdemona—dead. It seemed to be a great leading actress in a Shakespearean tragedy, one had to die.

Just one year later, my senior year, I won a Best Actress award from my peers for my performance as Lady Capulet in our outdoor classroom production of *Romeo and Juliet*, our amateur version of Shakespeare in the Park. She did not die, but she was not the lead, either. It was odd, to say the least, being the only brown girl in the principal cast, surrounded by white actors reading lines from an author that is often deemed to be the quintessential example of the "English" language. Apparently, my approximation of whiteness was convincing to someone. It was clear to me then—to be good at acting, as well, I needed to "speak Shakespeare." Up until then, I had never read or seen a Chicana/o/x play and the only example of a Mexican American author I had was the aforementioned Sandra Cisneros, then a resident of San Antonio. Esperanza never mentioned the Bard, but I figured she would have read him when she went to high school, too.

That senior year of high school, I auditioned for a prestigious theater program at an Ivy League University in New York City with Helena's monologue *from A Midsummer Night's Dream*. But, at the same time, I idolized the Cholas in my school. They always seemed so confident. Their eyeliner game was on point. And the red lipstick equated to power in my adolescent eyes. I wanted to emulate their poderosa attitude but as a kid, it was only ever a performance. So, when I prepped for my college prescreen, I channeled a chola Helena who was desperate to get her ex-novio back. I don't think it translated to the admissions committee. My application was unceremoniously rejected without comment. This Chicanita was not destined for a career in Elizabethan Drama. My early Shakespeare exposure was not over, though. When I was a sophomore in college, I was fortunate enough to attend that aforementioned Oxford Study Abroad program through UT's English Department. It took financial aid, scholarships, and my mother working a summer job teaching driver education. My parents were holding out hope that I would become a lawyer and they weren't thrilled about me leaving the country, but they supported it since it was only for the summer.

While living in Oxford, England, for six weeks, I was able to see *King Lear* and *Cymbeline* at the Globe and *Hamlet* and *Julius Caesar* in Stratford. It was a life-altering experience for a young woman from a working-class family whose only trips out of the country were to border towns for Spring Break and Summer excursions. Even so, I thought that would be the last of my intellectual forays into Shakespeare as an undergraduate. Shortly after I returned from Oxford, I registered for a Latina Literature course taught by Lisa Sánchez González, a visiting lecturer at the University of Texas. Then, I took a Tejana Narrative class with the esteemed poet Teresa Paloma Acosta and was introduced to Norma Cantú's *Canícula: Snapshots of a Girlhood en la Frontera*. This, also, was a life-altering experience for me, having suddenly discovered that there was an entire world of literature to study that more closely reflected my own experiences, and those of my community. I was so moved by these classes; I applied to the Chicana/o Studies doctoral program to study with María Herrera-Sobek and abandoned all my previous loyalties to the Western canon. I left my bulky, jade green *Norton Shakespeare* in the company of my collection of Jane Austin's complete works and various paperbacks of 19th c. British poetry on my bookshelf at my parent's home and moved to Southern California to pursue a Ph.D. at UC, Santa Barbara. There, I immersed myself in Chicana feminisms, embracing an Anzaldúan lens, studying with other amazing Chicana intellectuals, Chela Sandoval, Aída Hurtado, and Dolores Inéz Casillas, and researching literature and performances by Chicana cultural producers that focused on both violence and healing.

A decade and a dissertation on "Radical Storytelling in Chicana Narratives" later, and back in my hometown, teaching at the only four-year public institution on the Southside, I formed an alliance with two brilliant Shakespeareans: Katherine Gillen, an expert on issues of race, gender, colonialism, and economics in early modern drama and in Shakespeare appropriation, and Kathryn Vomero Santos, who specializes in the study of translation, race, and colonialism in Shakespeare and Shakespeare appropriation. I, myself, center Chicana/x cultural production and feminist theory in my research, with work that is deeply rooted in and accountable to my community. In San Antonio, we were all grappling with the important tasks of teaching first generation college students and training future teachers, and we all immediately saw the value in finding the intersections between our fields to better serve those students, each bringing unique experience and expertise that have been central to the development of the burgeoning field of Borderlands Shakespeare studies as a whole. As my colleagues and I state in the introduction to *The Bard in the Borderlands*, the Borderlands are "a site of ongoing humanitarian crises caused by the interplay of colonization, labor exploitation, anti-immigrant policies, militarization, environmental injustice, and socioeconomic inequity." For my part, I aim to read Borderlands Shakespeare through a critical lens I call cicatrix poetics that engages both literary trauma studies and Chicana feminist theory because works of Shakespearean appropriation, the border, and its art cannot be understood without attending to both the harm enacted upon its communities and the active resistance to such acts of violence that can be witnessed in the healing power of creative expression (Santos A. 2024).

Since our collaboration began, the BSC has grown an impressive network of collaborators, published a dozen articles, given numerous talks and workshops, and received funding from the Folger Shakespeare Library, the Renaissance Society of America, the National Endowment for the Humanities, and the Mellon Foundation. Using decolonial and community-accountable approaches, we hope to change the way Shakespeare is taught and performed and radically re-envision Shakespeare Studies, decentering white, European perspectives and valuing Chicanx, Indigenous, and Black perspectives and traditions, amplifying the world-making power of the border region's languages, traditions, and ways of knowing seeking to archive and circulate works of Borderlands Shakespeare. We are currently editing the third volume of the anthology, which includes I-DJ, a queer appropriation of *Hamlet* by beloved San Antonio author Gregg Barrios. Ultimately, we hope that the Borderlands Shakespeare Colectiva will generate scholarship, programming, and the creation of resources on multilingual Borderlands Shakespeare appropriations, creating leadership opportunities for emerging scholars, enhancing community collaborations that support Borderlands art and research, and creating avenues for scholarship that bridge the divide between early modern English studies and the multiple fields dedicated to the study of the Americas.

Another important milestone for me in this work was the collaboration with the Latino Bookstore at the Guadalupe Cultural Arts Center. As the only Latino bookstore in Texas, it shines as a beacon for San Antonio's historic westside community to access literature and arts that reflect the people it serves. Not only did we share the podium with beloved Texas author Ito Romo, we also invited a local K-12 teacher to reflect on her experience creating TEKS aligned lesson plans for multiple courses including ELL, history, arts, and with varying themes like ecocriticism and musical genres like corridos. In doing this work, I hope that I am upholding similar ideals that drove Anzaldúa's commitment to K-12 education. While I cannot reach out to Anzaldúa herself, to shake the hand of the writer who inspired me to tell my own story, I can give thanks for the helping hands of so many other Chicana mentors who have uplifted me and fortified me in my journey as an educator.

One of my earliest sources of inspiration was actually my grandfather, Romeo Santos, Sr., a farmworker who also served in World War II and then used the G.I. Bill to open a gas station on the West side of San Antonio. With a fourth-grade education, but a nimble mind, he supported his family of six and remained our beloved family patriarch into his nineties, recalling both his days in the fields and his days in the air force with a bittersweet nostalgia. For him, each of these experiences defined him as an "American." Although he was funneled into an Anglo unit in the military because of his light skin and English proficiency, his comrades would, nevertheless, often refer to him as "the Mexican." He spoke Spanish as his first language, but he was able to code-switch effortlessly, walking the tightrope of borderlands identity in a starkly segregated city and world at large. Due to racist school de facto segregation and normalization of corporal punishment in educational institutions, neither of my parents was encouraged, or even allowed to, speak Spanish at school. As Anzaldúa wrote in "How to Tame a Wild Tongue," and as I have come to believe, "Chicanas who grew up speaking Chicano Spanish have internalized the belief that we speak poor Spanish" an "illegitimate, a bastard language" (*Borderlands/La Frontera* 58). But the truth is that the Borderlands produces incredibly beautiful, multilingual, and multicultural works of art. The Pharr Community Theater's bilingual play, *The Tragic Corrido of Romeo and Lupe* by Seres Jaime Magaña is an excellent example. In it, struggles for worker's rights are candidly depicted, dramatizing the mid-twentieth century picket lines and boycotts, critiquing the harsh, sometimes fatal, conditions under which millions of farm workers continue to labor in the United States, a community that once included my grandfather and other ancestors. The play follows in the footsteps of farmworker's theater. Founded by Luis Valdez, El Teatro Campesino, the premier Chicano theater troupe of the United Farm Workers Union, began its performances in protest of the life-threatening working conditions in the fields for Mexican American and immigrant laborers (Valdez). *Romeo and Lupe*, centers on Rio Grande Valley agricultural workers who become "strangers in their own land" and must fight to protect their water source and their right to freely cultivate the seeds of their own homelands (Gillen and Santos, "Borderlands Shakespeare"). In their textbook for heritage Spanish language speakers, *Spanish in/of the United States: Español en los Estados Unidos,* Elena Foulis and Alexandra Rodriguez Sabogal excerpt a bilingual passage from *Romeo and Lupe*, stressing the importance of translanguaging as a mode of learning for borderlands communities. As an introduction, Foulis and Sabogal write, "*The Bard in the Borderlands* que destaca el trabajo de dramaturgues indígenas y chicanes, quienes adaptan las obras de Shakespeare para reflexionar sobre las realidades de la frontera entre México y Estados Unidos. Es así como las editoras…muestran una estructura que celebra los espacios bilingües y multiculturales, y descolonizantes." In the authors' note to the textbook, Foulis and Rodriguez Sabogal explain their reliance on "implicit language understanding, critical language awareness, and translanguaging strategies to encourage students to gain a deeper understanding of Spanish language variation, attitudes and the diversity of experiences...to recognize language as tied to identity, connection to communities."

The "linguistic terrorism" which Anzaldúa identifies at the border remains at issue in the contested border space between the US and Mexico and the ongoing humanitarian crisis whose language difference continues to grow considering the diverse peoples that seek refuge within the protection of degrading US amnesty laws. As vibrantly illustrated by Celeste de Luna in her "Tu Cuerpo es una Frontera," the embodied violence at the geopolitical border affects generations and continues to damage. Cantú and Hernández-Ávila write that the piece "is a political statement of how the bodies of Tejanas on the border embody the geopolitical and very real border. The children chained and holding US or Mexican flags stand on half-moons as if the angel from the Virgen de Guadalupe had stood up. It is a powerful image of a woman's body torn apart by the border, as a river runs through the body from her heart down to her legs" (229). In *Borderlands/La Frontera*, Anzaldúa describes the land as "una herida abierta, where the first world grates against the third and bleeds" (3). But violence at the border is not merely a metaphor, it is a lived experience, and ongoing trauma inflicted upon its people and its ecology (Tuck and Yang). Extending Anzaldúa's theory further Espinosa describes how, "[i]n the vein of Anzaldúa's keen view of the borderlands" how straddling the liminal space, "traversing the temporal borderlands of shakespeare both shores (historical, cultural, linguistic) reveals to us a space where the rigid borders that delimit Shakespeare's meaning and value can be traversed and ultimately effaced" (606-7). As Gillen and I have written about *The Tragic Corrido of Romeo and Lupe*, "Rather than conforming to the expected tone of the event, [a protester] references Anzaldúa's description of the border as 'una herida abierta' in her angry lament: 'This valley here is a grapefruit, anywhere you make a cut the nectar from the land spills out like an open wound. You cut deep into it. And you drain it of its soul.'" (64). Later in *The Tragic Corrido,* the protesters in *Romeo and Lupe* chant in unison, "We do not want your segregation, your discrimination, your dreams. Esta tierra no te quiere aquí. This is not your Magic Valley, this is the RGV" (251). Despite ongoing colonial violence, resistance continues to be a hallmark of borderlands art and culture, as evidenced in this act of public protest, one that mirrors the distinctly activist nature of Chicanx cultural production and performance specifically.

Like Magaña's *Romeo & Lupe*, Bill Rauch and Lydia Garcia's *La Comedia of Errors* is similarly rooted in the legacy of a distinctly Chicano theater history. Another work of Borderlands Shakespeare that was devised in collaboration with local bilingual community for the Oregon Shakespeare Festival, *La Comedia* opens with an "acto," a genre made famous by El Teatro Campesino in which short scenes are performed in service of political speech that seeks to educate about injustice and rally support for la causa. Many of the original actos performed by El Teatro Campesino would have been in Spanish, as their primary audience were their fellow farmworkers. In mainstream American theater, audience goers are assumed to be English speaking. In the bilingual *La Comedia*, language plays a key role and even the actors within the play are keenly aware of the linguistic divisions within which they perform their roles. There is no speech in the opening acto; it may rely on silent pantomime and props to relay the message, but the rest of the play directly emphasizes linguistic difference, even the character list is riddled with a smattering of varying linguistic identities. In the *Comedia* acto, the U.S. Mexico border is blurred. On one side, a destitute woman in poor health gives her newborns to the more affluent couple Egeón and Emilia, who also have newborn twins. Two Border Patrol officers then remove one set of twins and take Emilia over the border to the Mexican side. She waits until the officers leave, then crosses back into el otro lado in the U.S. to follow the babies. Egeón stays in Mexico to care for the other set of children. When questioned by the Sheriff about the incident decades later, Egeón replies, "No podrías darme tarea más dolorosa que hablar de mis dolores indecibles." (431). They all survive the cross again despite the dangers because he just wants to know if they are alive. The only reason Egeón is allowed to stay in the U.S. within the imagined world of the play is that La Vecina provokes the cast and audience members to revolt, chanting on his behalf. This act of civil disobedience exemplifies the power of art and storytelling to incite action for justice in marginalized communities. Enacting Shakespeare performance as a vehicle for social change, and centering hybrid language practices, the playwrights devise a stage in which linguistic difference is celebrated and an optimistic political viewpoint is possible, thereby resisting the colonial oppression of speaking and other ways of knowing and being in the Borderlands. Whose lives are deemed valuable in this context? Linking oppression to capitalism and exploitation, Drómio de México resists the romanticization of the western immigrant experience, deeming the U.S. "lleno de ladrones…who make their fortune at our expense" (440). Egeón expresses a similar sentiment later in the play, calling his experience "una pesadilla," or nightmare, in contrast to the mythic elevation of the "American Dream" that permeates mainstream narratives about the United States. Anzaldúa's vision for coalition-building, on the other hand, seeks to celebrate our collective dreams. She writes, "In gatherings where we feel our dreams have been sucked out of us, la nepantlera leads us in celebrating la comunidad soñada, reminding us that spirit connects the irreconcilable warring parts para que todo el mundo se haga un paíz, so that the whole world may become un pueblo" (Anzaldúa, *Light in the Dark/Luz en lo oscuro*, 149). Garcia and Rauch's *La Comedia* grapples with the devastating effects of family separation at the militarized borders, each concluding with un unsteady reconciliation that relies heavily on the decolonial imaginary of a just future while remaining cognizant of social conditions which make such reunion rare, if not impossible, for the majority of rent family units. And as Espinosa argues, "In ways both temporal and epistemological, this borderland dynamic creates a space for me not to speak to the dead—as I am, in many ways, expected to do—but rather to understand how the early modern, how Shakespeare, is not the incontestable focal point, but rather an element to which we, on the temporal and physical borderlands, can add nuance and layer with manifold meanings" (606).

It is impossible to comprehend the nuance of Borderlands Shakespeare without an understanding of the trauma experienced by fronterizos and the resilience that has characterized their cultural production. Histories of violence enacted in the name of the colonial project are particularly important to highlight here in the effort to adequately capture borderlands identity in the U.S. Kathryn Vomero Santos has demonstrated that border politics can be explored through deep analysis of the art, including Shakespeare adaptations, that arises from such contexts and that seeks to challenge Western, colonial imposition of geopolitical borders and the policing of citizenship, movement, language and identity. About border renderings of the bard's most famous soliloquy, "To be or not to be," she writes, "To appropriate the language and persona of Hamlet—to speak back through this canonical figure of white European selfhood—is to force the white gaze out of its self-centered mode of introspection so that it must bear witness to the racist colonial harm that has been inflicted on Black, Indigenous, and people of color who have been deemed expendable, exploitable, and not worthy of humanity" (Santos, "¿Shakespeare para todos?" 365). Indeed, Chicanx and Indigenous writers have brilliantly explored the use of canonical forms in innovative contexts, particularly those employed by Shakespeare. Kathryn Vomero Santos examines the soliloquy specifically "[a]s a canonical poetic form of expression with roots in Roman rhetoric and enduring associations with Shakespearean drama' and how it "takes on a new and indeed urgent purpose in the Borderlands, where it becomes medium through which to call for justice in the face of ongoing oppression" in border artist Guillermo Goméz-Peña's invocation of it (373).

Laurie Ann Guerrero composed her *Crown for Gumecindo* while she was grieving her grandfather and communing with students in El Paso whose friends and family were among the victims of the countless femicides at the border. In the book, Guerrero grapples with the crown of sonnets as part of a healing journey: "I had to write sonnets in defiance—with my sadness and fear and jealousy and loyalty and anger and fear and prejudice and speechlessness and ignorance and Texas pride and shame and fear and fear that I also inherited. I had to steal the crown" (213). The audacity with which she claims the form is reminiscent of the resistance to linguistic terrorism Anzaldúa describes, further noting her resolve to embrace her multiple identities and ways of expressing herself through language. Anzaldúa affirms, "I will no longer be made to feel ashamed of existing. I will have my voice: Indian, Spanish, white. I will have my serpent's tongue—my woman's voice, my sexual voice, my poet's voice. I will overcome the tradition of silence (*Borderlands/La Frontera* 59). Drawing on the legacies of both her literary and ecological ancestors, Guerrero continues, "[I]t was the sonnet, that vessel, that was the only thing I knew that was experienced enough to guide me through grief, what I have never known. What could I possibly try to understand of lost love that the sonnet didn't already know?... These sonnets functioned to help me understand the blessing of work. Something that my grandpa, Gumecindo, knew well" (207), her maternal grandfather and William Shakespeare each providing limbs of a crucial structure that allowed her creative work to continue through crisis. Guerrero's essay reminds me of one of the last conversations I had with my grandfather, Romeo Santos. He reverted mostly to Spanish towards the end of his life and when he told this story, it was with a haunting nostalgia for a childhood spent laboring, dropping out of school in the fourth grade to help support his family. He described how he was lauded as the strongest of all the juvenile workers in the fields, often continuing to work while his fingers bled from pulling at the ripe cotton bolls. Anzaldúa urges us to "recognize and acknowledge la herida" because "rupture and psychic fragmentation lead [us] to dialogue with the wound" (*Light in the Dark*, 89). When we write from the wound and we are "receptive, a new conocimiento/insight will flash up through the cracks of the unconscious" (Anzaldúa, *Light in the Dark*, 66), the cicatrix can activate a catalyst for creative expression (Santos, *Cicatrix Poetics*). In my work with Borderlands Shakespeare, I am dialoguing with my own wounds, those of my grandfather, and those of my unhealed ancestors, both Indigenous and European.

Next, I would like to highlight the striking cover image for the *Bard in the Borderlands* by Celeste De Luna, titled "Healing Borderland Hand" (2023). Commissioned by myself and my co-editors, De Luna's stunning linocut print harkens back to both the thriving world of printmaking during Shakespeare's lifetime and the importance of printmaking to the social justice struggles of the American Civil Rights Movement. De Luna's larger body of work engages the everyday experiences of fronterizos as well as the hybrid cultural Catholicism practiced in Borderlands communities, which are informed by thousands of years of indigenous spiritual practices and world views. Working with Celeste de Luna on the cover of the Anthology was one of the highlights of my career. Together, Kate, Katie, and I met with Celeste several times to discuss our shared vision for the cover. We wanted borderlands imagery that reflected both the violent colonial past and the enduring Indigenous roots of the space, both geographically and creatively. Her linocut print, while depicting common signs and symbols of the Borderlands, many of which are referenced in the plays in the anthology, also recalls a popular folk image, of La Mano Poderosa, that traveled along La Frontera in painted metal art pieces known as retablos beginning in the nineteenth century. The retablo tradition emphasized the local artists and devotions of Borderlands communities and reflected a "bottom-up" art-making tradition, very similar to the practice of theater-making that produces Borderlands Shakespeare performances. According to Chicano playwright Octavio Solis, he used the devotionals as inspiration for the title and methodology of his collection of personal essays because they are "at once visual and literary, they record the crisis, the divine meditation and the offering of thanks in a single frame, thus forming a kind of flash-fiction account of an electrifying, life-altering event" (10). His connection to trauma and healing in historical artmaking beautifully illustrates the importance of infusing contemporary culture-crafting with traditional practices in borderlands communities. De Luna's original artwork is inspired by La Mano Ponderosa, a common image among the folk in what is now Northern Mexico and the Southwest United States and which is often featured on the aforementioned retablos. Its origins are unclear, but it is thought to have originated in Spain and is connected to the cult of St. Ann (Torres). The hand graphically depicts the stigmata with lambs drinking from a chalice containing the blood of Christ. Above each finger is usually a representation of the holy family, baby Jesus, Mother Mary, Joseph, and Mary's parents, Joachim and Anne. Historically, devotees would often add their own elements to the art pieces, corresponding to bodily injuries for which they sought healing (Kilroy-Ewbank and Ortega). Chicana artist Santa Barraza has also created her own iteration of La Mano Poderosa, which vividly engages the iconography represented on the surviving codices inscribed by Florentine monks in the sixteenth century and famously visible on the ancient architecture throughout Mesoamerica. Interestingly, De Luna has remarked that she drew inspiration for the cover image not only from the plays themselves and the historical representations of La Mano, particularly Santa Barraza's version, but also from her embedded memories of one of Shakespeare's Lady Macbeth (*El Mundo Zurdo Conference*, 2024). The villain's iconic speech, at the beginning of Act 5 of "the Scottish Play" relays her guilty conscience at the murder of the King, but read within Borderlands frameworks, also points to the racial politics of colorism, and the idea of a staining that cannot be let out, the dark skin of las prietas, and what remains eternally unclean, born from the wounds of colonialism. "Out, damned spot! out, I say!—One: two: why,/then, 'tis time to do't.—Hell is murky!—Fie, my/lord, fie! a soldier, and afeard? What need we/fear who knows it, when none can call our power to/account?—Yet who would have thought the old man/to have had so much blood in him" (5.1). And the inky red blood of my grandfather stains the cotton white pages of this essay. The distinguishing factors of De Luna's Chicana feminist vision for La Mano are the Borderlands signs and symbols that imbue all of her work and the distinctly feminist politics of the image itself that imply the regenerative beauty of nature. The image features the river as an ecological stigmata, a barbed wire fence loosely threaded through the feminine fingers, resembling a scar, cotton blossoms hang overhead as clouds in the vast Texas sky, alluding to the legacy of enslavement that drove plantation economies in Texas. De Luna has replaced the holy family with a skull, La Virgen de Guadalupe, the Mesoamérican moon goddess, Coyolxoahqui, a green jay, and a cicada. To replace religious figures with ecological elements and spiritual iconography is to reflect the character of the land both pre- and post- colonially. Perhaps most striking of all, the blood of the stigmata in the original image is replaced by the Rio Grande River, symbolic of a potent site of colonial wounding for Borderlands communities. This wound, however, also has the potential to produce astoundingly beautiful works of art. The stakes could not be higher. The violence is real.

In conclusion, I would like to reflect briefly on my participation in El Retorno, 2024. My first time at the event, I was deeply moved by the community engagement and reverence shown at Anzaldua's gravesite. On her tombstone I placed my prayer beads and my hand in humility for everything she has given and continues to give to me. The speaker that afternoon was the beloved Chicana artist, Alma López, who shared her reflections on Anzaldúa's own version of un mano, and it allowed me to reflect on my work with the Borderlands Shakespeare Colectiva as a form of spiritual activism. In "To live in the borderlands means you," Anzaldúa writes that: "In the Borderlands / you are the battleground/where enemies are kin to each other; / you are at home, a stranger,/the border disputes have been settled / the volley of shots have scattered the truce/you are wounded, lost in action / dead, fighting back... To survive the Borderlands / you must live sin fronteras/be a crossroads (*Borderlands/La Fontera*). And now I have come to embrace that perhaps I am one manifestation of Anzaldúa's Trojan mula, hoping to bring new ideas with her to the ivory tower, and "boundary-crossing visions" with allies who share a dream of a more just and equitable world (208). After all, "As mestizas, we are negotiating these worlds every day, understanding that multiculturalism is a way of seeing and interpreting the world, a methodology of resistance" (*Anzaldúa Reader*, 209). I can embody a Donkey Lady Macbeth, with blood on her hands and a forked serpent's tongue. After all, "crossing cultural and class borders requires that one look at the blood in one's veins, examining the history of one's people" (*Anzaldúa Reader* 215). As a descendent of both colonizer and colonized, I am sitting with the discomfort of claiming to speak Shakespeare in the Borderlands. I am hoping that by highlighting artists, poets, and playwrights who are embracing, wailing against, and remixing canons, my work with the BSC can help to advance the broader social justice aims of Mexican American Studies, Chicana feminisms, Borderlands Studies, and Queer Studies. Decolonizing the canon is a lofty goal, but Chicanx cultural producers are up to the task. Their fearless creativity and willingness to burn down the master's house and remake it from the scraps gives me hope that Chicanx and Indigenous languages and cultures will continue to survive despite the forces attempting to silence them.

WORKS CITED

Anzaldúa, Gloria. *Borderlands/ La Frontera: The New Mestiza.* Aunt Lute Books, 1987.

—. "New Mestiza Nation." *The Gloria Anzaldúa Reader.* Duke University Press, 2009.

—. *Light in the dark/Luz en lo oscuro: Rewriting Identity, Spirituality, Reality.* Edited by AnaLouise Keating, Duke University Press, 2015.

De Luna, Celeste. "Healing Borderland Hand." linocut print. 2022.

De Luna, Celeste. Public remarks at the "Borderlands Shakespeare" panel. *El Mundo Zurdo: Society for the Study of Gloria Anzaldúa*, annual conference. Trinity University, 2024.

Espinosa, Ruben. "Beyond *The Tempest*: Language, Legitimacy, and La Frontera." In *The Shakespeare User*, ed. Valerie M. Fazel and Louise Geddes. Palgrave, 2017. 41-61.

—. "'Don't it make my brown eyes blue": Uneasy assimilation and the Shakespeare–Latinx divide." *The Routledge Handbook of Shakespeare and Global Appropriation*, 48-58. Routledge, 2019.

—. "Traversing the Temporal Borderlands of Shakespeare." *New Literary History*, vol. 52 no. 3, 2021, p. 605-623. *Project MUSE*, https://dx.doi.org/10.1353/nlh.2021.0028.

Foulis, Elena and Rodríguez Sabogal, Alexandra, *Español en los Estados Unidos*, 2024. https://ohiostate.pressbooks.pub/spanishintheus/front-matter/foreword/ licensed under a Creative Commons Attribution-NonCommercial-NoDerivatives 4.0 International License, except where otherwise noted.

Gillen, Katherine. "Shakespeare and la Herida Abierta: Twin Skin, Colonial Wounds, and Cicatrix Poetics of Borderlands Theatre." *Shakespeare/Skin: Contemporary Readings in Skin Studies and Theoretical Discourse.* Eds. Munro, L., Massai, S., Cooper, F.K. and McMullan, G., Bloomsbury Publishing, 2024.

Gillen, Katherine, and Adrianna M. Santos. "Borderlands Shakespeare: The Decolonial Visions of James Lujan's Kino and Teresa and Seres Jaime Magaña's *The Tragic Corrido of Romeo and Lupe.*" *Shakespeare Bulletin 38*, no. 4: 2020, p. 549-571.

Gillen, Katherine, Adrianna M. Santos, and Kathryn Vomero Santos. *The Bard in the Borderlands: An Anthology of Shakespeare Appropriations en La Frontera, Vol. 2*, ACMRS Press, 2024.

Gillen, Katherine and Kathryn Vomero Santos, "Where Curriculum Meets Community: Shakespeare in San Antonio." In *Situating Shakespeare Pedagogy in US Higher Education: Social Justice and Institutional Contexts.* Greenberg, Marissa, and Elizabeth Williamson, eds. Edinburgh University Press, 2024.

Guerrero, Laurie Ann. "Stealing the crown." *Latinx poetics: Essays on the art of poetry.* Ed. Herrera, Juan Felipe. University of New Mexico Press, 2022.

Hernández-Ávila, Inés, and Norma Elia Cantú, eds. *Entre Guadalupe y Malinche: Tejanas in literature and art.* University of Texas Press, 2016.

Herrera, Cristina. *ChicaNerds in Chicana young adult literature: Brown and nerdy*. Routledge, 2020.

Hernández-Ávila, I. and Cantú N.E., eds. "Celeste De Luna." *Entre Guadalupe y Malinche: Tejanas in literature and art*. University of Texas Press, pp. 229-233, 2016.

Kilroy-Ewbank, L. and Ortega, E. "Retablo of La Mano Poderosa/The All Powerful Hand," Smarthistory, February 15, 2022, accessed May 24, 2024, https://smarthistory.org/retablo-all-powerful-hand/.

Montaño, Jesus. *Young Latinx Shakespeares: Race, Justice, and Literary Appropriation*. Springer Nature, 2024.

Puente, Josue, and Stephanie Alvarez. "Texas Resistance: Mexican American studies and the fight against Whiteness and White Supremacy in K-12 at the turn of the 21st Century." *Association of Mexican American Educators Journal* (2021).

Saldaña, Lilliana Patricia. "The Struggle for Mexican American Studies in Texas K-12 Public Schools: A Movement for Epistemic Justice through Creation/Resistance." *Association of Mexican American Educators Journal*, vol. 15, no. 2, 2021, pp. 9–35.

Sánchez, George J. "Opening the Humanities to New Fields & New Voices." *Daedalus* 151.3 (2022): 82-93.

Santos, Adrianna M. *Cicatrix poetics, trauma and healing in the literary Borderlands: beyond survival*. Palgrave Macmillan, 2024.

Santos, Kathryn Vomero. "¿ Shakespeare para todos?." *Shakespeare Quarterly* 73.1-2 (2022): 49-75.

Santos, Kathryn Vomero."The Oppressor's Wrong, or, What's Hamlet to the Borderlands?" *Latino Studies* 22.2 (2024): 353-75.

Shakespeare, William. *The Norton Shakespeare*. Edited by Greenblatt, S., et.al. Third edition. New York, NY: W.W. Norton & Company, 2016.

Solis, Octavio. *Retablos: Stories from a life lived along the Border*. San Francisco, CA: City Light Books, 2018.

Torres, K. *Made in the Americas?: Deciphering the enigma of the powerful hand*. 2011. Diss. University of Delaware.

Tuck, Eve and K. Wayne Yang, "Decolonization is not a Metaphor," *Tabula Rasa, 38*, 2021, 61–111. Available at: https://doi.org/10.25058/20112742.n38.04.

Valdez, Luis. *Luis Valdez early works: Actos, Bernabé and pensamiento serpentino*. Arte Público Press, 1990.

THE CONCEPT OF NEW TRIBALISM AND THE ROOTS OF IDENTITY

HOW TO CONNECT TO TERRITORY AND BUILD POLITICAL COALITIONS

DIEGO SÉVAL

To introduce this reflection, I would like to start with Ana Mendieta's *Siluetas* (1973-1980). In her *Siluetas*, the artist draws a shape of herself, blends it in a variety of natural landscapes, and then photographs her mark. The artist invites us to rethink the links between the self and the territory, in opposition to an essentialist conception of the territory as the "natural environment" of an individual or a community, determining and fixing its own characteristics. Ana Mendieta was born in Cuba but was sent to Iowa at the age of twelve as part of Operation Peter Pan. If we consider her "uprooting" from Cuba to the United States, we can read the *Siluetas* series as an attempt to reappropriate and anchor herself in a territory to which she was sent, a territory to be understood in the geographical as well as the social, cultural, and emotional senses of the term. However, the *Siluetas* are ephemeral, decomposing over time and eventually being erased. What's interesting in Mendieta's work, then, is that she seeks to inscribe herself in a territory, underlining the need to put down roots while revealing the fragility and active, creative part of this rooting.

From this perspective, Mendieta's work shows similarities with Gloria Anzaldúa's preoccupations when she tries to redefine the roots of identity in the sense that people speak of the geographical and socio-cultural background from which they come from as "their roots." Using the botanical notion of "root" to describe the subject's links to their environment would suggest that the latter plays the role of an essence, necessary to the subject's life and development. In other words, the environment would be what gives the subject, whether individual or collective, their substance. This is the case, for example, in the Romantic conception of the nation, as in Fichte's *Addresses to the German Nation* (1807), where he raises the point that national identity derives as much from a shared genetic past as from a specific culture, defined by the idea of the spirit of the people (*Volkgeist*), in opposition to an external Other. Moreover, the nation encloses different individuals within borders with *a* single history, culture, and language, erasing others by doing this.

That said, in the *mestiza* situation of Anzaldúa, or in a migratory context that links different and unequal geographical and cultural spaces, the rooted conception of identity and connection to environment is problematic. In view of the many past and present dispossessions, Anzaldúa affirms the importance of being able to reconnect, both materially and spiritually, with the territory understood as a geographical place and space. However, she opposes the nationalist anchoring that produces exclusion and violence. Thereby, how can we continue to use the image of roots and relate to them when we come from so many different, and sometimes antagonistic, backgrounds? And how can we break with a conception of "roots" which is closed and exclusionary while maintaining its importance for existence and political action? In my opinion, the significance of Anzaldúa's work lies in proposing a third way of linking the self to its environment, founding a sense of belonging, and creating political coalitions. This prevents us from falling into either of two symmetrical pitfalls: a romanticism of the soil (as in the theory of *Lebensraum*) or an idealized nomadism that hinders putting down roots (as in Deleuze and Guattari's *A Thousand Plateaus*). The issue is to rethink individual and community anchoring so that we can try to answer the following question: how can we build coalitions, aware of the impasses of both nationalism and certain forms of identity politics, in order to regain political agency, both locally and globally?

A NEED FOR ROOTS?

First of all, we can analyze the situations where one can feel a "need" for roots. In *Light in the Dark/Luz en lo oscuro* (2015), Anzaldúa talks about the negation, dispossession, and plundering that characterize the colonial situation vis-à-vis cultures, practices, and knowledges of colonized peoples:

> La negación sistemática de la cultura mexicana-chicana en los Estados Unidos impede su desarrollo, haciéndolo este un acto de colonización. As a people who have been stripped of our history, language, identity,

> and pride, we attempt again and again to find what we have lost by digging into our cultural roots imaginatively and making art from our findings. (Anzaldúa, *Light in the Dark*, 48)

In other words, colonization is defined as an uprooting that cuts individuals off the possibility to anchor themselves in a territory and a past, preventing them from a sense of belonging. Using the image of *Coyolxauhqui* Anzaldúa describes the fragmentation that characterizes both the colonial situation and transnational immigration or adoption (*Light in the Dark* 68-69). Because of violence, loss, and mobility, some people have no obvious, accessible links to what might constitute "roots" with which to anchor themselves. Coyolxauhqui's severed head, her mutilated body, and the coherence broken by her dismemberment are all images that symbolize the initial violence that gives birth to subjects who are a product of colonization, literally cut off from their genealogical roots, their culture, and the vision of the world offered by the latter. As a result, the world experienced is a fragmented one, torn between the imposition of hegemonic categories and knowledges and the search for wholeness.

Starting from this suffered fragmentation, Anzaldúa posits a need for roots, understood as a need for coherence and attachment. On this point, the author echoes Simone Weil's observation, made during her exile in London at the time of World War II:

> To be rooted is perhaps the most important and least recognized need of the human soul. It is one of the hardest to define. A human being has roots by virtue of his real, active, and natural participation in the life of a community, which preserves in living shape certain particular treasures of the past and certain particular expectations for the future. This participation is a natural one in the sense that it is automatically brought about by place, conditions of birth, profession, and social surroundings. (*The Need for Roots* 70)

Anzaldúa shifts the way in which rootedness is conceived, thinking of it in terms of situations where it is not possible to relate to an environment in which one is a "natural part." In other words, roots are not given elements but something to be constructed or reconstructed, using all the resources of memory and imagination, both individual and collective.

However, Anzaldúa points out certain dangers inherent in this approach, such as claiming purity and authenticity and reproducing the same logic as nationalism. This can take the form of rejecting a part of oneself, such as refusing bilingualism. On the other hand, there are also attempts to recover one's roots, often fantasized, and to become the stereotype of a lost or distant culture. In the relentless search for a fixed identity anchor, we can sometimes turn into a "border patrol," to use the author's words, i.e., exercising control and deciding who is authentic enough and who is not. Falling back into the ways of closed nationalisms creates internal dissension and reproduces exclusion (*The Gloria Anzaldúa Reader* 112-113).[1,2] So, while Anzaldúa recognizes the importance of roots, she does point out certain dangers, inherent to the search for roots, that lead to a return to the very logic inducing exclusion: the definition of territorial and cultural anchorage by exclusive and unitary criteria, which cannot integrate differences. If a person does not meet these criteria, they are deemed inauthentic and cannot be part of the community. So, how to develop an anchoring on which to build a sense of belonging without falling into its exclusionary and nationalistic downward slides?

EL ÁRBOL AND THE RHIZOME

In *Light in the Dark* Anzaldúa attempts to combine two images that, at first, seem contradictory: *el árbol de la vida*, which represents ancestral verticality, and the *rhizome*, a networked horizontality never taking root. Anzaldúa refers directly to Deleuze and Guattari's rhizome, a type of stem made up of invisible, subterranean branches that produce horizontal structures on the surface in all directions. This rhizomic form contrasts with the vertical, arborescent root. The rhizome marks a rupture with the idea of a genetic axis or deep structure that could always account for so-called "superficial" variations and movements (in a deterministic scheme). In short, by using the concept of rhizome, Deleuze and Guattari are trying to draw a model for conceiving reality in terms of flows, multiplicities, and networked planes:

> Don't sow, grow offshoots! Don't be one or multiple, be multiplicities! Run lines, never plot a point! [...] A rhizome has no beginning or end. The tree is filiation, but the rhizome is alliance, uniquely alliance. The tree imposes the verb "to be," (but the fabric of the rhizome is the conjunction," and... and... and..." This conjunction carries enough force to shake and uproot the verb "to be." (Deleuze and Guattari 24-25)

Despite the use of the rhizome concept, Anzaldúa continues to use the metaphor of the tree, notably via the image of "*el árbol de la vida*." More precisely, the author represents things as follows:

1. Anzaldúa, Gloria. *Light in the Dark/Luz en lo oscuro. Rewriting Identity, Spirtuality, Reality*, AnaLouise Keating (ed.), Duke University Press, Durham, 2015, pp. 68-69: "Some immigrants are cut off from ethnic cultures. Como cabezas decapitadas, they search for the 'home' where all the pieces of the fragmented body cohere and integrate like Coyolxauhqui. Many urban, multiethnic people, as well as others adopted out of their racial group, have mixed or tangled, distant or mangled roots."

2. Anzaldúa, Gloria. "En Rapport, En Opposition" in *The Gloria Anzaldua Reader*, AnaLouise Keating (ed.), Duke University Press, Durham, 2009, pp. 112-113: "Para que sea 'legal,' she must pass the ethnic legitimacy test we have devised. And it is exactly our internalized whiteness that desperately wants boundary lines (this part of me is Mexican, this Indian) marked out. [Si no califica, if she fails to pass the test, le aventamos mierda en la cara, le aventamos piedras, la aventamos]."

> Roots represent ancestral/racial origins and biological attributes; branches and leaves represent the characteristics, communities, and cultures that surround us, that we've adopted, and that we're in intimate conversation with. (*Light in the Dark* 67)

In this scheme, Anzaldúa retains the conception of roots as what fixes individuals to a past, synonymous with origins (both temporal and biological). From this base grows the tree, whose branches and leaves represent cultural traits, social ties, and existential hazards. One might think that Anzaldúa is reproducing an essentialist conception of identities determined by roots. However, she blends the image of the tree with that of the rhizome and thus attempts to form a theory of identity and of its material and spiritual anchorage that does not reject the idea of root but rethinks it to avoid the logic of nationalism and racism. In view of the dispossessions described earlier, rejecting all roots can be seen as a form of privilege (following the example of first-world digital nomads working in countries of the global South) or a romanticization of mobility that glosses over the difficulties experienced by immigrants. By retaining the image of the tree, Anzaldúa shows that it is necessary for the subject to cultivate an anchorage and that pure uprooting is a violence that cuts emotional and spiritual ties on which to structure one's life and relationship with the world. However, she modifies the way we think about anchoring, asserting that the elements considered to define it (geography, class, race, culture, nationality, etc.) are never fixed and totally decisive. Anzaldúa has no biologizing conception of roots:

> Maybe identity depends more on which community you identify with how you are reared, and less on the drops of blood in your veins. But roots are important; who was here on this continent first does matter. (*The Gloria Anzaldúa Reader* 287)

Here, we find again the median position that Anzaldúa tries to hold: countering closed conceptions of identity that posit the primacy of blood while recognizing the importance of roots (politically and culturally). In the American context, as she said, this means acknowledging the Indigenous presence that preceded the colonial period. Without the idea of roots, it is difficult to claim this priority and thus to account for the dispossessions. Basically, the paradoxical image that emerges is that of a tree with a rhizomic base. The roots imagined by the author are intertwined, tangled, distant, or mutilated, not linear.

A NEW TRIBE TO CONNECT WITH OTHERS AND CREATE COALITIONS

How, then, does Anzaldúa rethink social ties, political coalitions, and inter-individual relations on the basis of this anchorage? With the concept of "new tribalism," the author attempts to think of attachment and community as an alternative to the ways the concept of nation proposes it:

> We looked for something beyond just nationalism while continuing to connect to our roots. If we don't find the roots we need, we invent them, which is fine because culture is invented anyway. We have returned to the tribe, but our nationalism is one with a twist [...] I call this the New Tribalism. It's a kind of mestizaje that allows for connecting with other ethnic groups and interacting with other cultures and ideas. (*Interviews/ Entrevistas*185)

What's interesting in this quotation is that Anzaldúa acknowledges the imaginary and created dimension of any root. This doesn't mean the elements that define roots are not real, since it has concrete effects on the way we identify ourselves and access civil rights, but that it isn't a given, unquestionable "nature." It is because culture is invented that the author emphasizes the created dimension of roots. By paying attention to the dangers described above, we can use art or philosophy as means for recreating roots, forging an emotional, intellectual, and spiritual community that recognizes itself in shared symbols, experiences, and references. In an interview from 1991, Anzaldúa recalls how she looked for roots once her feminist commitment had been established:

> So here we go as feminists—wanting to be practical, wanting to make a difference, wanting to make some changes. We're looking at everything that gives us strength: having roots, having a historical past that we can connect with [...] we've dug into the past for a history and models and women and stories that can give us some sort of ground to walk on, some sort of foundation, some sort of place to take off from and also to find positive stuff there that will feed us, that will inspire us. (*Interviews/ Entrevistas* 159-160)

Here, Anzaldúa describes an experience shared by many people who are part of a minority: the emotion and connection that can come from simply reading or watching a movie that links us to other people and other stories of this group. Rootedness is understood here as the emotional and spiritual awareness of being connected to people who are distant from oneself, both geographically and historically. In other words, the subject puts down roots in multiple territories and connects them actively in their own existence. Putting down roots is a way to feel ourselves grounded and, so, to gain power.

The tribes Anzaldúa seeks are no longer characterized in biological (kinship) or culturalist (ethnicity) terms. The author tries to move the basis of belonging to a more spiritual, chosen, and relational space. So, it's about giving precedence to what enables us to feel connected to others rather than what constantly erects borders. In the words of AnaLouise Keating, "new tribalism" is Anzaldúa's attempt to think about belonging and political coalitions without falling into the pitfalls of assimilation, which denies difference or separatism, which prevents any connection (*The Anzaldúan Theory Handbook* 189). I quote Anzaldúa in an early interview where she is already criticizing nationalism as a violent way of relating to others and an ideology that justifies the erection of closed, excluding, and discriminating borders:

> I'm a citizen of the universe. I think it's good to claim your ethnic identity and your racial identity. But it's also the source of all the wars and all the violence, all these borders and walls people erect. I'm tired of borders, and I'm tired of walls. I don't believe in the nationalism [...] People are dying every day. And then people talk about being proud to be American, Mexican, or Indian. We have grown beyond that. We are specks from this cosmic ocean, the soul, or whatever. (*Interviews/ Entrevistas* 118)

The challenge is to understand that nationalism is a misguided form of belonging because it asserts the superiority of the self over others and advocates a conditional attachment in which love for the nation and its members is matched by distrust or hatred of outsiders—the logic of "us" versus "them" as Anzaldúa puts it. This logic is echoed in the rigid forms of identity politics, where a minority group is defined only in terms of some of its elements (often the most privileged in terms of class or race) and reproduces, excluding boundaries. Anzaldúa, therefore, seeks to fight all closed identifications that jeopardize alliances. The goal of new tribalism, then, is to rediscover a sense of attachment and interconnection.

Finally, why does choosing the notion of "tribe" help us to rethink political and affective ties? Here, Anzaldúa develops a thought of political struggle and coalition against violence and oppression. The tribe is the structure where we can gather and take care of each other when we know that outside, we won't be able to, finding only negation and discrimination. However, if this tribalism is qualified as "new," it is precisely because it is no longer naturalized, in the sense that the tribe would be a group defined by a unique determining essence. Anzaldúa understands the tribe as an active grouping in a context of political antagonism, a group in which to feel connected to others and gain agency. Furthermore, the goal is also to understand that we are linked to other forms of life. That is why Anzaldúa gives such a crucial place to spirituality—and not institutionalized religions—in order to understand what connects us within and despite our differences. Being part of certain tribes (defined by class, race, gender, sexual orientation, culture, nationality...) should not prevent us from thinking globally and losing sight of what binds us together: "To partake of the new tribalism, you don't have to be connected to your home-ethnicity; other root systems will suffice" (Anzaldúa, *Light in the Dark*, 68). Here, Anzaldúa clearly shows that she no longer prioritizes local and ethnic roots. We need to rethink rootedness and the nature of the roots that make it possible. Roots must once again become what they are, i.e., the foundation which, by providing a grounding, enables a being to grow and develop, also spiritually. With the paradoxical image of a tree with rhizomic roots, Anzaldúa sees the growth of a being as the result of networking and welcoming multiplicity. Far from denying internal dissension, the aim is to work to ensure that differences and power relations—a source of misunderstanding and injury—do not get in the way of coalition. It is necessary to go beyond national borders to extend political action and thought. We cannot think about, criticize, or struggle against ecocidal capitalist logics nor those of coloniality if we don't take into account the "global thinking" Anzaldúa describes, if we don't understand that we are interconnected and that what happens far from us affects us too.:

> The point may not be to move beyond a nationalistic search for indigenous roots but rather to undertake transformative work that processes and facilitates evolving as a social group, becoming an extended tribe, and developing a new tribalism. What's important is negotiating alliances among the conflicted forces within the self, between men and women, among the group's different factions, and among the various groups in this country and the rest of the world. (*Light in the Dark,* 75-76)

WORKS CITED

Anzaldúa, Gloria. *Interviews/Entrevistas*. Edited by AnaLouise Keating, Routledge, New York, 2000.

—. *The Gloria Anzaldúa Reader*. Edited by AnaLouise Keating, Duke UP, Durham, 2009.

—. *Light in the Dark/Luz en lo oscuro. Rewriting Identity, Spirituality, Reality*. Edited by AnaLouise Keating, Duke UP, Durham, 2015.

Deleuze, Gilles and GUATTARI, Félix. *A Thousand Plateaus. Capitalism and Schizophrenia*. University of Minnesota Press, Minneapolis, 1987 [1980].

Keating, AnaLouise. *The Anzaldúan Theory Handbook*. Duke UP, Durham, 2022.

Weil, Simone. *The Need for Roots*. Routledge, New York, 2002 [1949].

LIVING IN THE SHADOWS AS UNDOCUMENTED COLLEGE STUDENTS AND THEIR COLLECTIVE HEALING THROUGH A CREATIVE ART EXPRESSIONS GROUP

DOING WORK THAT MATTERS

MÓNICA TORREIRO-CASAL, YANEYRY DELFIN MARTINEZ, AND KAREN MIRANDA CHAVEZ

This essay originates from our presentation at the Society for the Study of Gloria Anzaldúa's El Mundo Zurdo in 2024. In response to this year's theme of *Les Atravesades en Comunidad: Coalition Building as Light in the Dark*, we found it very relevant to share our mental health initiative creating a healing space for our undocumented students on campus at the University of California in Davis. Attending the El Mundo Zurdo conference was unfortunately problematic for two of our team members due to their immigration status and challenges traveling to Texas. Nevertheless, we creatively used media to make it possible for all of us to present and be part of the conference virtually. This was our Anzaldúan response, by bringing light to the dark of their living-in-the-shadows realities. In our presentation, we described the creation and execution of the healing group through creative art expressions for our undocumented students on campus. This work was informed by Mónica's clinical experiences as a psychologist working with undocumented populations in the community and specifically in university counseling settings.

Indeed, despite the importance of providing psychological support for our undocumented and other minoritized students on campus, very little has been done in academic settings to support these communities. Thanks to student protests and advocacy, the first AB540 (Nonresident Assembly Bill) and Undocumented Student Center in the nation was established at UC Davis to meet the needs of undocumented students. The Center opened in 2014 as the first dedicated physical space for these students in the country. Mónica began working with the Center in 2015, initially as a clinician and later as a faculty partner and collaborator. Mónica's involvement with the community of undocumented students and the Undocumented Student Center on campus contributed to the creation of the healing through creative art expressions group prioritizing the cultural and emotional needs of undocumented students while fostering solidarity.

The development of the program was consistent with Anzaldúa's belief in the transformative power of art as a venue of resistance and reclamation of identity (*The Gloria Anzaldúa Reader* 95). Throughout the essay, the first-person singular represents Mónica's voice; only in the testimonios, the first-person singular means the other authors of this manuscript, Yaneyry and Karen. They are Mónica's former students who participated in the healing group and coordinated the program's implementation and evaluation. Their involvement was inspired by a research pedagogy, which emphasizes the active participation of the communities of interest and aligns with Anzaldúa's concept of *Nepantla*, a state of in-between spaces where individuals can empower themselves as self-agents of change, working toward social justice and collective transformation (*The Gloria Anzaldúa Reader* 100). My intention was also to create opportunities for undocumented students to engage in meaningful research connected to their realities, guide them, foster mutual learning and growth throughout this process.

UNDOCUMENTED STUDENTS LIVING IN THE SHADOWS

Undocumented college students are presented with unique challenges because of the systemic oppression, discriminatory practices and policies against this population of *atravesados* living in the shadows. The political climate in the U.S. fragments souls, minds, and spirits. This fragmentation permeates every aspect of their lives and makes it difficult to form meaningful connections (with others and themselves), pursue their academic goals, and envision a stable future. Anzaldúa's poem *"To Live in the Borderlands"* captures and speaks to the realities of those who cross and pass over and the reminder that to survive you must live *"sin fronteras and be a crossroads"* (*Borderlands* 216-17). Inspired by Anzaldúa's *Light in the Dark / Luz en lo Oscuro* (2015), we (Monica, Yaneyry and Karen) are reminded of the importance of doing work that matters in the context of academia and in Monica's role as a scholar-activist, which often feels detached from communities. This work with undocumented students not only reflects a commitment to activism; it also embodies a pedagogy of resistance. Additionally, Anzaldúa highlights the necessity of shared narratives and collaborative efforts in creating change, emphasizing that work done within communities is essential for personal and societal empowerment (*Light in the Dark* 1-50). Ultimately, Anzaldúa sees this work as not just important but essential for nurturing resilience and solidarity among people. Therefore, our program was designed to foster a community space of hope and nurture connections among its participants.

It was work done in the community and with the community of undocumented students. Moreover, the program encompassed student's intersectionalities and contributed to the development of healing *en y con comunidad.* The healing group intended to contribute to transform the lived experiences of undocumented college students on campus who are forced to live in the shadows as part of their daily reality. The program facilitated a safe space for self-exploration and healing of *las "heridas abiertas"* and the *agravios* (Anzaldúa, *Light in the Dark* 32-38) that these students face. Students were exposed to different artistic expressions that included poetry, journaling, traditional healing practices and silk printing. Each session was guided by different collaborators, writers, artists and student interns at our TANA *(Taller del Arte del Nuevo Amanecer)* part of the Chicana/o/x studies department at UC Davis.

Indeed, in *Borderlands/La Frontera*, Anzaldúa emphasizes the importance of community work as a form of social engagement and transformation. She advocates for building inclusive, supportive spaces that honor diverse identities and experiences, particularly those of marginalized groups (159). Furthermore, Anzaldúa highlights that meaningful community work should be rooted in authenticity and connection, addressing systemic inequalities and fostering collective healing (*Light in the Dark* 32). The healing through creative expressions group follows these principles, providing tools for expressing and healing through creative arts. The program also highlights the importance of offering alternative healing practices within the context of Westernized psychological and educational models, which often fail to meet the specific needs and realities of our community of underserved undocumented students and other marginalized populations.

THE EMOTIONAL WELL-BEING AND HEALING THROUGH CREATIVE ART EXPRESSIONS PROGRAM

The program funding was possible with the UC Davis Health Initiative grant in collaboration with the AB540 and Undocumented Student Center on campus and TANA part of the Chicana/o/x department. This support allowed us to recruit participants, hire undocumented students to help develop and evaluate the program, and compensate students for their involvement. Many undocumented students prioritize work over self-care, making it essential to advocate for funding that helps them to be able to attend this type of initiatives. In addition, the program follows an inclusive and community-based research practice and methodology. The main objective of this art-healing project was to decrease the stigmatization around mental health, the lack of access to mental health services for undocumented students and to provide a "safe environment" for them. The program exposed students to different modalities of creative arts to heal through artistic expression and develop new skills to help with their emotional well-being. The development, design and implementation were informed by Mónica's clinical experiences working with undocumented students on campus and her teaching of Chicanx and Latinx psychology classes to undergraduate minoritized and marginalized students. Her work emphasizes community-based research, critical, and transformative approaches to education, scholarship, and activism (Torreiro-Casal et al.; Flores and Torreiro-Casal) and the healing through creative art expression group encompasses those principles.

Certainly, undocumented students often fear navigating institutional systems, lack access to therapy and the appropriate mental health support attuned to their specific needs and ecological realities. In consonance with Anzaldúa's understanding of activism as integral to the process of healing and transformation, community engagement is essential for nurturing resilience and solidarity (*Borderlands* 134). Our methodology embodies a pedagogy of resistance, transformative community work, and advocacy to make their realities visible.

Building on this foundation, once the program curriculum and facilitators were established, we disseminated information about the healing group through our campus partners and various media outlets. As part of the initial recruitment we developed a survey to ask students questions such as: "Why are you interested in being a part of this program" and "what do you hope to gain by participating?" students revealed that their motivations to join were financial constraints and need, mental health stigma, as well as a desire to find a community on campus and learn healthy coping mechanisms. In both years of implementation, there was a consensus that students were experiencing heightened mental health strain due to the financial need and burdens of maintaining academic performance and friendships amidst the aftermath of the Covid-19 pandemic. In the students' own words:

> I am interested in this program, if I am being transparent, because of the compensation. I am unable to get a job because of the fact that I am undocumented, so this type of stipend program would help a lot financially. This compensation would help me pay for some of my tuition that my financial aid doesn't cover. (First year, Psychology major)

> Coming from a family that highly stigmatizes mental illness, it was difficult for my family to understand and support me. As someone from a low income home, it was difficult to pay for treatment with a therapist of my choice and after meeting with a community clinic therapist, I didn't feel like she was truly understanding me so I decided to deal with

> my mental health myself until I could financially support myself and receive the correct treatments for myself. (Third year transfer, Sociology & Chi Studies major)

> I am interested in being part of a community where we collectively find a way to express ourselves especially during these difficult times. With COVID-19, it is difficult to meet new people and step away from my computer/work. I think this would be a nice way to give myself a break and prioritize myself and my well-being. It is often difficult to put myself first when I have so much work so I am excited to take advantage of this opportunity. (Third year, Political Science major with a Public Health Emphasis)

> I find myself often feeling burnt out and I do not know what the best outlet to release stress is…I have not engaged in any self care activities during my time at UC Davis and would like to learn how to find ways to take care of myself while not feeling guilty. (Third year, Mechanical Engineer major)

In addition to seeking interpersonal healing, students also emphasized their struggles with self-confidence tied to various dimensions of their identity including: the burden of academic expectations, their undocumented and first-generation status, as well as their cultural heritage and sexuality. One student particularly mentioned their experience impacted by their personal intersectionality:

> As an EOP and AB540 student, resources to practice self-care are scarce, and healing can seem challenging without support. I have recently come out to my parents about two summers ago, and the hardships that are tied to a Hispanic household have taken a toll on my self-esteem and confidence. (Fifth year, Civil Engineering major with an emphasis in Sustainability in the Built Environment)

In response to their life experiences, students also communicated their interest and participation in the program as their initiative to build back up their self-confidence and seek professional support, including mentorship. One student shared:

> Connecting through art with others takes vulnerability, and I want to build my confidence in sharing a part of myself within my art for others to see and understand. (Spring' Quarter 2024, Political Science & Chicanx Studies major)

Overall, students collectively emphasized their internal longing for a safe environment to alleviate stress and socially connect with peers of similar backgrounds and experiences. These responses underscore yet again the critical importance of initiating and sustaining such programs aimed at addressing the unique disparities and barriers faced by undocumented and mixed-status college students.

The healing group consisted of two cohorts per year during the winter and spring quarters for two academic years. Once students were selected based on their availability, they attended five group sessions during winter or spring quarters. In the first session, participants were introduced to several healing strategies, including breathing exercises, meditation, traditional healing remedies, and the use of music as a healing tool. In the second session, participants had the opportunity to learn about poetry written by Nicaraguan poet Dr. Leon Salvatierra, a former undocumented individual. This session included a self-experiential journaling exercise. In the last three sessions, participants explored the history and process of silk screening as part of the Chicana/o/x movement. During these sessions, they worked on creating their own silk-screening art, which was exhibited at the AB540 and Undocumented Student Center in its first year and in an art exhibition titled "Healing Through the Arts: La Cultura Cura" hosted by the Chicana/o/x Department. Once students completed the program, we evaluated the outcomes through a questionnaire, where students shared their insights and impressions:

> The best part of the program personally was seeing a group of students create a community, starting the first minute we all stepped in the room. I really enjoyed being able to cope and relate to fellow students who are/have gone through similar experiences. (Winter '24 cohort)

> The best of the program is connect with my friends and made me feel in family, doing art and help each other, make jokes, exchange out stories, cultures, goals, etc. (Winter '24 cohort)

> I enjoyed spending time with people in my community that made me feel safe. It also helped my anxiety knowing I would be able to get some financial aid and food. (Spring '24 cohort)

> My favorite moment was when we ate as a group and talked. I also really enjoyed the printmaking session. I learned many new techniques, and it was great to hear people's ideas and make art together. I also enjoyed the music played during the sessions. It brought positive vibes. Overall, it was fun. (Spring '24 Cohort)

The observations shared by some of the participants emphasize the sense of community and connection fostered by the program. They highlight the relevance of meeting peers who share similar experiences and the supportive environment that feels like *familia*. The program not only facilitates artistic expression but also provides a safe space with a positive atmosphere and creativity, contributing to their overall sense of belonging.

NUESTROS TESTIMONIOS

In the following section, Yaneyry and Karen, who are Mónica's former students contributing to this manuscript, share their testimonios, reflections, and insights about the program, as well as details of their involvement. It is especially important to include their testimonios to validate their experiences, as a source of invaluable knowledge often neglected in academic spaces. In sharing a testimonio, we heal by liberating ourselves. As Anzaldúa suggests, testimonios are vital for making visible the otherwise invisible, especially the lives and struggles of those who occupy the "borderlands" (*Borderlands* 20).

Yaneyry's Testimonio: I transferred to UC Davis my junior year and spent the first quarter becoming acquainted with the institution as a whole and learning, for the first time in my life, what it meant to be on my own. Looking for resources and support, I found the AB540 and Undocumented Student Center and it is through this center that I learned about the mental health initiative for undocumented students. Having been diagnosed with depression during my senior year of high school, my journey with therapy has been frustrating. I have struggled to find a therapist with whom I felt comfortable enough to disclose being undocumented and where my status didn't overshadow my mental health needs. Often, I found myself educating therapists about the nuances of my situation, which left little room for the healing and understanding I was seeking. I grew tired of the inevitable question of "Why can't you get documentation?" which created barriers rather than fostering connection. In light of these challenges, I shifted my focus toward self-help options and support groups. I sought spaces where I could engage with others who understood my experiences without requiring explanations of my existence. This desire led me to participate in the mental health initiative for undocumented students. I joined the Winter Cohort of 2021, and the impact of that experience continues to resonate with me today. Throughout the program, I not only learned holistic techniques that have since become integral to my mental health practice, but I also connected with a community of fellow students who were both inspiring and supportive. Here, I was surrounded for the first time with students who all shared similar struggles and triumphs, and who truly understood and related to the complexities of my experiences.

Additionally, being part of this initiative, both as a participant and a researcher, has been an enlightening journey. While the program had a profound impact on my own life, being involved in documenting and presenting its benefits has allowed me to witness its positive effects on others. My research role highlighted to me not only the critical importance of providing effective mental health services tailored specifically for undocumented students but the scarcity and lack of availability of these services. Through this experience, I've come to understand how vital it is for institutions to offer support that acknowledges the unique challenges faced by undocumented individuals. In a country where the undocumented are silenced, this initiative is a space where undocumented students can find their voice, share their stories, and cultivate colors of resilience.

Karen's Testimonio: Having managed to escape a life of violence and poverty, my family was truly blessed to live in the fulfillment and comfort of family union, yet we simultaneously lived in the constant fear and anxiety of family separation. Growing up in an immigrant household, witnessing the selflessness and sacrifices of my parents for the wellbeing of their daughters, it was instinct to adopt their values and dreams. The dream of attaining education, though pure and steadfast at first, was constantly struck and beat down by anti-immigrant rhetoric, legislation, and violence that has only continued to increase throughout past years. Going into university amidst the 2020 elections, the beginnings of the Covid-19 pandemic with my father bedridden, having been given an eviction notice, triggered overwhelming stress, anxiety, immense sentiments of not belonging, and paralyzing fear of failure that followed me throughout the upcoming years and provoked me to live in a survival mode, to tirelessly pursue academic validation in hopes it would prove my worth, despite the expense it would have on my physical, mental, and emotional wellbeing.

Dedicating my time to the student coordinator position immensely shifted the trajectory of my academic career and the perspective I hold of my scholar identity. It was not until I sat in my first Chicanx Studies class and took the initiative to go to therapy with a therapist specifically trained to help undocumented students on our campus that I truly felt valued and motivated to pursue my dreams through inclusive opportunities. Because of my status, I, along with thousands of others, was excluded from countless leadership and professional development opportunities, especially paid opportunities. Equitable opportunities, such as this program, are critical in addressing this inequity! As the student coordinator, I was finally given the same opportunity as my documented peers to develop my skills with professional guidance. Through this position, I had the opportunity to conduct a literature review, help compose a research article, attend research conferences, and network with professionals across campuses and departments. Being trusted and challenged to coordinate and facilitate the program's group sessions not only helped develop my leadership and my self-confidence, it also helped heal a part of me that felt utterly alone in my struggles and doubted my ability to succeed. From conducting a literature review on my communities to standing in the same room with several other students who shared my identities, this whole experience finally opened my eyes and heart to a community of individuals that understood each other on such unique and intricate levels. Serving my community, communicating so freely with them about topics that we have all been accustomed to hide, liberated me from that paralyzing fear and taught me the empowerment of courageously embracing my identities. Conducting and presenting this work, witnessing the hope it fosters within the eyes and hearts of the undocumented students in the program and audience at conferences, firmly consolidated my desires to center my work and career on service, giving back to the underserved and underrepresented communities, uplifting the spirits of those I serve and motivating them to positively shift their perspectives with which they perceive themselves so that they too may have the courage and opportunity to pursue and attain their dreams.

The testimonios of Yaneyry and Karen capture the complexity, the struggles, and the self-determination, love, and care of these students who know what living in the shadows means. This is a reminder that our work matters and we need to continue supporting each other in our multiplicity of identities and circumstances.

LET'S CONTINUE DOING THE WORK THAT MATTERS

The healing through Creative arts expressions group illustrates a small-scale initiative at UC Davis that carries significant systemic implications. It is a call for institutional awareness and understanding of the unique and often overlooked needs of our undocumented students, urging a deeper recognition of their challenges and experiences within academic environments. Additionally, it serves as a call for accountability, demanding that institutions not only acknowledge these needs but also take meaningful action by aligning their policies, practices, and resources with the lived reality of these students and other marginalized communities. The creation of the group on campus was critical and impactful, as it directly challenges the marginalization and invisibility of these students within academic spaces. The group fosters solidarity among those who are historically oppressed and disenfranchised.

The current political climate, along with Westernized and patriarchal normative institutions, urge scholar-activists to invest their energy and resources in doing meaningful work with and for the community, *doing work that matters.* Our healing group initiative embodies this approach, highlighting the importance of providing resources and support for undocumented students to navigate their educational journeys in institutions of higher education.

The ongoing efforts to continue the program reflect this vision and underscore the importance of continuing this work, not just for our undocumented students, but for the development and implementation of other initiatives to include all marginalized communities. Our ongoing program aims to continue healing *heridas abiertas* and to demonstrate the importance of valuing the human, cultural, and linguistic capital of our undocumented students. We are reminded of Anzaldúa's legacy, *let's continue, si vale la pena*; our undocumented students embody the essence of Anzaldúa's inspirational legacy.

WORKS CITED

Anzaldúa, Gloria. *Borderlands/La Frontera: The New Mestiza*. Aunt Lute Books, 1987.

—. *The Gloria Anzaldúa Reader.* Edited by AnaLouise Keating, Duke University Press, 2007.

—. *Light in the dark/Luz en lo oscuro: Rewriting Identity, Spirituality, Reality.* Edited by AnaLouise Keating, Duke University Press, 2015.

Flores, Y., and M. Torreiro-Casal. *Chicanx and Latinx Psychology: A Decolonial Approach*. Great River Learning, 2022.

Torreiro-Casal, M., Y. Flores, A. Medel-Herrero, and N. Deeb-Sossa. *The Praxis of Latinx and Chicanx Research Methods*. Kendall Hunt Publishing, 2024.

THE DESTRU/CREACIÓN OF SONGWRITING

ATRAVESADES EN COMUNIDAD

RACHEL YVONNE CRUZ

I stare up at the moon, Coyolxauhqui, and its light in the darkness.
I seek a healing image, one that reconnects me to others.

-Gloria Anzaldúa, Light in the Dark/Luz en lo Oscuro

My approach to songwriting embodies a cycle of *destru/creación*—a process of destroying and recreating, where intimate, personal experiences of love and loss are broken down, reshaped, and transformed into collective artistic expressions. Songwriters traverse pain and memory, reconstructing their realities through music. This act mirrors what Anzaldúa calls "the Coyolxauhqui process after the dis-membered Aztec moon goddess... After being split, dismembered, or torn apart la persona has to pull herself together, re-member and reconstruct herself on another level" (*The Gloria Anzaldúa Reader* 279). Songwriters navigate this complex process, sharing deeply personal narratives with which listeners connect on a visceral level. Why do I say songwriters and not composers? Because songs carry words, and words hold memory. Much like Anzaldúa's writing, songwriting bridges individual and communal experiences, offering a way to traverse *nepantla*—the space where identities are fractured, reimagined, and reclaimed. As a Queer, Chicana/x singer/songwriter, the Coyolxauhqui process resonates deeply within me.

I began songwriting long before I fully grasped the weight of that identity—the power a songwriter holds to shape and transform emotions into melody, to turn personal truth into part of someone else's story. The act of songwriting reflects what Anzaldúa describes as the development of mestiza consciousness, a way of thinking and creating that is fluid, a shift from what might be considered rational "to divergent thinking, characterized by movement away from set patterns and goals and toward a more whole perspective, one that includes rather than excludes. The new *mestiza* copes by developing a tolerance for contradictions, a tolerance for ambiguity.... nothing is thrust out, the good the bad and the ugly, nothing rejected, nothing abandoned.... she turns the ambivalence into something else.... an intense, and often painful, emotional event which inverts or resolves the ambivalence... It is work the soul performs" (*Borderlands* 101). According to Anzaldúa, the new mestiza is one who embraces contradiction, straddles multiple realities, and refuses to be confined by rigid categories. Songwriting is rarely linear; songs are layered, shaped by multiple influences, embodying both personal memory and collective history. When I write songs, I am the new mestiza.

Music has always been a part of me—an ever-present companion, usually comforting, yet at times unsettling, like a voyeur lingering in the shadows. Though I only recently became familiar with Anzaldúa's work, many of her ideas had long been embedded in my music. The way I sing and the songs I write emerge from gut-level, emotional responses rather than intellectual reasoning, from a place of *conocimiento*[1]—a deeper awareness that comes from lived experience. Upon being introduced to Anzaldúa, I recognized others like me, *mujeres* navigating *nepantla*, living at the crossroads of identities and histories. Through *la facultad*,[2] that heightened perception that allows us to understand everything more profoundly, I began to see my work through a new lens.

My songs *Hermanas del Alma* and *Hay Un Lugar / Somewhere There's a Place* are not just personal expressions but acts of *destru/creación*, transforming memory, trauma, and longing into something that can be voiced, carried, and ultimately released into the world. These songs exist in tension—between past and present, solitude and connection, pain and healing. *Hermanas del Alma* explores the bonds of sisterhood and coalition-building, the ways we find

1. "Like mestiza consciousness, conocimiento represents a nonbinary, connectionist mode of thinking; like la facultad, conocimiento often unfolds within oppressive contexts and entails a deepening of perception" (Anzaldúa, *Borderlands,* 320).

2. La facultad, as coined by Anzaldúa is "the capacity to see in surface phenomena the meaning of deeper realities, to see the deep structure below the surface. It is an instant 'sensing,' a quick perception arrived at without conscious reasoning" (Anzaldúa, *Borderlands*, 321).

ourselves reflected in others. *Hay Un Lugar*, on the other hand, is a song of searching, yearning for belonging beyond imposed boundaries. It is both a plea and a promise, a declaration that such a place exists—"*Hay un lugar, donde libre estaremos, a renacernos guiados solo por amor*" (A home awaits us, where we can remake ourselves guided only by love).

This work explores how *Hermanas del Alma* and *Hay Un Lugar* reflect the new mestiza consciousness—how they have fractured and reformed over time, just as I have been broken and remade alongside them. These songs were not written in isolation; they were shaped by lived experiences, refined through performance, and expanded by the voices of those who embraced them—embracing me in the process. They reflect the ongoing nature of *destru/creación*—how music, like identity, is never static but constantly evolving. Most importantly, the work traces the communal nature of songwriting—how songs begin as deeply personal expressions and evolve toward completion through sharing, listening, and recognition of the lived experiences of others. Through songwriting, memory and meaning take shape, weaving together personal truths with collective journeys. These songs, like identity, remain in motion—fracturing, reforming, and revealing new possibilities, inviting us to listen, reflect, and rebuild. What begins as a solitary process transforms through performance; this is where I find connection with others like me—*atravesades en comunidad.*

SONGWRITING AS *DESTRU/CREACIÓN*

My songwriting process embraces what Gloria Anzaldúa described as the Coyolxauhqui Imperative,[3] "an ongoing process of making and unmaking," (*Light in the Dark* 20) where experiences of heartbreak, loss, and identity struggles are broken apart and reconstructed into new forms of understanding. In *Light in the Dark/Luz en lo Oscuro* (2015), Anzaldúa explains that this imperative is an act of healing, a way of reassembling fractured parts of the self to create something new, something whole. This philosophy of continuously making and unmaking, or *destru/creación*, reflects the fluid nature of the songwriting process (19-21).

My song *Hermanas del Alma* is deeply rooted in this idea, particularly in its exploration of coalition-building through shared experience. The chorus, "*mujeres extranjeras, compartiendo la misma alma*," captures the bond that forms between women who, though shaped by different paths, recognize themselves in one another. This connection echoes Anzaldúa's concept of *nos/otras*, where understanding emerges not from sameness, but from the ability to bridge differences and find strength in collective struggle. Anzaldúa developed her

3. Coyolxauhqui (goddess of the moon) Imperative is the "path of the artist, the creative impulse, ... attempt to heal wounds. It's a search for inner completeness" (Anzaldúa, *Borderlands*, 320). Anzaldúa often associated this imperative with her desire to write and the writing process itself.

concept of *nos/otras* by splitting the word *nosotras* (feminine Spanish for "we") into two. She does this to acknowledge the tension between unity and division—*nos* implies "us," while *otras* implies "others." In doing so, she offers *nos/otras* as both a philosophy and praxis, one that generates new ways of understanding across differences. As she explains, "We contain the others, others contain us.... generating previously unrecognized commonalities and connections... enabling us to acknowledge, bridge, and sometimes transform the distances between self and other" (*The Gloria Anzaldúa Reader* 322–323).

The lyric "*Tú eres mi hermana del alma, cada vez que te encuentro siento que estoy mirando en un espejo...*" captures the profound experience of seeing oneself reflected in the life of another and affirming a shared experience of love, pain, and resilience. This act of recognition is a process of *desatravesades atravesando*—crossing through boundaries, connecting with others, and forging new ways of being in community. The movement between separation and connection requires breaking apart and rebuilding, much like the Coyolxauhqui process. This continual reshaping—both of the self and in relation to others—mirrors the transformative nature of songwriting, where personal narratives evolve through sharing, listening, and collective understanding.

Hermanas del Alma Lyrics

Verse 1
Tú eres mi hermana del alma
Cada vez que te encuentro siento
Que estoy mirando en un espejo.
El amor que tú sientes, yo siento.
Y el dolor que tú sientes
es el dolor que yo siento.
Vidas diferentes, lugares tan lejos uno del otro.
Mujeres extranjeras, compartiendo la misma alma.

Coro
Te conocí by the waves in your hair,
Te conocí by the curves that make you,
Te conocí by the look in your eyes,
By all the things that make me who you are.

Verse 2
Tú eres Latina como yo.
Naciste muy lejos de mí,

pero la vida que tú vives es la vida que yo vivo.
El amor que tú sientes, yo siento.
Y el dolor que tú sientes
es el dolor que yo siento.

NEPANTLA AND THE IN-BETWEEN SPACES

Anzaldúa's concept of *nepantla*—the liminal space between identities, realities, and understandings of self—deeply informs my songwriting process. *Nepantla* is a threshold, a state of transition where old ways of being no longer fit, yet new ones have yet to fully emerge. Anzaldúa describes, it is an unsettling and disorienting space, however one of immense creative and transformative potential. "Nepantla is *tierra desconocida*, and living in this liminal zone means being in a constant state of displacement—an uncomfortable, even alarming feeling. Most of us dwell in *nepantla* so much of the time it's become a sort of 'home.' Though this state links us to other ideas, people, and worlds, we feel threatened by these new connections and the change they engender" (*The Gloria Anzaldúa Reader* 243). The tension of *nepantla*—between stability and upheaval, fear and possibility—is where transformation begins.

My song *Hay Un Lugar* was born from *nepantla*—from my own experience of feeling suspended between worlds, caught between conflicting expectations and realities. The song captures the search for a place where love, identity, and belonging can exist without restriction. The opening line, "Somewhere there's a place where people who live the way that I do can live in harmony," expresses the deep longing for such a space. *Nepantla* is not a passive place; it is a space of conflict, where one can confront their proverbial demons. The journey through nepantla is not straightforward—it requires bravery, facing hardship, uncertainty, and change. The lyric, "Through the darkness of the storm, that's where life transforms," speaks to the challenge of working through the conundrum of being caught between worlds, the struggles that must be endured to reach a place of self-definition. *Nepantla* is not a place to remain but a passageway that must be navigated on the road to finding self. The act of transformation requires enduring this in-between space, using the storm as fuel for growth–metamorphosis.

The imagery of flight in *Hay Un Lugar*—"Souls soar high above the tethers of earth's embrace"—evokes the liberation that emerges after passing through *nepantla*. In my songwriting journal, I sketched a dove—how I have always envisioned souls, likely influenced by my Catholic upbringing, where the dove symbolizes the Holy Spirit. To me, this image represents the soul breaking free from earthly constraints, ascending beyond limitation, and finding release. Much like the *Coyolxauhqui imperative*, in which fragmentation is necessary for transformation, *nepantla* is not a place to remain but a rite of passage—an essential stage of transition—perhaps a death—that ultimately leads to rebirth.

When I began writing this essay, I returned to a passage in *Light in the Dark/ Luz en lo Oscuro* that articulated an experience I had long struggled to name:

> You face divisions within your cultures—divisions of class, gender, sexuality, nationality, and ethnicity. You face both entrenched institutions and the oppositional movements of working-class women, people of color, and queers. Pulled between opposing realities, you feel torn between "white" ways and Mexican ways, between Chicano nationalists and conservative Hispanics. Suspended between traditional values and feminist ideas, you don't know whether to assimilate, separate, or isolate. (126-127)

This feeling—the tension of existing between multiple worlds, never fully belonging—defined my experience as a doctoral student at The University of Texas at Austin, one of the very places Anzaldúa referenced in the passage above. It was there that I earned both my master's and doctoral degrees, navigating the contradictions and pressures of academia while carrying the weight of expectations from multiple communities. This feeling of being suspended between identities, of searching for a place where I could exist fully, was what led me to begin writing *Somewhere There's a Place*. The song would take over 30 years to evolve into its current form—its final form, for now. When I first wrote it, I only had the first two stanzas. Though I hadn't yet encountered the term *nepantla*, the song was already my response to it—my way of articulating the liminality of my existence in academic spaces, in life, and in familial settings where I was not always seen, where my work was not always valued.

Writing *Somewhere There's a Place*, which later became *Hay Un Lugar/ Somewhere There's a Place*, was an attempt to imagine the possibility of belonging—to create a space where I did not have to choose between conflicting expectations, where I could simply exist, whole and unfragmented. For me, this place took shape in song. *Hay Un Lugar* was not just an imagined destination; it was an act of world-building, a way of forging a space where my existence, my love, and my identity needed no justification. Much like *nepantla* itself, my approach to songwriting is not a static process. It is an act of creation and recreation, a space where the self is broken down and reassembled. *Hay Un Lugar* expresses this movement—the passage through uncertainty toward transformation. The song does not simply long for a place of belonging; it enacts it, carving out space through lyric and melody. In offering these songs to others, I find my way through the storm. And in doing so, I join others who are also moving through *nepantla*, forging new realities and new ways of being—through music, through words, through community.

Hay Un Lugar / Somewhere There's a Place Lyrics

Verse 1

Somewhere there's a place
Where people who live
The way that I do
Can live in harmony.

Verse 2

I'll take you to a place
Where dreams align in grace
And hearts find their homes
Guided by love alone.

Coro

Hay un lugar
Donde libre estaremos
A elegir cómo vivir
Y amar sin cesar.
Hay un lugar
Donde te llevaré
A renacernos guiados
Solo por amor.

Verse 3

Through the darkness of the storm,
That's where life transforms.
Two hearts unchained
In a new world untamed

Verse 4

Al ritmo de la tempestad
Baila la luna con el sol
Yo lo oscuro, tú la luz
Alumbrando nuestro ser.

Verse 5

Somewhere there's a place
Where we can be free
Free to live and to love
The way that we please

Verse 6
Sometime in our life
The world is gonna change
Souls will soar high above
The tethers of earth's embrace.

CHIAROSCURO: LIGHT, SHADOW, AND THE TRANSFORMATIVE PROCESS

The term chiaroscuro stems from the Italian words *chiaro* (meaning "clear" or "bright") and *scuro* (meaning "obscure" or "dark"). "The technique focuses on shadows and a single source of light to achieve photorealistic depth and tone" (Taggert, para. 3). Though originally a term from Renaissance painting, I first encountered it in a voice lesson—not as a visual concept, but as a way to describe the tonal balance my teacher wanted me to achieve. She described my voice as rich and romantic, dark—like chocolate—but emphasized that for it to carry without becoming heavy, I needed to blend in brighter tones. This balance between warmth and clarity, depth and brightness, was essential to achieving *bel canto*—beautiful singing—where both vocal colors or timbres had to coexist to create resonance and fluidity. The interplay of light and dark in the voice, as I was learning, mirrored the artistic principle of chiaroscuro, revealing that contrast is not opposition, but a necessary tool for achieving a beautiful sound that will carry without amplification.

Over time, the concept of *chiaroscuro* reached beyond vocal technique and into my songwriting, once again, albeit inadvertently, aligning with Anzaldúan concepts of *Light in the Dark/Luz en lo Oscuro.* For Anzaldúa, *chiaroscuro* (she didn't use this term) is not simply about contrast but about the necessary coexistence of opposing forces—pain and healing, visibility and obscurity, past and present. Rather than seeking to erase darkness and pain, Anzaldúa invites us to openly receive it, recognizing that areas of discomfort are not voids but spaces of possibility and growth. Chiaroscuro thus becomes a process in which light and dark work in complement—light does not eliminate darkness but emerges through it.

> A paradox: The knowledge that exposes your fears can also remove them. Seeing through these cracks makes you uncomfortable because it reveals aspects of yourself (shadow beasts) you don't want to own. Admitting your darker aspects allows you to break out of your self-imposed prison. But it will cost you. When you woo el oscuro, digging into it, sooner or later you pay the consequences—the pain of personal growth. Conocimiento will not let you forget the shadow self, greedy, gluttonous, and indifferent; will not let you lock the cold 'bitch' in the basement anymore. (Anzaldúa, *Light in the Dark*, 132).

Anzaldúa's words resonate in the way *chiaroscuro* manifests in my work—as a reckoning with the shadow self, the aspects of experience that demand acknowledgment rather than repression. This idea is embedded in my songs, where the negotiation between light and darkness is not just thematic but structural, shaping the movement of melody, harmony, and lyrics. "*Al ritmo de la tempestad, baila la luna con el sol. Yo lo oscuro, tú mi luz, alumbrando nuestro ser.*" The moon dances with the sun, both radiant, yet the sun burns infinitely brighter—moving in tandem, yet only the moon illuminates the night.

Musically, *chiaroscuro* emerges in the interplay between tension and release, dissonance and resolution, minor and major tonalities, silence and sound. It is the moment in a canción where sorrow and resilience meet, where the voice cracks before soaring. In storytelling, this same dynamic unfolds—histories of erasure persist alongside acts of reclamation, and narratives of oppression remain inseparable from resistance. Understanding *chiaroscuro* in this way moves beyond binary thinking; it shifts the focus from simply overcoming darkness to recognizing it as an essential force that gives light its depth and meaning.

This balance between light and shadow is central to *Hermanas del Alma* and *Hay Un Lugar*. In *Hermanas del Alma*, the song's thematic shifts mirror the complexities of relationships—how love and grief, connection and loss, exist within the same space. The structure itself embraces contrast, moving between warmth and melancholy, intimacy and distance, much like the experience of recognizing oneself in another. In the lyrics of *Hermanas del Alma*, the line "*...el amor que tú sientes, yo siento, y el dolor que tú sientes es el dolor que yo siento...*," encapsulates this shared experience, where the light of love is always accompanied by the shadow of pain. The song constantly negotiates these spaces, where the act of reflection becomes reciprocal: "*Te conocí* by the waves in your hair, by the curves that make you, and by the look in your eyes, by all the things that make me who you are; make you who I am."

The song captures the beauty and challenge of seeing oneself in another, a mutual reflection that underscores the complexities of deep connections. It illustrates the coexistence of love and struggle, and light and dark, continuously reshaping the experience of how one sees or is being seen. Similarly, in *Hay Un Lugar*, the storm symbolizes the darkness we must navigate before undergoing a metamorphosis into our authenticity. The music intensifies with each verse, gaining momentum until it reaches the chorus, where it transitions from the weight of a minor key to the brightness of C major. This mode mixture, shifts between minor and major, acts as a light switch, shifting the journey from struggle to triumph as the song evolves. The shift represents not just a change in tone but the emergence of strength and renewal, marking the culmination of the journey through darkness into light—overcoming.

This is *chiaroscuro* in motion, light cutting through darkness, illuminating what was left in silence, a symbol of re-engagement, a return to songwriting after a period of absence. Shadows stretch across a dark room filled with memories and songs long forgotten waiting to be rediscovered and reimagined. The guitar, resting against the chair, its strings barely catching the light, waits. It is both an invitation and a confrontation, a reminder that the music, like the self, can only remain dormant for so long. Its presence mirrors the way music lingers within me—persistent, even in silence. This is the essence of *chiaroscuro*—not simply contrast, but coexistence. Darkness does not erase light; it gives it depth, definition, meaning.

My understanding of *chiaroscuro*—light in or through the dark—began as a lesson in classical vocal technique, a method of balancing timbres to create resonance and strength. My voice teacher once described my sound as rich and romantic, yet powerful and poignant, urging me to balance my dark tones with bright ones so that my voice would carry. This balance—of warmth and clarity, weight and brilliance—is the foundation of *bel canto*, the art of beautiful singing. Over time, however, the concept of *chiaroscuro* extended beyond vocal technique, becoming a framework for how I understand identity and approach songwriting and personal transformation.

Light and darkness, joy and sorrow, past and future—all exist in constant negotiation. In music, this plays out in the interplay between tension and release, dissonance and resolution, minor and major tonalities. In storytelling, it manifests in the juxtaposition of struggle and triumph and winning and losing. And in life, it is the negotiation between what we leave behind and what we carry forward. Whether it be in songwriting or in life, I chose to coexist with the shadows, the struggle, the pain and recognize their presence as part of the process. The act of creation—of finding light within the dark—and a part of the artistic endeavor. The guitar in the corner is waiting. The music is waiting. And so, I turn back to the work, to the process of *destru/creación*, back to the journey. ¡*Siempre adelante!*

CONCLUSION: *LA FACULTAD*

> Cada *arrebatamiento* is an awakening that causes you to question who you are, what the world is about. The urgency to know what you're experiencing awakens *la facultad*, the ability to shift attention and see through the surface of things and situations. With each *arrebatamiento* you suffer *un susto*, a shock that knocks one of your souls out of your body, causing estrangement. With the loss of the familiar and the unknown ahead, you struggle to regain your balance, reintegrate yourself (put Coyolxauhqui together), and repair the damage. You must, like the shaman, find a way to call your spirit home. (Anzaldúa, *Light in the Dark*, 125)

When she died, my first *hermana del alma*, I felt it. Part of me died with her. And in that moment, any chance to reckon, to make sense of what never made sense, to salvage or heal, vanished. There was no confrontation, no resolution—only an insurmountable finality. I felt it—a shift deep in my chest, sudden and unshakable. It wasn't grief. It wasn't relief. It was something unfinished, something unresolved. The weight of the unspoken, the unsung, pressed down on me. It was her transition, her soul entering the body of a dove … perhaps.

The songs we sang had been silent for decades, not forgotten but set aside—an unintentional burial of memory and meaning. I convinced myself that leaving them behind would allow me to move on, to create something new, to step into another version of myself. But silence does not erase. The past lingers—unspoken, waiting, insistent. And so, when the weight of all that was left unsaid became unbearable, I turned back and quite literally "faced the music."

> Every paroxysm has the potential to initiate you to something new, giving you a chance to reconstruct yourself, forcing you to rework your description of self, world, and your place in it (reality). …You honor what has ended, say good-bye to the old way of being, commit yourself to look for the 'something new,' and picture yourself embracing this new life. But before that can happen, you plunge into the ambiguity of the transition phase, undergo another rite of passage, and negotiate another identity crisis. (Anzaldúa, *Light in the Dark,* 125-126)

Because what's one more identity crisis? At this point, I've had enough of them to form a catalog—each one pushing me further into *nepantla*. Through songwriting, I engaged in the process of *destru/creación*, transforming personal experiences of loss, love, and identity into expressions of healing and liberation. *Hermanas del Alma* and *Hay Un Lugar* are not just compositions; they are testimonies to the transformative power of music, where personal and collective journeys toward connection, freedom, and resilience intertwine. These songs personify *nepantla*, *la facultad*, and *chiaroscuro*, weaving together light and dark, struggle and redemption, in both their lyrics and melodies. Each act of songwriting is an *arrebatamiento*, an emotional upheaval that forces an awakening, a reckoning with the past and the present. Anzaldúa describes this process as both painful and necessary, a moment when the soul is dislodged, forcing one to reconstruct themselves, to find a way to "call your spirit home."

Through songwriting, soul-building, and encountering *hermanas del alma*—mirror images of myself reflecting even my most secret struggles and joys—I've found profound connections that drive this journey of collective healing and deliverance. These songs, once left in the quiet, have been reawakened through performance, through community, through recognition. And in that reawakening, I, too, have been transformed. And together, we move forward, *atravesades en comunidad*—one song at a time, one love at a time—we soar.

WORKS CITED

Anzaldúa, Gloria. *Borderlands/La frontera: The New Mestiza.* 4th ed., Aunt Lute Books, 2012.

—. *Light in the Dark/Luz en lo oscuro: Rewriting Identity, Spirituality, Reality.* [Kindle Version], edited by AnaLouise Keating, Duke University Press, 2015.

—. *The Gloria Anzaldúa Reader.* Edited by Ana Louise Keating, Duke University Press, 2009.

Taggart, E. *How Chiaroscuro Emerged from the Dark to Become one of the Most Iconic Painting Styles.* My Modern Met, 2022. https://mymodernmet.com/chiaroscuro-painting-technique/.

A VISUAL INTERPRETATION OF GLORIA ANZALDÚA'S UNPUBLISHED FABLE, NEPANTLA

IMAGERY AND ANALYSIS

NOREEN M. GRAF

On October 23, 1991, Gloria Anzaldúa was audio-recorded reading her unpublished fable, *Nepantla*. Introducing her work, Anzaldúa stated, "This is a poem, not a poem. This is a fable that I need help with. I need you to help me with it. I'm going to read it, and afterwards when you see me, tell me what you think I should work on."

Thirty-one years later, I take up her invitation to help flesh out her fable by offering a visual interpretation consisting of ten drawings inspired by her fable. Because Anzaldúa also engaged in the visual arts and created several sketches and painted versions of the dismemberment state of Nepantla, such a venture seems congruent with her belief in art as additive and supplemental to her work.

According to Marcos de R. Antuna , *Nepantla*, in Aztec culture, translates to the everyday (every moment) changes that are ordinary and constant. Anzaldúa, however, writes about *Nepantla* as a state of extraordinary transformation. While Anzaldúa may have been "historically and philosophically inaccurate" (Antuna), there is wide acceptance of Anzaldúa's interpretation and use of the term. "And I now call it Nepantla, which is a Nahuatl word for the space between two bodies of water, the space between two worlds … And that is what Nepantla stands for" (Anzaldúa, *Borderlands*, 56).

Anzaldúa's categorization of the work as a fable compels me to first understand this deliberate categorization. The Greek rhetorician Aelius Theon, who trained orators in the 1st century AD, defined a fable as "a fictitious story picturing a truth" (Patillon). Many fables depict relationships between humans and gods. They are stories which typically contain symbolism, anthropomorphized animals, and lessons that may have a moral intent. Thus, by framing *Nepantla* as a fable, Anzaldúa teaches us through a symbolic story. Prieta, the main character in Anzaldúa's fable, has been used as a representation of herself in many of her publications (Anzaldúa, "La Prieta,"198-209). Like her other stories, this fable reflects Anzaldúa's experiences and is intended to assist in our understanding of the entire process of transformation.

The purpose of this essay is to reimagine Gloria Anzaldúa's unpublished fable *Nepantla* through textual analysis and visual interpretations inspired by the narrative. The paper begins with a summary of the fable and is followed by a discussion of key components.

SUMMARY OF ANZALDÚA'S NEPANTLA FABLE

The *Nepantla* fable begins with Prieta, who has blue skin, arriving at a bridge where she meets the chalk-skin guard who doesn't allow her to cross into *Nepantla* because she has green hair. She circles around the perimeter, looking for another way to cross the river, and meets a group of people who are waiting to cross. They ask her to join them, but she declines, stating, "each must cross alone" (Anzaldúa, "Nepantla"). Prieta's body is spray-painted to look as if she is wearing clothes and she realizes that when she crosses, she will need actual clothes. She then meets another blue-skinned woman who gives Prieta the clothes from her body. Prieta puts the clothes in a bag and holding the bag over her head, enters the river. On the other side, she is met by the faceless chalk-skins, who dismember her and gouge out her eyes. When she awakens, in pieces, she reconstructs her body and finds a new piece of herself, which she presses into her forehead. Everything looks so different, and she has trouble even recognizing herself. She has transformed: "I am no longer the one who crossed the river, yet I am still me, only I am more me." Prieta then senses she is being watched and feels threatened by snarling dogs. She can no longer stay in Nepantla and "sprints towards eyes far ahead in the distance" ("Nepantla").

VISUAL INTERPRETATION METHODOLOGY

The methodology for my process of visual translation of the *Nepantla* fable begins with my own transcription of the fable from the recorded reading. I then attend closely to Anzaldúa's written words. Descriptions with the most amount of detail became my initial sketches of the story and were my most literal translations of her work. This was followed by a kind of visual listening, which was an internal process scrutinizing my sketches, where I determined if my preliminary images reflected the tone and meaning of the fable. I allowed additional images to emerge where I believed a vacancy existed. Once I achieved a sense of unity and coherence, I completed the sketch and added color inspired by Mexican folk art, particularly alebrijes, which feature vivid colors and fantastical designs (Oaxacan Alebrijes).

Once the drawings were nearly finalized, I grounded the images in my artwork in scholarship. For instance, I had instinctively introduced spiritual companions—the snake and the fish—into Prieta's journey through Nepantla. These elements emerged organically during the creative process, and it was only through subsequent research into Aztec mythology and Anzaldúa's writings that I came to fully comprehend their deeper significance, which I will expand upon below. While this method deviates from my customary artistic and intellectual practices, it resonates with Anzaldúa's attunement to the metaphysical realm (Anzaldúa, *Light in the Dark*). Ultimately, it is my sincerest hope that my visual interpretations faithfully honor both her work and intentions.

The resulting mixed-media drawings of the Nepantla fable integrate numerous references to Aztec folklore. Some of these references are directly drawn from Anzaldúa's naming of objects and beings in the story, such as the moon (Coyolxāuhqui), the dog (Itzcuintli), the eye (ixtli), the lizard (Cuetzpallin), and the chalk-face (Cihuacóatl). Others were incorporated to align with the story's tone and suggested imagery, including the skeleton (Miquiztli), the serpent (Coatl), the fish (Yemaya, the ocean mother), and the new state of awareness (Ollin) (Miller and Taube). These are discussed further as they occur in the fable.

FOUR PHASES OF THE NEPANTLA JOURNEY

Anzaldua's fable is perhaps the only place she puts all the components of a voyage into, and out of, Nepantla within a single work. An examination of the fable reveals four key phases, mirroring the classic structure of mythic storytelling (Vogler). I explore the story through the four phases: Arrival and Entry into Nepantla (four images), Dismemberment and Reconstruction (two images), Transformation (two images), and Reentry and Reintegration (two images). Each image reflects a transcribed passage from the fable. They are positioned accordingly. Following each set of images, I detail the artistic choices and symbolism I used in these sets of images.

Phase One: Arrival and Entry into Nepantla

Anzaldúa spends most of the story describing the difficulty of entry into *Nepantla*. Four drawings are associated with the entry and arrival into *Nepantla*. They depict Prieta's arrival at the bridge, her meeting with other travelers, the meeting of a woman who gives her clothes, and her crossing of the river.

Image 1. Arrival at the Barrier Bridge

Image 2. Meeting Others Wanting to Cross

Image 1 depicts Anzaldúa as she is confronted by the chalk-skin guard. She is denied entry, "We don't want anyone with green hair here. They don't want anyone with green hair where I come from either (Anzaldúa, "Nepantla").

Image 2 depicts Prieta meeting others who are waiting to cross the river. Anzaldúa writes, "They ask me to cross with them. I squat beside them saying each must cross by herself. Each must find her community on the other side."

Image 3 shows the blue-skinned woman who gives Prieta her clothes. "First, she steps out of her pants and hands them to me. While I'm stuffing them into a plastic nap bag, she takes off her camisa" (Anzaldúa, "Nepantla").

Image 4 shows Prieta crossing the river holding the bag of clothes over her head. The moon lights the way, "I walk into the shadowed part of the river. The water is lukewarm, but I shiver and tremors course down my body. I am scared, scared, so scared" (Anzaldúa, "Nepantla").

Image 3. Receiving Clothing

Staying true to the fable, in images one and two I depict a blue-skinned woman with green hair. She wears my vision of Aztec-painted clothing and stands at a bridge, waiting to cross. In addition, I chose a traditional long hair braid to represent the unchanged self. Other additions are the companions in the water of a fish and snake who accompany Prieta as she crosses the river. Below, I

Image 4. Crossing the River

examine elements of the drawing in relation to Anzaldua's prior writings, Aztec culture and folklore, and various literary references.

The Bridge. As in this fable, Anzaldúa's writings about the process of getting to *Nepantla* often use the metaphor of a bridge associated with crossing borders: "Bridges are thresholds to other realities, archetypal, primal symbols of shifting consciousness. They are passageways, conduits, and connectors that connote transitioning, crossing borders, and changing perspectives. Bridges span liminal spaces between worlds, spaces I call Nepantla, a Nahuatl word meaning tierra entre medio" (Anzaldúa, *Borderlands,* 243).

Blue Skin. In the fable, Anzaldúa uses blue skin to symbolize people of color. The only Aztec reference to blue skin comes from the burial rituals where persons who died by water had blue dye poured on their foreheads before their burial. (Balderas and Balderas). Skin color plays an enormous role in Gloria's writing: "Because of the color of my skin, they betrayed me. The dark-skinned woman has been silenced, gagged, caged, bound into servitude with marriage, bludgeoned for 300 years, sterilized, and castrated in the twentieth century" (*Borderlands*, 25).

Green Hair. In terms of the hair, Anzaldúa further uses color to symbolize difference as a reason for exclusion. I chose to open the story with Prieta's hair in a traditional braid, and as the story progresses towards transformation, the hair changes dramatically. As Maine reminds us, "Hair is never just hair. It has consistently served as a second, nonverbal language to express critical sentiments, telling the story of women's lives like nothing else does" (122). Hair also plays roles in gender identities and the politics of sexuality and race, signaling compliance with societal norms or resistance and subversions (Sigal). Anzaldúa writes, "My mother used to tell me, 'Don't let your hair grow long; don't let your hair be messy, otherwise people will think you're dirty or rebellious.' Hair is controlled just like women's voices are controlled, like our sexuality is controlled" (*Borderlands*, 38).

Miquiztli the Skeleton. In Anzaldúa's fable, she refers to a "chalk-face" multiple times. This figure prevents her from crossing the bridge and later dismembers her. Initially, I considered depicting the chalk-face as a white border guard symbolizing racial oppression. However, I chose to move beyond this more literal interpretation to better align with the overarching theme of transformation. Since *Nepantla* is defined as a fable by Anzaldúa, I chose to anthropomorphize the skeleton, *Miquiztli*, white as chalk, to symbolize the border guard, who turns away the blue-skinned woman because of her green hair. *Miquiztli*, the Aztec skeleton, symbolizes death and rebirth (Miller and Taube). Throughout Mesoamerican history, death has been seen as connected to the continuity of life and as a regenerative process with supernatural implications that illustrate the transformation which occurs between old endings and new beginnings (Balderas and Balderas).

The idea of a "chalk-face" appears in Aztec folklore. *Cihuacóatl* is described as having a face white as chalk. Or, in *Borderlands*, as covered with chalk. According to Miller and Taube, *Cihuacóatl* represents a unification of the feminine (sexuality and fertility) and masculine (male sexuality and warfare) principles and is frequently depicted as an old woman with a skull face.

Coatl the Serpent Anzaldúa doesn't place the serpent in the fable *Nepantla*, but I found the serpent (*Coatl*) trailing the blue-skinned woman in my sketches and decided, upon conducting research, that it made a good addition because of its reference to rebirth. I use the serpent as both a spiritual guide and protector of Prieta as she travels into *Nepantla*.

Coatl is a sacred creature in Aztec mythology. *Coatl* is the symbol of the earth and the personification of *Coatlicue*, mother of the gods. She is viewed as the patron of fertility, life, and death, and the guide of transformation and rebirth (Miller and Taube). *Coatl* represents the power of the female (Aigner-Varoz). Anzaldúa writes, "*Coatlicue* is one of the powerful images, or 'archetypes' that inhabits, or passes through, my psyche. *Coatlicue* is the mountain, the Earth Mother who conceives all celestial beings out of her cavernous womb, goddess of birth and death, *Coatlicue* gives and takes away life, she is the incarnation of cosmic processes" (*Borderlands,* 56).

Anzaldúa further writes directly of Coatl:

> In pre-Columbian America, the most notable symbol was the serpent. The Olmecs associated womanhood with the Serpent's mouth, which was guarded by rows of dangerous teeth, a sort of vagina dentata. They considered it the most sacred place on earth, a place of refuge, the creative womb from which all things were born and to which all things returned... the destiny of humankind is to be devoured by the Serpent. (*Borderlands,* 94)

Anzaldúa's strong connection to the serpent may have originated from her childhood when she was bitten by a rattlesnake and watched her mother use a hoe to cut it to pieces. Anzaldúa writes, "In the morning I saw through snake eyes, felt snake blood course through my body" (*Anzaldúa, Borderlands*, 47). And finally, she concludes, "The serpent, mi tono, my animal counterpart... Always when they cross my path, fear and elation flood my body. I know things older than Freud, older than gender" (*Borderlands,* 47). The snakebite symbolically initiates Anzaldúa into shamanism, and the snake-as-metaphor for hidden knowledge remains a consistent motif throughout the author's work (Dahms).

The Moon. In image four, Prieta is moving towards the moon. In her work published in *Light in the Dark* (2015), Anzaldúa references the Moon as follows: "I stare up at the moon, Coyolxauhqui, and its light in the darkness. I seek a healing image, one that reconnects me to others" (304). The Coyolxauhqui imperative is to heal and achieve integration. "Then fragmentations occur, you fall apart and feel as though you've been expelled from paradise" (312). "What I call the Coyolxauhqui imperative is basically an attempt to heal the wounds. It's a search for inner completeness" (292).

The River. In *Borderlands*, Anzaldúa writes about the dangerous crossings of rivers: "Without benefit of bridges, the 'mojados' (wetbacks) float on inflatable rafts across el Rio Grande, or wade or swim across naked, clutching their clothes over their heads. Holding onto the grass, they pull themselves along the banks with a prayer to Virgen de Guadalupe on their lips: Ay virgencita Morena, mi madrecita, dame tu bendición" (33). Anzaldúa further describes the people crossing, "Faceless, nameless, invisible, taunted with 'Hey cucaracho' (cockroach). Trembling with fear, yet filled with courage, a courage born of desperation. Barefoot and uneducated, Mexicans with hands like boot soles gather at night by the river where two worlds merge..." (Anzaldúa, *Borderlands*, 34).

Fish. While not written into the fable, I included a fish as a second spiritual companion. The Nahua word for "fish" is *michin*. The Aztecs viewed fish as a symbol of the world of water and fertility (Karttunen). Yemaya, a goddess associated with oceans and waters, is referenced by Anzaldúa in her poem *Yemaya*: "I come to you, Yemaya, ocean mother, sister of the fishes." ("Yemaya" 73). Anzaldúa's connection to water and fish is evident, "I, like the ocean, am water, am wind, am fish" (*Borderlands* 4th ed. 242).

Phase 2: Dismemberment and Reconstruction

Two art pieces are related to the process of dismemberment and reconstruction.

Image 5 shows Prieta, naked, on the other side of the river being confronted by a chalk-skin: "I stand there trembling, covering my nakedness with my hands, and I press my thighs together to hide the trickle going down my legs. They know I have wet myself" (Anzaldúa, "Nepantla").

Image 6 depicts Prieta using her mouth to put her limbs back in place: "I wiggle my torso through the grass like a worm, grope for my arms, and using my mouth, I push them back into their sockets" (Anzaldúa, "Nepantla").

Image 5. Confronted by the Chalk-face

Image 6. Reconstructing the Body

Dismembered Body. Anzaldúa refers to being in *Nepantla* as a state of discomfort, often described as painful, requiring dismemberment—a process of being pulled apart before reconstruction: "It is very awkward, uncomfortable, and frustrating to be in that *Nepantla*, because you are in the midst of transformation" (*Borderlands*, 122).

As in the fable, Anzaldúa tells us that before transformation can occur, there is a dismemberment and reconstruction of the self. She states, "We are currently undergoing disintegration and reconstruction, pulled apart, dismembered, then reconstructed—a process I envision symbolized by Coyolxauhqui" (*Light in the Dark*, 74). In Aztec mythology, Coyolxauhqui, goddess of the moon, was cut into pieces, and her head was thrown into the sky by the Aztec god of war, Huitzilopochtli, revealing her head as the moon (Tuana and Scott).

Anzaldúa writes about the dismemberment of Mexican culture in relation to the mutilated body:

> I stop before the dismembered body of la diosa de la luna, Coyolxauhqui, bones jutting from sockets. The warrior goddess with bells on her cheeks and a serpent belt calls to mind the dominant culture's repeated attempts to tear the Mexican culture in the U.S. apart and scatter the fragments to the winds. (*Borderlands* 56)

Anzaldúa also explains the reconstruction process as more than simply putting parts back in place. It allows for the reordering of pieces to create a new self: "Coyolxauhqui is my symbol for the necessary process of dismemberment and fragmentation, of seeing that self or the situations you're embroiled in differently. It is also my symbol for reconstruction and reframing, one that allows for putting the pieces together in a new way" *(Light in the Dark*, 74). Anzaldúa also illustrated her concepts of Nepantla, the Coatlicue state, and Coyolxāuhqui with a particular emphasis on the dismembered state. Her drawings are housed at the Nettie Lee Benson Latin American Collection at the University of Texas at Austin.

Phase 3: Transformation

In *Light in the Dark/Luz en lo Oscuro*, Anzaldúa and Keating discuss the spiritual aspect of *Nepantla*, stating, "In *nepantla* you sense more keenly the overlap between the material and spiritual worlds; you're in both places simultaneously—you glimpse *el espíritu*—see the body as inspirited" (54).

For Anzaldúa, *Nepantla* was, "where I struggle with my creations...." (*Borderlands* 2). She named not one *Nepantla*, but numerous ones: "I am conscious of various *Nepantlas*—linguistic, geographical, gender, sexual, historical, cultural, political, social—when I write" (2). For Anzaldúa, her writing became automatically infused with both ordinary and spiritual realities, which made healing and transformation possible. *Nepantla* was a place where she experienced culturally inherited ideas and identities that formed her roots (Tuana and Sullivan). She described this alternate dimension as a place where a person feels lost. Time and meaning are suspended.

Anzaldúa discusses what is necessary for change to take place:

> You remove the old bridge from your back, and though afraid, allow diverse groups to collectively rebuild it.... You don't build bridges to safe and familiar territories; you have to risk making *mundo nuevo*, have to risk the uncertainty of change. And *nepantla* is the only space where change happens. Change requires more than words on a page; it takes perseverance, creativity, ingenuity, and acts of love (*Light in the Dark* 125).

Two images reflect the transformation of Prieta, in her hair, skin, and physical form have all been transformed.

Image 7 shows Prieta holding a piece of herself: "I find my hands, pick up my eyeballs, rinse them in the river, put them back in my face. I see a new piece of myself I don't recognize, never knew, or had forgotten. I press it into my forehead" (Anzaldúa, "Nepantla").

Image 8 depicts the transformed Prieta. Behind her are skeletal creatures that welcome her. Her body and face have changed: "I catch a glimpse of a face in a store window. Watch its color recede and realize that it is my face. I no longer look the same. Light radiates from me, and my body hums" (Anzaldúa, "Nepantla").

Image 7. Finding a New Piece

Anzaldúa writes, "To be healed, we must be dismembered, pulled apart" (*Light in the Dark* 29). When Anzaldúa is torn apart and grappling on the ground to find parts of herself and reconstruct her body. Although she doesn't recognize the piece, she instantly identifies it as an authentic part of her being. The transformation is therefore coming to know and recognize herself or paying attention to what was already present in her. When she is torn apart, she can find herself. Below is an examination of the images present in the drawings as they relate to Aztec culture and Anzaldúa's work.

<u>Ollin.</u> My challenge was to visually represent the new piece that was an old piece, and I chose Aztec iconography that lies at the center of the Aztec calendar, *ollin*. In the Nahuatl language, *ollin* or *olin* means movement from some applied force or quake/earthquake (Brinton 1885). Thus, the force of being torn apart creates the movement necessary to reconstruct the self, and I chose this imagery as the new piece Prieta presses into her forehead. *Ollin* appears at the center of the Aztec calendar stone. In the very center is the face of a god, which is framed by a graphic symbol, indicating the date *naui olin*. The Aztecs believed the past had consisted of four fifty-two-year cycles, and at the end of each cycle, the sun

Image 8. Transformation Achieved

was destroyed. They believed they were living in the fifth and final cycle, *naui olin*, during which time the universe would be destroyed. It is interesting to note that during this time, the Spanish Conquest occurred (Klein).

In the fable, once Prieta has achieved transformation, her skin and appearance change. In her writing, Anzaldúa states, "In relinquishing your old self, you realize that some aspects of who you are—identities people have imposed on you as a woman of color and that you have internalized—are also made up" (*Light in the Dark* 138).

Face. At the end of the fable, Prieta doesn't recognize her face and watches its blue color recede as light radiates from her body. I reflect this in the image with a color gradation from blue to light yellow. Anzaldúa views the face as, "the world knows us by our faces, the most naked, most vulnerable, exposed, and significant topology of the body" (*Light in the Dark* 89).

> During the dark side of the moon, something in the mirror catches my gaze. I seem all eyes and nose. Inside my skull, something shifts. 'I see' my face. Gloria, the everyday face; Prieta and Prietita, my childhood faces; Gaudi, the face my mother and sister and brothers know. And there in the black, obsidian mirror of the Nahuas is yet another face, a stranger's face.

> *Simultaneamente me miraba la cara desde distintos* ángulos. *Y mi cara, como la realidad, tenía un carácter múltiple.* (*Light in the Dark,* 67-68)

Lizard. In the fable, Anzaldúa writes of approaching lizard-like creatures. The lizard *Cuetzpallin* symbolizes unisexuality and possesses mysterious energies (Cuetzpallin). Anzaldúa states, "But I, like other queer people, am two in one body, both male and female. I am the embodiment of the *hieros gamos*: the coming together of opposite qualities within. Half and Half" (*Borderlands* 41). Anzaldúa has written about the gender border, and for this reason, when she indicates a physical transformation, I created a lizard-like creature that also has chameleon features. "Some of us are forced to acquire the ability, like a chameleon, to change color when the dangers are many and the options few" (*Light in the Dark* 125). But Anzaldúa goes on to examine change as a choice, "Living in *nepantla*, the overlapping space between different perceptions and belief systems, you are aware of the changeability of racial, gender, sexual, and other categories, rendering the conventional labelings obsolete" (70).

Phase 4: Returning and Reintegration

The final two art pieces show the leaving and integration process.

Image 9 illustrates Prieta, still in the form of a lizard, climbing over the wall and running from the dogs. "The sun rises. I hear footsteps behind me. On the sidewalks,

Image 9. Running From the Dogs

I hear the dogs snarl. I turn around. Nothing, no one. Yet from that empty terrain I had crossed earlier and the unexplored land up ahead" (Anzaldúa, "Nepantla").

Image 10 shows Prieta, in the human form of Anzaldúa, walking out of *Nepantla*: "But I know I can't stay in *Nepantla*. Slapping my thighs hard to give me courage, I sprint toward the eyes far, far ahead of me, in the distance" (Anzaldúa, "Nepantla").

Both the dog and the eyes are mentioned directly in the closing of the fable. Exploration of these symbols provides further insight.

Dog. The dog is considered the animal of the dead. *Itzcuintli* is the dog who carries the souls of the dead to the afterlife. At times, a dog would be placed next to a dead body because it was believed that after four years, the dog would carry the soul to the underworld, the home of the dead (Beyer). "The violence against us, the violence within us, aroused like a rabid dog. Adrenaline-filled bodies, we bring home the anger and the violence we meet on the street and turn it against each other. We sic the rabid dog on each other and on ourselves. The black moods of alienation descend, the bridges we've extended out to each other crumble. We put the walls back up between us" (Anzaldúa, "La Prieta" 229).

Anzaldúa writes of her connection to death and dogs: "I dig a grave, bury my first love, a German Shepherd. Bury the second, third, and fourth dog. The last one retching in the backyard, going into convulsions from insecticide poisoning. I buried him beside the others, five mounds in a row crowned with crosses I'd fashioned from twigs. No more pets, no more loves—I court death now" ("La Prieta" 225).

Image 10. Leaving Nepantla

Eyes. The Nahuatl (Aztec) word for "eye" is *ixtli*. It symbolizes vision and insight. (Karttunen). Anzaldúa often references eyes and vision in her work to represent self-awareness, perception, and the process of understanding one's identity and reality, especially in relation to cultural, spiritual, and personal transformation (*Borderlands 4th ed.*). Anzaldúa states, "I will overcome the tradition of silence. My eyes are the eyes of a woman half-dead, caught in a thunderous swirl, but they hold a fiercely shining hope" (*Borderlands 4th ed.*, 81). In *Light in the Dark/Luz en lo Oscuro*, Anzaldúa also discusses "el espíritu," referring to a spiritual vision or insight that allows her to see beyond the material world. This kind of vision, rooted in the metaphysical, plays a key role in her process of self-healing and spiritual growth.

While Anzaldúa ends the fable with Prieta running out of *Nepantla*, I include a final drawing of transformed Gloria Anzaldúa, aglow with color, and with the skeleton following as a tribute.

CONCLUSION

Gloria Anzaldúa's *Nepantla* fable narrates a deeply transformative journey that challenges the boundaries of identity, culture, and spirituality. Through the fable's metaphorical language and rich Aztec imagery, Anzaldúa explores the painful yet necessary processes of dismemberment, reconstruction, and transcendence. Each phase of Prieta's journey—from the initial denial at the border, through the painful fragmentation, to her ultimate transformation and reintegration—mirrors the personal, cultural, and spiritual struggles that Anzaldúa faced as a woman of color, a queer writer, and a borderlander.

The artistic interpretation of *Nepantla* in this essay seeks to honor the complexity of Anzaldúa's vision, weaving together visual symbolism, mythological references, and personal history. The inclusion of Aztec icons such as Coyolxauhqui, Coatlicue, and Ollin reflect Anzaldúa's grounding in Mesoamerican spirituality, while the imagery of the serpent, the skeletal figures, and the chameleonic lizard signify the constant negotiation between life, death, and rebirth. These interpretations aim to capture the depth of *Nepantla's* themes—exile, alienation, self-discovery, and, ultimately, transformation.

At its heart, Nepantla serves as a powerful allegory for those who find themselves on the margins, constantly negotiating between worlds. Anzaldúa's fable, like her larger body of work, offers guidance for navigating the liminal spaces in which we exist, urging us to embrace the discomfort of Nepantla, which precedes transformation.

WORKS CITED

Aigner-Varoz, Erika. *Metaphors of a Mestiza Consciousness: Anzaldúa's Borderlands/La Frontera.* Conference Proceedings. MELUS, 2000, pp. 47-62.

Antuna, Marcos de R. "What We Talk About When We Talk About Nepantla: Gloria Anzaldúa and the Queer Fruit of Aztec Philosophy." *What We Talk About When We Talk About Nepantla: Gloria Anzaldúa and the Queer Fruit of Aztec Philosophy*, vol. 17, 2018, pp. 159-163.

Anzaldúa, Gloria. *Borderlands/La frontera: The New Mestiza.* San Francisco, Aunt Lute Books, 1987.

—. *Borderlands/La frontera: The New Mestiza.* 4 ed., Aunt Lute Books, 2012.

—. *Light in the Dark/Luz en lo oscuro: Rewriting Identity, Spirituality, Reality.* Edited by AnaLouise Keating, Duke UP, 2015.

—. "Nepantla." University of Arizona Poetry Center, 1991, https://voca.arizona.edu/track/id/65533.

—. "Yemaya." *This Bridge We Call Home: Radical Visions for Transformation*, edited by Gloria Anzaldúa and AnaLouise Keating, Routledge, 2002.

—. *"La Prieta." This Bridge Called My Back: Writings by Radical Women of Color.* Edited by Cherrie Moraga and Gloria Anzaldúa, 2nd ed., Kitchen Table: Women of Color Press, 1983.

Balderas, Adelina, and Carlos Balderas. *Mesoamerican Death and Continuity: Cultural Perspectives.* U Texas P, 2018.

Beyer, Hermann. "The Symbolic Meaning of The Dog in Ancient Mexico." *American Anthropologist*, vol. 10, no. 3, 1908, pp. 419-422.

Brinton, Daniel G. *The Annals of the Cakchiquels.* U Pennsylvania P, 1885.

"Cuetzpallin: The Sacred Lizard Day in the Aztec Calendar." *Symbol Sage*, https://symbolsage.com/cuetzpalin-aztec-symbol/. Accessed 27 February 2025.

Dahms, Elizabeth A. *The Life and Work of Gloria Anzaldúa: An Intellectual Biography.* U Kentucky, 2012.

Karttunen, Frances. *An Analytical Dictionary of Nahuatl.* UOklahoma P, 1983.

Klein, Cecelia F. *The Aztec Calendar and the Sun Stone.* U Texas P, 1976.

Maine, Miliann. *Hair: A Cultural History.* U California P, 2018.

Miller, Mary, and Karl Taube. *An Illustrated Dictionary of the Gods and Symbols of Ancient Mexico and the Maya.* Thames & Hudson, 2003.

Oaxacan Alebrijes: Art, Legends and Meaning. Oaxaca Auténtico, https://oaxacaautentico.com/en/oaxacan-alebrijes-art-legends-and-meaning. Accessed 6 September 2024.

Patillon, M. *Aelius Théon: "Progymnasmata."* Paris, University of France, 1997.

Sigal, Janet. *Hair and Identity: Gender, Sexuality, and Race.* Routledge, 2018.

Tuana, Nancy, and Shannon Scott. *In Aztec Mythology: Coyolxauhqui and Huitzilopochtli.* U Texas P, 2020.

Tuana, Nancy, and Shannon Sullivan. *Nepantla: Writing (from) the In-Between.* Pennsylvania State UP, 2020.

Vogler, Christopher. *The Writer's Journey: Mythic Structure for Writers.* 3rd ed., Michael Wiese Productions, 2007.

LAS MESTIZAJES/ LOS MESTIZAJES

YAEL VALENCIA ALDANA

LAS MESTIZAJES/ LOS MESTIZAJES

To those that slip in between
the los and the las, the el and the la
Los atravesados, las mestizajes,
los mestizajes.

To those who slip
across snake thin land, sometimes
thick with muddied water, sometimes
wide and cyan-clear, a place of squint-eyed
wisdom.

To those who step on slips of land
dusty and straight, verdant and clammy
mita and mita.

To those between the el and the la
the los and the las, dwell. beneath
and above and within
shadow.

To those where mita and mita meet,
Queer, to those between the los
and the las, the el and the la.
Where the half-dead dwell.
Where those who traverse dwell.
Where those who pass over dwell.

To those who are half-breed, half mongrel
half mulato, half perverse, half troublesome
but whole.
To those in between the los
and the las, slip between the el
and the la
Los atravesados, las mestizajes,
los mestizajes, whole.

To those Los atravesados,
las mestizajes, los mestizajes,
above and below the midline
whole.
To those that slide between
the los and the las, the el and the la
whole.
To those who slide in between
the los and the las, the el and the la
intertwine. Los atravesados
las mestizajes,
los mestizajes.

IN NAME ONLY

HOCICONA, PELEONERA

YOU WANT TO KILL ME

AMALIA ORTIZ

IN NAME ONLY

I once went to a college
they called "Hispanic serving,"
but the lessons they taught
were White culture preserving.

Dark skinned with an accent?
Not on our main stage!
angry brown girl stereotyped
to dismiss righteous rage

I worked for a nonprofit
that claims "social justice,"
but overworking, underpaying
workers always fucks us.

How we treat other
speaks more than our main goal.
Community shouldn't cost
my mental health and soul.

In name only
In name only
You say you we stand together,
then, you leave me standing lonely.

In name only
In name only
You say you stand for something,
but you're really a big phony.

I thought I knew a Christian.
He professed "Love one another!"
But he could barely tolerate,
let alone love his queer brother.

"No handouts for the poor,
and not in my backyard!"
Equity is not charity.
So, down with your old guard!

I've had fake ally friends
who pledged me their support,
bled my emotional labor,
and in crisis left me short.

But check their social media,
and boy, they sure look woke!
Self-serving, lip-service shit sandwich–
Eat it all and choke!

In name only
In name only
You say you we stand together,
then, you leave me standing lonely.

In name only
In name only
You say you stand for something,
but you're really a big phony.

Performative allies
Anti-racists steering POC to wreck?
Performative allies
Social justice with your boot on workers' necks?
Performative allies
Fake feminist ignoring other women's screams?
Performative allies
Fuck your ends, and fuck your means!

In name only
In name only
You say you we stand together,
then, you leave me standing lonely.

In name only
In name only
You say you stand for something,
but you're really a big phony.

Ew! Your performance is showing!

HOCICONA, PELEONERA

I've seen a lot of violence.
I've felt a lot of pain.
Now, if I don't stand up to it,
I felt it all in vain.

I've stood up to some enemies.
I've stood up to some friends.
And if my peace is threatened,
I'll stand up once again.

I hear a word of insult.
I see a cruel act.
The powerless should rally
when the powerful attack.

So, we must fight together,
and we must hold the line.
If community's the body,
las mujeres are the spine.

They call me "hocicona."
When I'm pissed, I won't shut up.
My mouth is a volcano.
Cross my gente, it erupts.

They call me "peleonera,"
'cause they think I like to fight,
but I'm not fighting for my ego.
I'm just fighting for what's right.

¡Hocicona! ¡Peleonera!
¡Luchadora, ¡Soldadera!
¡Adelita!, ¡Mujer fuerte!
¡Poderosa! ¡Muy valiente!

Hocicona, Peleonera
Luchadora, Soldadera

I've seen a lot of violence.
I've felt a lot of pain.
Now, if I don't stand up to it,
I felt it all in vain.

Mothers stand up for our children.
Sisters stand up for their friends,
and when our peace is threatened,
we must stand up once again!

They call me "hocicona."
When I'm pissed, I won't shut up.
My mouth is a volcano.
Cross my gente, it erupts.

They call me "peleonera,"
'cause they think I like to fight,
but I'm not fighting for my ego.
I'm just fighting for what's right.

¡Hocicona! ¡Peleonera!
¡Luchadora, ¡Soldadera!
¡Adelita, ¡Mujer fuerte!
¡Poderosa! ¡Muy valiente!

Hocicona, Peleonera
Luchadora, Soldadera

YOU WANT TO KILL ME

you want to kill me
strangle me slowly
hunt me down and cage me
deny my dignity

you want to kill me
brainwash my family
bind us in slavery
steal our humanity

the church, the State
the job I fucking hate
the KKK, the NRA
the fascist USA

just give it to me straight
stop lying to my face

I know you want to kill me.

you want to kill me
feeding me toxins
control my options
walls shrunk & boxed in

you want to kill me
shallow, bombastic
blank mind, fake body
choke me with plastic

the one percent who raise the rent
the fucks who take without consent
corruption in the government
politicos misrepresent

just give it to me straight
stop lying to my face

I know you want to kill me.

Oh, no!

you wanna kill me
don't feel like dyin'
you wanna kill me
I'm multiplyin'

bureaucracy, hypocrisy
democracy don't work for me
from GMOs to student loans
my HMO, the status quo

just give it to me straight
stop lying to my face

I know you want to kill me.

"NOW LET US SHIFT" INTO THE LIGHT

A GENERATIVE AUTOHISTORIA-TEORÍA PERFORMANCE

AVERY C. CASTILLO, ESTHER MEDINA DE LEÓN, CHRISTEN SPERRY GARCÍA AND LESLIE SOTOMAYOR II

INTRODUCTION

Hearkening the work of the *Teatro Chicana* (2008), we uncover a healing light that is contagious and produces the energy necessary for the work that must be done through storytelling, performance, coalition building, and seeing that *beyond our brokenness lies our wholeness.* As *autohistoria-teorístas,* authors of our individual stories, we, four women, offered our autohistoria-teorías (Anzaldúa, *Light in the Dark*) as a collaborative performance during the 10th El Mundo Zurdo conference in San Antonio, Texas. Our collective autobiographical storytellings were offered for expansion of Anzaldúa's autohistoria-teoría where the storytelling process encompasses spaces for the life story and self-reflection with potentials of "redrawing, "exposing limitations, and creating new stories for individual and collective transformations (Anzaldúa, *Light in the Dark*).

In *"Now Let Us Shift" Into the Light: A Generative Autohistoria-teoría Performance*, we explore the body, cultural memories, and generational traumas. We embody Anzaldúa's spiritual teachings as mindbodyspirit (Facio) through autohistoria-teoría to create a hybrid four-woman short play encompassing a prologue, four 10-minute individual autohistorias, and a conclusion with generative dialogue between performers and audience members. With each individual performance, and with repetition in some way of the word "shift[ing]," we acknowledge that the storytelling process through autohistoria-teoría is one way to "attempt to heal wounds or search for inner completeness," which defines Anzaldúa's Coyolxauhqui Imperative.

We each bring our own performance styles and stories of different chapters in our lives, yet the performance as a whole exemplifies the necessities for collective listening and the healing and building up of individual and community lights within the dark. What is revealed through this storytelling and creative essayist experience is the healing kindness we can give to ourselves, our mothers, and grandmothers; how the suturing of broken pieces and healed scars can reveal new pathways for remembrance, appreciation, and a re-writing of the self for collective healing and coalition building as nepantlera travelers of light through the dark (Lockhart). The alchemy of testimoniando (Roncero-Bellido) encompasses the theorizing of the self, the theorizing as collective voices and the theorizing in relation to the self and each other. This collaborative autohistoria-teoría performance sutured four women together by first opening with joined voices and mantras, next taking turns sharing our individual stories, and finally, re-joining again in one unified voice at the end of the performance.

SOMOS MUJER / WE ARE WOMAN

Our beginning—we stand together while facing the audience and holding hands, speaking in parts and in unison:
(*De León and García*)
(*Castillo and Sotomayor*)

Un-
broken

Like the time we cried
in the back room
when we thought no one
was watching

Somos mujer / See me

Breaking through
the worlds not meant
for us

Somos mujer / See me

We are not meant to be here
but where else

Could we go?

Un-
broken

Our light

Somos mujer / See me

Un-broken

Healing.
Loving.
Lighting darkness.

See me (*all*)
Somos mujer (*all*)

See me (*all*)
Somos mujer (*all*)

FLESH & NEEDLE

BY AVERY CASTILLO

Anzaldúa writes in metaphor of a "cactus needle embedded in the flesh" to imagine a wound which cannot be soothed, sutured, or entirely healed until it is comforted with ink stains on paper and eased by the reclamation that the wound will somehow always be there. As a chronically ill artist, poet, and writer, I acknowledge bodily turmoil through self-exploration of a cyclical and ongoing disease progression by gently shifting (invisible) wounds towards healing light to find voice, joy, and purpose. I embrace the vulnerabilities of childhood chronic illness and continual physical pain by not shying away from the truth of my exponential decay. Under the framework of Anzaldúa's Coyolxauhqui Imperative and autohistoria-teoría, wounds are sites for exploration and are conduits for seeing others' pain with empathy and compassion. Similarly to Leah Lakshmi Piepzna-Samarasinha's written letter to Gloria titled "So Much Time Spent in Bed," I also write and perform out of a "nepantla place," situating the in/visible chronic illness experience as a gift not only for self-healing but to acknowledge such a path possible for others. In my autohistoria, I perform out of my ongoing wound[ing] laying groundwork for others to visibly confront their own cactus needles in flesh. This is my testimonio.

"Along the sea / halo all around / bright raw fibers emerge. / In my imagination / I walk no matter age, storm, or sea." *—erasure poem inspired by Gloria Anzaldúa's Light in the Dark/ Luz en lo Oscuro*

You can't do this.
You can't.
You can't do it.
Do it, you know
you shouldn't
because you'll
hurt yourself
or worse
fail and look stupid
like you don't know
what you are doing.
Do you even know
what you are doing?

I try. I always try.

Who am I?
If I don't
cry and fight
and cry and try
again and again.

Oh, please...

But I—I believe
in me. I say it out loud:
I   believe   in   me.
I say it out loud to make it true:
I believe in me.

Just don't.

I have to
believe in something.
I must believe
in me—
        who else will?

No one.

I don't believe You
even though
You are me
and you are
Mean & why?
Why do I believe
in You the most?
Why are You
the loudest
voice in my head?

Because I know you
your purest and most
vulnerable parts of you
I know your dreams and how
far-fetched and ridiculously
hopeful they are. I know how scared
you are to be happy and lonely
at the same time. I know how you want
to save yourself and love the world.
It's a useless, tireless waste of energy.
Energy you don't have to spare.

Listen to me:
You
can't
do
it.

~

This inner dialogue is pure.
I am not ashamed
to confess: I lose
small pieces of myself
every day
to the pain
in my bones—bones
that should be
strong
dense
flexible
rejuvenating
instead
they are
brittle
necrotic
locked
dying.

This feeling of running out
of time
out of
a language
I know *so* well
but cannot translate
between you and I
it's suffocating.

Most of the time
my heart beats too fast
there is a burning down my throat
& my head feels as if there is a Queen Bee
raising an army to swarm out of me…except
there is no escaping

out of me: I   am   alive.

Just look into my eyes
I want you to know
I have not known a day without
pain—physical pain
the debilitating kind
the kind that's sharp and dull
burning and throbbing
here   there   all   at   once
I am achy all the time.

I was three years old
when the fevers set in
then the rash
swollen ankles
knees
hips
hands
wrists
shoulders
elbows
neck
        this body   on fire

I'd say as a child
        I am achy hot.

Don't you know the feeling?
No, probably not.
I'd have to remind myself
                no, they don't know
what it feels like for a warm
rainstorm to creep down
drizzle inside this body
my telltale sign of a nearing flare
readying to consume me
a downpouring of
achy hotness
swelling

icky
tired

Me versus me

I am both
myself & *Other*

Once through the storm
I remember my mother
smiling at me
I remember
smiling back—a language
only we speak of hope and survival

It takes less energy to smile
I force my lips straight
ignite tight muscles
in cheeks to pull
lips upward and show teeth

If I don't smile
this face will crumple
revealing a ruin
I know I will not come back from
so through the grief

I smile

I am not ashamed to confess: I have lost
a part of me I will never know—
risk taker
adventurous friend
Woman
I grieve
this healthier version
of Self

I remind myself:

I believe in me

Right now
alive with you
telling You there is hope
there is love for You to choose
this moment to be free
to be free on this stage
with you, with you, with you
with all you

I remind myself
this is not a dream
I am awake
I am alive

We are love
& it is okay to light the match
to see a new way
through this pain and decay

So, today I plant
these rheumatic feet
on solid ground &
now with all of me I shift

I am shifting

I am shifting

I am shifting
into new light

HERIDAS, INNOCENCE VEILED, I AM ESTHER

By Esther Medina De León

My written word elicits emotional and cognitive responses, facilitating an understanding of my lived experiences as a mother and a woman as I navigate what I have termed "self-inflicted chaos." My writing explores embodied experiences and the process of healing wounds through memory and words. As Gloria Anzaldúa describes it, the Coyolxauhqui Imperative, es un "camino"—a journey that was necessary to traverse and comprehend the precise nature of her experiences. This journey necessitates confronting personal traits, habits, and preconceived notions of identity, culminating in my realization I had previously suspected, that "This is and was not how I, or my children were supposed to live" (Anzaldúa, Light in the Dark). In preparation for the performance, and in performing, sharing these words opened past wounds prompted reflection on the consequences of participating in bad relationships subjecting myself to men's questionable behaviors, of bearing witness to my child's pain because of his decisions and unnecessary incarceration. The "susto" being a factor, albeit a needed factor, in our family's emergence of healing and restructuring frames of thought and being. I knew I had to heal, addressing my own wounds so that they could heal and be who they should be. Coyolxauhqui experience—I understood I had stumped their "psychological growth," but also understood that my own experiences and psychological growth were not nurtured nor supported growing up. Rewriting our own narrative—I wasn't passing on my resilience, perseverance, desire for stimulation for a better life. In performing our testimonios, blending storytelling and of analogous to Playback Theatre, a concept conceived by Jonathan Fox, which is an interactive improvisational theatrical form that "illuminates life and incites dialog," fostered my own healing through the recounting of our personal experiences (Wager et al.) and through comadrazgo. The process of self-reflection and identity exploration described in the text often leads to realizations about one's identity. The use of testimonio and Playback Theatre as tools for storytelling and dialogue can be powerful in creating spaces for healing and collective understanding. These approaches allow for the sharing of personal narratives in a way that resonates with others, fostering empathy and potentially catalyzing social change through the recognition of shared experiences and challenges.

(Heridas)
You see this scar right here?
(as I point to the scar across the top of my forehead)
I got this in a gang fight
(and then I wink)

No te crees!
I got it from not listening to my mom
when she said don't swing on the laundromat tables
BAM!
I was about 5
One of my first acts of defiance (*smirk*)

I remember riding in a car
vaguely the hospital where my grandma used to work
her laughing at me

they made fun of me...
mis primos
for having to have that bandage around my head
and then later for seeing the stitches
"you look like a baseball"

I later broke my collar bone
from playing and climbing on the station wagon
don't really remember that one
there are pictures somewhere

This one, appendix, (*point to my abdomen/right*)
when I was about 8
we were staying at the Ronald McDonald House
my little brother was already in the hospital
fighting his losing battle with Leukemia
I remember my mother getting mad at the doctors
I vaguely remember her saying they touched me wrong
But who knows...I was a kid

This one right here,
(as I point to the places where I got the cholecystectomy)
gallbladder removal,
Of course none of the doctors knew what was ailing me
until I was in immense pain

(Pointing again to my head, more to the right)
this right here, you can barely see

I got hit.
First time getting hit like that…
it bled like crazy.
He wanted me to go to the hospital,
to call the police,
turn him in,
I said, "no"
he said, "cover it"
I said, "for what? Aren't you proud of your work?"
As if it was aesthetic

that was the last time
I settled for a fool
They were all fools (*roll eyes*)
who had mad potential
but wasted my time and energy
and actually brought out the ugly in me

So many scars
those were a few that stood out

Wearing my wounds like battle scars
Como—proudly boasting
"I can handle my own"

The scars that remain
on my heart
in my mind
are tougher wounds
I deal with on a day-to-day basis

(Innocence veiled)
my heart hurts...wounds constantly ripped open
it's unfair
it's unfair
how it feels so helpless
how i feel so helpless
nothing to my name
no way to help
despair

heart crumbling
seeing my boy.......there....where he shouldn't be
instead of at home with us
he's there
when the real person behind this is out free
i hate this
i hate it
i wish it would all go away
tears stain my face
thoughts swirling in my head
safety compromised for the lack of consideration
from the police, from the media
makes me hate this place this city
for my son to be judged
dealt the wrong hand
wrong place wrong time
here, he was guilty until proven innocent
name splashed everywhere
his side never spoken
i hate this
i hate this
where are those "friends" those "buddies"
no one in sight, no one speaking up for him
my boy my baby
mijo lindo, my heart! my heart crumbles my heart aches for him
always dealt the wrong hand, always in the wrong place the wrong time
always has those "friends" who do him wrong
I HATE this I HATE IT! I hate it here in this place we call home
where you are guilty until proven innocent
where they don't care if they put your life in danger
where they destroy families for the sake of "doing their job"
I hate it.

(I am Esther)
I am Esther
A work in progress…

I wear many hats
have several aspects to my identity
She/her/ella.

Your local LatinaLibrarian.

In a society that is fixated with labels—I call myself, Chingona

Soy, Latina, Chicana, Tejana. Soy Mexican-American
Soy Hispanic.
I am indigenous to where I am from, I am indigenous in my roots.
Soy mujer. A mother, a sister, before that, a daughter.
I am the granddaughter of immigrants, of field/farm workers.
Second-generation coming from my father's side.
Possibly 3rd on my mother's.
I am First-Gen—
as a student, a graduate student, as faculty, as tenured faculty.
I am a librarian.
The only Latina librarian, of 2 Latino faculty at my library.

I grew up in a low-socioeconomic household.
A fractured family.
My mother in and out,
my dad doing the best he could

I am a middle child
The second oldest out of four siblings,
but third to receive degrees.
I was the first to have children
but have never been married.

We travel borders.
in life. in work. in the conversations we have.
Navigating everything...
I am first-gen in everything I do.
Not always right; mostly wrong;
but NEVER GIVE UP—
I persevere.
I am resilient.

I see many things.
interpret things differently.
I see a half, a whole, minimally,
depending on where I'm at

and what I'm doing—holistically

my being, my identity, my experiences
have led me in all different kinds of directions
and the many hats I wear and have worn...
in Anzaldúan thought—mestizaness—shifting from one identity to another...
Neplanta—of being torn, not necessarily fitting in—of finding myself as if I do not belong to any one dynamic...
of that Coatlicue state—where I think most of my "growing up" has occurred
though I didn't realize it at the time
these stages in my life where I had to learn,
I made myself go through things,
only to come out at the end
more poderosa...
.....

LA CASA TRACT

BY CHRISTEN SPERRY GARCÍA

I am from a mythical place called San Dijuana. It is where San Diego, CA, USA and Tijuana, BC, Mexico meet. No matter where I live within this beautifully liminal, fraught, purely-impure, and contradictory space that Anzaldúa (2009, 2012, 2015) refers to as nepantla. I am an artista and Chicana who creates "una mestizada" through art and performance (Anzaldúa, Light in the Dark, *47). La Casa Tract is a zine-based performance that is an example of one of my nepantla life episodes. Living between a romanticized vision of el rancho en Mexico and my abuelos 1960's track home in x, I piece together my Coyolxauqui—fragmented experiences (Anzaldúa,* Light in the Dark*) of tasting Mexican food on the Southwest and Midwestern borderlands wherein chiles secos, McCormick chile powder, and canned Chile de Las Palmas form an incomplete wholeness—mi autohistoria-teoría.*

Not el rancho en México, a track home, a 1960s tract home **en San Diego**
i'm not gonna to tell you a story about my abuelitos
who lived on the rancho in Mexico
because they lived in a 1960s tract en San Diego
i'm not gonna to tell you about the visits to
el rancho and setting foot on mythical Mexican land

instead, i will tell you about my abuelitos backyard en la frontera en San Diego
non-native southern California trees that mi bisabuelita would climb up
taking off the old palmas in a pink velour jumpsuit
from the desert named "killer"
One-orange tree (that jonny couldn't resist picking)
under the balcony, a large dusty brown wooden rosary hung
dusty weathered white plastic lawn table y chairs

Unas Vergüenzas: Mom's Enchiladas Wisconsianas vs Abuelita's Enchiladas Californianas

when i was 13 years old, my mom taught me how to make enchiladas
i did not know this at the time but they were el estilo de Southern California
because not all of the usual ingredients were available in Wisconsin
she adapted the chile recipe to using a can of tomato sauce and a couple of tablespoons of mccormick chile powder
the tortillas were not fried in oil, just dipped directly in the sauce
from a tortilleria on the South side of Milwaukee there called el rey
she used a brick of grated monterey jack cheese
but in the Midwest, they were exotic and favored by all bland palettes
my mom catered Mexican foods to the very bland taste of my Midwestern dad
when i moved back to the California borderlands
my abuelita showed me how to make her enchiladas
tortillas from el indio, our family restaurant
dipped in oil and then in a canned sauce, chile de las palmas
She found chile de las palmas that tasted like nana's salsa para enchiladas

Comida AUténtica de Mi Abuelita

mi abuelita was the best cook of
Mexican, California, Chicana, So Cal, Mexican American, American, familia food
i dreamt of her
frijoles refritos
enchiladas de queso con black olives on top
tostadas con carrots y todo
chiles rellenos
empanadas de pina
fideo
tacos
enchiladas de pollo con salsa de tomate y canela
chocolate con molinillo, (no, we did not drink abuelita brand)

Better Homes y Gardens

all those years
i would see her referencing this cookbook
i thought it was a book from her mamá
maybe it was a Sonoran recipe book or a cookbook from her suegra from Guadalajara
un día, I asked her what that special book was that she referred to
she pulled out a book titled……… Better Homes and Gardens Mexican cookbook?
nana gave it to her when she joined a Los Angeles bank in the 1970s
QUE?
the editorial board was from Iowa?
HUH?
what kind of comida Mexicana was she making all of these years?
it wasn't *authentic*?
a cookbook made in Iowa that claimed to be Mexican food?
our comida de familia
Sonora/Guadalajara/California —-> Nana —-> Abuelita —> Iowa -—> California borderlands
Better Homes y Gardens de familia García

PULLING AT MY UMBILICAL CORD (BRINCANDO EL CHARCO A CUBA)

BY LESLIE C. SOTOMAYOR II

I bridge intersections of my lived experiences with my knowledge of fragmented pieces of my mother's lived experiences that have often been too painful and difficult to articulate into conversations. Homing in on other sensibilities and ways of knowing (Pitts), I tap into imagined pláticas, dream-like memories from childhood voices, whispers through telephone lines, historicized contexts, and realities that overlap and have been transmitted, transcending into my psyche, spiritual realms, and border crossings between myself, my mother, Cuba and the U.S.

2011 when presented with the opportunity to go to Cuba I was terrified.
I was scared as I recalled the many stories I had heard since I was carried in my mother's womb......

Assassinations
Disappearances
Tortures
militant state
despised their own

Severed, exile, displaced: madre y familia
She only had one sister out of eleven siblings in the USA.

Vamos a brincar el charco...un grupito de 6 somos> Cuba—

Fear, reluctance:
three young children
no money of my own
no finances
housewife
What would my husband say? love of education, art and feminism

DIS[**RUPTURE**]ION

¿Dónde está el maní? All was provided: My condition was simple:

maternal family
two in Havana
five days con la familia

Querida mami,
Yo se que el país donde naciste y tuviste tu niñez fue también un lugar de trauma, de tristeza y de sufrimiento—Cuba no te cuido. Pero mami, por favor, yo necesito ir y conocer Cuba y a mi familia. Yo quiero ver de donde eres.

Solo fuiste tres veces:
1979
1995
2010

Despite not having her blessing, I went to Cuba the following month and it changed my life in many ways.

U.S.A.>>>>>>Mexico>>>>>>Havana.

//////////GATE KEEPERS///////////

Miedo ...susto: Gu(sana)!

?

?

?

Gu(sana)!

?

?

What if algo happens and I am imprisoned?
Would the US oficina de interes fight for me?
What if I fall off the grid?
What if I run out of dolares?
What if I need to call and I can't?
What if I fall sick?

José martí airport under dim lights, military brigades
holding large guns, a stale dense air encapsulated within

dreary painted walls as makeshift long lines greeted full flights of passengers from everywhere around the globe. As we went through the lines and gatekeepers who didn't dare smile, once crossing the metal detectors.

[there was one loop conveyor belt spitting out packages and luggage]

Tres Zonas:

1. Americans with their blue passports in hand.
2. Cuban citizens.
3. and everyone else.

*Cubans are taken through a whole section of tedious inspections of all luggage and packages where their belongings are itemized and taxed as they are grilled about everything.

I have my golden ticket: a blue american passport.

Caribbean heat
Crowded
Cafe
......and there I knew I was home—on a land that somehow recognized me and embraced me warmly.

Contradictions
Amazing
beautiful abandoned
wounded
old cars
polluted air
palm trees
Fidel's cielo
crashing ocean

La mar no se le olvida.

I remember one day going into el Museo de la revolution and I could barely make it through half of the exhibits, me tuve que ir.

I kept seeing so much archival with the year stamps of the time frame of when my mother was living in Cuba—I kept a running timeline automatically through my head:

1959 she was about 15 year old, communist education reform and propaganda; my mother as a young teenager seeing huge ditches on her way home from school with bodies, bicycles in it; military men enforcing curfews; armed men going through their homes; wondering where loved ones had disappeared to, accused of not upholding the communist regime because her essay in school spoke against it; civilians being assassinated; newspaper images of violence, death; she was thrown in jail, Guanabaco; sent to the other side of the country; her family couldn't visit her.

SOLITARY CONFINEMENT: 1962
SOLITARY CONFINEMENT: 1963
SOLITARY CONFINEMENT: 1964
SOLITARY CONFINEMENT: 1965
SOLITARY CONFINEMENT: 1966
SOLITARY CONFINEMENT: 1967

I thought I was going to vomit over all of the little enshrined cases documenting violence, concentration camps and stripping of human dignity. Tears welled up. I felt guilty.

NUESTRA CONCLUSION

In *Now Let Us Shift*, Anzaldúa writes, "This is your new vision, a story of how conocimiento manifests, but with one flaw: It doesn't work with things that are insurmountable or with all people at all times... But it works with las nepantleras, boundary crossers, thresholders who initiate others in rites of passage, activistas who, from a listening, receptive, spiritual stance, rise to their own visions and shift into acting them out, hacienda mundo nuevo (introducing stage)." And so, when we set off to co-create this performative piece, we began by holding space and sharing parts of our vulnerable stories. Stories and circumstances that changed us in some way. With intention we listened to each other's hearts, sitting in the pauses, silences, tears and wounds. It is from those places that we began to suture our stories together to see, feel, witness, acknowledge, not only each other's pain but also our similarities as mujeres. Lockhart describes this conjuring of bodily writing and knowledge through Anzaldúa's "*Tlilli, Tlapalli*/The Path of the Red and Black Ink," where she situates the embodiment of writing through the flesh to emerge. We gathered our brokenness in our hands and began to create a visual mural with our words, egging and flowing between each other. We collectively envision our individual stories coming out of darkness, the shadows, and into the light. This performance was an offering to those in the audience who reciprocated with their own vulnerability and holding space with us. It was and is our hope that the sharing of our fragmented stories reveals the camino, the shift, the stitching of our light as one. The more stories told, the brighter our pathways to wholeness become.

We close our testimonio journeys by holding hands, facing the audience, and speaking in unison to the audience:

We are shifting.

We are shifting.

We are

shifting

into the light.

WORKS CITED

Anzaldúa, Gloria. *Borderlands/La Frontera: The New Mestiza*, 4th ed. Aunt Lute Books, 2007.

—. *Light in the dark/Luz en lo oscuro: Rewriting Identity, Spirituality, Reality.* Edited by AnaLouise Keating, Duke University Press, 2015.

Facio, Elisa, and Irena Lara. *Fleshing the Spirit: Spirituality and Activism in Chicana, Latina, and Indigenous Women's Lives*. The University of Arizona Press, 2014.

Garcia, Laura E, et al. *Teatro Chicana: A Collective Memoir and Selected Plays.* University of Texas Press, 2008.

Lockhart, Tara. "Writing the self: Gloria Anzaldúa, textual form, and feminist epistemology." *Michigan Feminist Studies*, vol. 20, 2006, http://hdl.handle.net/2027/spo.ark5583.0020.002.

Piepzna-Samarasinha, Leah Lakshmi. *Care Work: Dreaming Disability Justice*. Arsenal Pulp Press, 2018.

Pitts, Andrea. J. "Gloria E. Anzaldúa's Autohistoria-teoría as an epistemology of self-knowledge/ignorance." *Hypatia*, vol. 31, issue 2, Spring 2016, pp. 352-369. DOI: https://doi.org/10.1111/hypa.12235.

Roncero-Bellido, Ana. "Testimoniando y comadreando Across Borders: Latina/s Anónima/s in Telling to Live: Latina Feminist Testimonios." *Chicana/Latina Studies: The Journal of Mujeres Activas en Letras y Cambio Social*, vol. 20, issue 1, Fall 2020, pp 26-55.

Wager, Amanda Claudia, et al. *Art as a Way of Listening: Centering Student and Community Voices in Language Learning and Cultural Revitalization,* 1st ed., vol. 1. Routledge, 2023. https://doi.org/10.4324/9781003302186.

A CREATIVE WORK: REFLECTION ON OUR COALITION-BUILDING ZINE WORKSHOP

BRIANNA GLASS AND DANIEL ALEJANDRO GONZÁLEZ

Zine View 1

ARTISTS' STATEMENT

The image above is of our collaborative individual zine (Zine View 1). It contains the shared reflections of our 2024 El Mundo workshop, *Coalition Building Through Zines*. In our workshop, we contemplated who we are, how we collaborate, and how we can build vibrant and directed coalitions. We reflected on these concepts with our words and drawings as we produced individual zines. The individual zines convey, in chronological order, what stood out in our workshop.

BUILDING COALITIONS

The point of our workshop, *Coalition Building Through Zines*, was to introduce critical reflection and creativity by building networks and coalitions. We wanted our participants to first look at themselves individually and consider their social identities as a way to give them more awareness about their place and impact in the world. We decided to facilitate our critical questions with zines, a creative format that folds into a small book. We provided materials for zine-making, such as scraps of magazines, pens, pencils, colored pencils, colored markers, bone folders, glue sticks, and scissors. We divided up the two-and-a-half-hour workshop into four sessions, with two sessions of zine-making and the remaining two dedicated to sharing and dialogue. As presenters, we wanted the participants to think critically and to have honest encounters with themselves, a peer, with a small group, and finally, the entire room of participants. The zine making process and dialogue were geared towards creating coalitions by developing effective communication and understanding ourselves and each other while fostering working relationships that would expand outside the conference. We also wanted to acknowledge the slow process of coalition building, showing that there is work to be done internally, with a peer, small groups, and finally, the communities we live in and serve. Anzaldúa showcases the continuous building of coalition by looking within herself through introspective, creative poetry and addressing broader concepts of community, relationships, and belonging. It is through the participants' dialogue and zine creating that "Perspectives from cracks offer us different ways of defining the self, of deciding group identity" speaks to the intricacy of ourselves, complex and nuanced (Anzaldúa 85).

At the end of the workshop, about 25 zines were created. The participants either kept them or gifted them to participants they met at the workshop. In our rehearsal of this workshop just with ourselves, we uncovered new clarity about coalition dynamics. This resulted not only from self-reflection but also in how we interacted with each other, how we presented ourselves to each other, and what that meant for our dialogue and moving towards building coalition. It is a process that we thought would offer clarity in a group setting so we can start "Recognizing and engaging in the nos/otras imperative (of removing the slash)" and move towards building coalition (Anzaldúa 85).

FIRST SESSION: INDIVIDUAL ZINE AND CRITICAL REFLECTION

Zine View 2

In our first session, before dialoguing with others, we wanted participants to consider who they are and how they might fit into and impact the community. We asked them to think about different parts of their identity and social statuses. We posed the question: In what ways are we atravesadas, and in what ways are we not? We asked participants to think through their social positions, power, and privileges alongside with less powerful aspects. This first zine making session is illustrated in the above picture (Zine View 2). The preliminary questions allowed participants to visually map and return to them later. This process resembles Anzaldúa's visual mapping and drawings in her book *Light in the Dark/Luz En Lo Oscuro*. We encouraged participants to write and draw visuals they thought represented themselves. After asking those preliminary questions, we gave participants twenty minutes to think and create their own zines. While the participants worked on their zines we, the facilitators, gave examples of how our social positions are framed within society, giving them ideas of what to think about in their own exploration of self.

SECOND SESSION: SHARING ZINES

Zine View 3

After the participants created their zines about their social positions and identities, (we, the facilitators, also created individual zines so we could participate in this session), we asked participants to find a peer to share with. After introductions, participants presented the zines they created to another participant. They read through their peer's zine, asked questions, and learned more about the creator and their process. Doing so ensured participants shared space, offered visual elements, and identified similarities and differences. This exchange resulted in a vibrant dialogue laden with vulnerability and trust. This session lasted around forty minutes, as everyone was really active in their conversations. The above illustration (Zine View 3) shows a few words that stood out while exchanging and sharing zines.

THIRD SESSION: ARTFULNESS, IMAGINING, AND COALITIONS

After one-on-one discussions, we reconfigured the groups into four to five participants for the last session. The discussion about positionalities continued and expanded into a larger group dynamic. For this element, we asked participants to create a zine reflecting their group dynamics and how they would achieve coalition. We looked at service and implementation as Anzaldúa guided us to consider coalitions with, "The new tribalism is about working together to create new 'stories' of identity and culture, to envision diverse futures" (Anzaldúa 85). The zines offered us a visual template to imagine working together, vital coalitions, and organizing Nepantlera projects that might come. The zine spread above portrays a group of four working collaboratively imagining how their coalition can thrive.

Zine View 4

FOURTH SESSION: SHARING THEIR COALITION ZINES

After thirty minutes, we asked each group to present themselves and their zine about how they build coalitions. We were surprised that participants went a step further to name and imagine a physical space to represent how each of them could utilize their various skills, expertise, and social positions. They then named the communities they would serve in these spaces. It was a surreal moment for us because we envisioned this last session as a simple acknowledgment of the group's social positions, marginalizations, and how they could work together generally. This advanced dialogue and energy spread between groups and into our shared imaginations. After closing remarks and thanks, participants continued in dialogue, shared their zines with new people in the workshop, and discussed future projects they could envision together.

CONCLUSION: ANZALDÚA AND ACHIEVING COALITION

Creating our individual zines allowed us the space to process and come together in dialogue and see the successes of our workshop. One participant's comment that kept coming back to us was, "I wish this workshop was offered earlier in the conference." This was referenced again in another conversation concerning how they could stay in contact with other participants and how they could incorporate creative, critical dialogue and zine making into their lives. We received a lot of positive feedback and embraced the rituals of writing down emails, phone numbers, and Instagram handles. But, ultimately, the ritual felt different for us, our sense of community, service, and building effective coalitions envisioned by Gloria Anzaldúa, her family, and Les ATRAVESADES en Comunidad.

Zine Collage created by Brianna Glass

WORKS CITED

Anzaldúa, Gloria. *Borderlands: La Frontera*. San Francisco, Aunt Lute Books, 1999.

—. *Light in the dark/Luz en lo oscuro: Rewriting Identity, Spirituality, Reality.* Edited by AnaLouise Keating, Duke University Press, 2015.

Martinez, Aja. *Counterstory: The Rhetoric and Writing of Critical Race Theory. Conference on College Composition and Communication*. National Council of Teachers of English, 2022.

Sleeter, Christine. *Un-Standardizing Curriculum: Multicultural Teaching in the Standards-Based Classroom*. New York: Teachers College Press, 2005.

CONTRIBUTOR BIOGRAPHIES

Sonya M. Alemán (editor) is an associate professor in the Race, Ethnicity, Gender, and Sexuality Studies Department and Mexican American Studies program at the University of Texas, San Antonio. She is also Director of UTSA's Women's Studies Institute. She received her BA from St. Mary's University, an MA from the University of Texas, Austin, and a PhD from the University of Utah. A Chicana from south Texas, she studies mainstream media representations of communities of color, alternative media content produced by communities of color, and manifestations of race, racism, and whiteness in the media. In addition, she is invested in improving the educational experiences of students of color. She draws on critical race theory and Chicana feminism to inform both her scholarship and pedagogy. She developed and teaches Texas' first class based on the life and career of Tejano singer Selena Quintanilla. She served as Editor of *Chicana/Latina Studies* from 2017-2022. She is published in *Critical Studies in Media Communication*; *Frontiers: A Journal of Women's Studies*; *Review of Research in Education*; *Race Ethnicity & Education*; and *International Journal of Qualitative Studies in Education.*

Yael Valencia Aldana (editor), an Afro-Latinx/e poet and writer, is the author of *Alien(s)*. Aldana, her mother, her mother's mother, and so on are descendants of the Indigenous people of modern-day Colombia. Her poem "Black Person Head Bob" won a Pushcart Prize, and her work has appeared in *Torch Literary Arts, Chapter House Journal*, and *Slag Glass City*, among others. She teaches creative writing in South Florida and lives near the ocean with her son and too many pets. Find her online at YaelAldana.com.

Avery Castillo is a Mexican American poet, artist, and editor from South Texas. She is currently pursuing an MFA in Creative Writing from the University of Texas Rio Grande Valley. She holds a degree in English from Texas Tech University. Her work can be found and/or forthcoming in *Huizache, Latino Book Review, Boundless 2024: The Anthology of the Rio Grande Valley Poetry Festival, Equatorial Magazine*, and elsewhere.

Rachel Yvonne Cruz (editor) is an assistant professor at The University of Texas at San Antonio and a leading scholar in Mexican American music. She received her BA from The University of Notre Dame (Indiana) and the Master of Music and Doctor of Musical Arts Degrees from The University of Texas at Austin. In 2022, she pioneered a Mexican American Music concentration, currently the only program of its kind in the U.S. housed specifically within a Mexican American Studies (MAS) program. The MAS Music concentration focuses on cultivating future activist scholars to use music as a guardian of culture and history and a catalyst for social change. Cruz's commitment to preserving the contributions of Chicanas/xs and gender and sexual non-conforming musicians through traditional and creative scholarship—research and writing, original compositions, and recordings, notations and arrangements of others' work— has driven her to create a program of study that elevates these artists' voices within the historical narrative and secures their enduring legacy. Cruz is the award-winning author of *The Art of Mariachi: A Curriculum Guide*, and is contracted for her upcoming book, *Latinx Music and the Arts: A Celebration of Generations and Genres*. A passionate singer, songwriter, and educator, her greatest pride lies in her students' achievements, having mentored numerous ensembles and soloists to national recognition. She resides in San Antonio, TX, with her wife, Deborah, and their beloved fur babies, Chloe, Maggie, and Guero.

Esther Medina de León is an associate librarian at Texas Tech University. De León received her MA in Library Science from University of North Texas in Denton, and graduate certificates in Women's and Gender Studies and Advanced Digital and Social Media from Texas Tech. She is currently pursuing a graduate certificate in Indigenous and Native American Studies at Texas Tech University. As a Mexicana/Latina/Chicana academic, she utilizes her positionality to make spaces for others (in all realms), so that our culture is seen, remembered, shared, known, represented.

Yaneyry Delfin Martinez holds a BA in sociology and Chicana/o/x studies from the University of California, Davis. They are currently pursuing a Master's in Public Sociology at Cal Poly Humboldt, where they are collaborating with the

Social Justice Center to establish a Dream Center. Additionally, Martinez serves as an ESL tutor for recent Afghan refugees and is conducting research that examines the experiences of undocumented students with Academic and Career Services, focusing on how these interactions impact their navigation of higher education.

Rebecca Esho Greenslade (she/her) works as an existential-feminist psychotherapist. She is the founder of Gaia Therapy Project, the Feminist Therapy Network. Her writings explore the interstices between embodied philosophy, psychotherapy, spirituality and liberatory feminisms; she is currently undertaking PhD research that considers how a spiritualized feminist psychotherapeutics can intervene in contemporary modes of alienation. Greenslade is a Zen practitioner in the White Plum lineage and Buddhist chaplain-in-training with Upaya Zen Center.

Christen Sperry García is originally from the San Diego/Tijuana borderlands, and her visual and written work is informed by lived experiences and Chicanx and Latinx theories. García is co-founder of the Nationwide Museum Mascot Project that has performed at over forty art museums and galleries including Museo de Arte Contemporáneo Lima, Peru; Museo Jumex, Mexico City; Museum of Contemporary Art San Diego, CA; Hammer Museum, Los Angeles, CA; and Museo de Arte Moderno, Bogotá, Colombia. García has published in peer-reviewed journals including *Art Education*, *The Drama Review*, and J*ournal of Curriculum and Pedagogy*. She is Associate Professor in the Department of Art Education at Florida State University.

Brianna Glass is community educator, zine maker, and artist. To access the local communities' Funds of Knowledge, she avidly explores race, gender and class. Her teaching praxis "thoroughness" is informed by bell hooks, Gloria Anzaldúa, and Judith Flores Carmona. Brianna currently works at the urban downtown public library in San Antonio where she assists patrons with digital literacy questions and teaches basic computer lessons. In 2023-2024, she was named NonProfit Technology Enterprise Network's (NTEN) Digital Fellow for San Antonio. She represented the San Antonio Public library and her Digital Fellowship sought to bridge the digital divide at San Antonio Senior Centers, where she and colleagues taught accessible classes on all things digital. To assist bicultural and bilingual seniors in their learning, she creates bilingual how-to zines, like keyboard shortcuts, how to create a strong password, etc. The zines she creates can be found at community events and at the library, free to take and share.

Christina Gómez Hernández is a first-generation college graduate, an emergent bilingual, and a self-identified XicanA. She passionately advocates for dual language education and Mexican American Studies. With 24 years of experience in bilingual/ESL education, Gómez Hernández has served as a one-way dual language teacher, campus instructional coach, Emergent Bilingual (EB) coach, specialist, and coordinator. She earned my doctorate in Educational and Community Leadership from Texas State University. Her dissertation, titled *The Gibbous and Crescent of la Luna: Emergent Bilingual Educator Experiences in the K-12 Public School System as Student and Educator*, focused on the experiences of emergent bilinguals in public schooling as students and as dual language educators. Her dissertation was awarded the NACCS Tejas Foco 2024 Dissertation Award for research.

Noreen Graf is a professor at the University of Texas, Rio Grande Valley where she teaches about disability in the School of Rehabilitation. She recently received her MFA in creative writing where she studied the work of Gloria Anzaldúa.

Mark A. Hernández is a program coordinator and a clinical mental health counseling graduate student at The University of Texas at San Antonio. He holds a BBA in finance from Texas A&M University, a BA in philosophy from D'Youville University, and an MA in systematic theology from the Oblate School of Theology. Growing up along the border of Eagle Pass, Texas, and Piedras Negras, Coahuila, he was influenced by the male-dominated structures that perpetuate injustice in U.S. colonial and Roman Catholic narratives. These narratives separated him from the inner-feminine healer, Mesoamerican Indigenous anthropology, and from developing an inclusive consciousness of belonging. His introduction to the writings of Gloria E. Anzaldúa marked a significant shift in his conocimiento and inspired his passion for healing fragmented parts of the self. Anzaldúa's auto-historia-teoría, Indigenous, and embodied storytelling guides his research and advocacy.

Salvador Herrera is an assistant professor of Latinx literature and cultural production in the University of Oregon's department of English. His research analyses transborder aesthetics to theorize queer life. His work is informed by Chicana feminism, world-systems theory, psychoanalysis, and aesthetic decipherment. Herrera maintains research interests in queer theory, trans studies, New Materialism, and border studies as they coalesce around questions of reproduction and the erotic.

Alina Lugo holds an MA in world cultures and literatures from the University of Houston. Her topics of interest include comparative cultural studies, as well as language and identity. She's a freelance writer for *Diáspora*, an editor for Purple

Ink Press, and an English-language tutor. She has been heavily involved in intercultural communication and community outreach projects. In her spare time, she loves making handmade crafts and writing poetry.

Laura Lopez is an associate professor of English at the University of the Incarnate Word in San Antonio, Texas. Her teaching and scholarly interests focus on literary representations of social justice, gender and cultural identity formation, and belonging in Latinx literature, Latinx young adult literature, and contemporary American literature.

Karen Miranda Chavez holds a BA in psychology and Chicana/o studies with a minor in education from the University of California, Davis. Chavez's academic pursuits are guided by the desire to give back to underrepresented and underserved communities, to voice the diverse experiences of first-generation students but also promote social justice, life wellness, and help decrease mental health stigma.

Amalia Ortiz is a Tejana playwright and author of two award-winning books of poetry. She was awarded the 2020 American Book Award for Oral Literature, and appeared on three seasons of Russell Simmons Presents Def Poetry on HBO. She and her band, Las Hijas de la Madre, were awarded a City of San Antonio Artist Grant and a Democratizing Racial Justice Artist Residency from the Mellon Foundation to complete their new project Diatribas Punk.

Christian Ramirez earned a dual PhD in sociology and Chicano/Latino studies from Michigan State University. He is currently an assistant professor of sociology in the Department of Psychology and Sociology at Texas A&M University, Corpus Christi. His areas of research include migration, identity, and decolonial theory. He is particularly interested in the historical legacies of rebellion forged by Indigenous and African communities in the Americas.

María José Ramírez-Jiménez. Maestrante en Estudios Latinoamericanos en la Universidad Nacional Autónoma de México (UNAM). Licenciada en Letras Hispánicas por la misma casa de estudios. Editora, reportera y escritora. Sus textos han sido publicados en *Tierra Adentro, Marabunta, ERRR Magazine, Enpoli, Hipérbole Frontera y MilMesetas*. Dirige "Poderosas. Círculo de lectura de escritoras latinoamericanas." Participó en *Voces indómitas. Antología de narrativa breve escrita por mujeres* (Crisálida ediciones, 2022) y *Vagón rosa rosa rosa* (Ediciones Periféricas, 2024).

Adrianna M. Santos is an associate professor of English at Texas A&M University, San Antonio, and the author of *Cicatrix Poetics, Trauma and Healing in the Literary Borderlands: Beyond Survival* (Palgrave, 2024). She earned a BA in English from University of Texas at Austin and MA and PhD in Chicana/o studies from University of California, Santa Barbara. She has published in *Chicana/Latina Studies*, *Latina Critical Feminism*, and *Shakespeare Bulletin*. With Norma E. Cantú and Rita Urquijo-Ruiz, she is co-editor of *Interplanetary Nepantla: El Mundo Zurdo 8* (Aunt Lute, 2022). With Katherine Gillen and Kathryn Vomero Santos, she is co-editor of *The Bard in the Borderlands* (ACMRS Press, 2023).

Diego Séval is a PhD student in philosophy (Université Toulouse Jean Jaurès and Paris 8), working under the supervision of Jean-Christophe Goddard and Nadia Yala Kisukidi. He is currently teaching philosophy in high school, in parallel to his doctoral dissertation. His areas of research are border and decolonial studies, and Latin American philosophy.

Leslie Sotomayor II was born in New Jersey with a strong connection to her ancestry through her Cuban and Puerto Rican parents. As a first-generation bilingual Spanish and English McNair scholar, she received her dual PhD from The Pennsylvania State University in art education and women's, gender & sexuality studies. She is a writer, artist, curator and scholar centering underrepresented themes in her work. Sotomayor's studio art process is painting, collage work and installations.

Mónica Torreiro-Casal holds a PhD in counseling psychology and MFT. As a former clinician, she has worked extensively in the community and university counseling services (domestic violence, addictions, LGBTQIA, undocumented immigrants and school settings). Torreiro-Casal teaches Latino/Chicano psychology and mental health classes at the Chicana/o/x department at University of California, Davis and for the UC Davis Latinx health study abroad program in Oaxaca, Mexico. She conducts research on immigration and mental health and mentors' students on community-based research projects. Torreiro-Casal enjoys traveling, music, dancing, biking and spending time with family.

Romana Radlwimmer (editor) is a professor of romance literature at the Goethe University of Frankfurt. Before, she held research and teaching positions at the Universities of Salamanca, Lisbon, Augsburg, and Tübingen. She has been visiting the Mexican–US Borderlands since 2009, when she first participated in the International El Mundo Zurdo Conference, but most intensely when being a Fulbright Scholar in the Latina/o Studies Program at the University of Missouri–Kansas City (2015-16). She was an elected forum member for Literatures of the United States in Other Languages than English of the Modern Language Association (2018–2023). She is the author of the monographs *Wissen in Bewegung: Latina-Kulturtheorie / Literaturtheorie / Epistemologie (Moving Knowledges: Latina Cultural Theory / Literary Theory / Epistemology)*(2015) and *Gloria Anzaldúa's Hemispheric Performativity. Pieces, Shuffles, Layers* (2023), and the editor of *Transborder Matters: Circulaciones literarias, transformaciones culturales mexicanas y chicanas* (2020).

OUR MISSION Founded in 1982, Aunt Lute Books is an intersectional, feminist press dedicated to publishing literature by those who have been traditionally underrepresented in or excluded by the literary canon. Core to Aunt Lute's mission is the belief that the written word is critical to understanding and relating to each other as human beings. Through the centering of voices, perspectives, and stories that have not been traditionally welcomed by mainstream publishing, we strengthen ties across cultures and experiences, promoting a broader range of expression, and, we hope, working toward a more inclusive and just future.

LAND ACKNOWLEDGMENT We, Aunt Lute Books, acknowledge that we do our work of uplifting marginalized voices and striving toward justice via the written word on the unceded ancestral homeland of the Ramaytush Ohlone who are the original inhabitants of the San Francisco Peninsula. As the indigenous stewards of this land and in accordance with their traditions, the Ramaytush Ohlone have never ceded, lost, nor forgotten their responsibilities as the caretakers of this place, as well as for all peoples who reside in their traditional territory. As Guests, we recognize that we benefit from living and working on their traditional homeland. We wish to pay our respects by acknowledging the Ancestors, Elders and Relatives of the Ramaytush Community and by affirming their sovereign rights as First Peoples.

You may buy books from our website.

www.auntlute.com

aunt lute books

P.O. Box 410687
San Francisco, CA 94141
books@auntlute.com

This book would not have been possible without the kind contributions of the Aunt Lute Founding Friends:

Anonymous Donor	Diana Harris
Anonymous Donor	Phoebe Robins Hunter
Rusty Barceló	Diane Mosbacher, M.D., Ph.D.
Marian Bremer	Sara Paretsky
Marta Drury	William Preston, Jr.
Diane Goldstein	Elise Rymer Turner

www.ingramcontent.com/pod-product-compliance
Lightning Source LLC
Jackson TN
JSHW071944170526
102459JS00038B/124
* 9 7 8 1 9 5 1 8 7 4 1 1 7 *